Deleuze and World Politics

The central argument of this book is that the univocal ontology and corresponding immanent metaphysics of the French philosopher Gilles Deleuze (1925–1995) can provide a theoretical perspective capable of accounting for the complex nature of world politics.

Drawing on a wide variety of Deleuze's writings, it develops a thorough investigation of his ontology and metaphysics as they pertain to core questions of world politics such as power, identity, hierarchy, space, time, territory and the state.

The book explores the dynamics of contemporary world politics and issues by focusing on the 'anti-' or 'alter-globalization movement' (AGM). It analyses several approaches to social and political theory which deal explicitly with the AGM including global governance theory, international relations, social movement theory, Marxism, and post-Marxism. These are contrasted with a larger Deleuzian theory which can be of use when addressing the diffuse and often paradoxical aspects of world politics.

Deleuze's work poses a major challenge to traditional understanding of global politics and this book will be of considerable interest to researchers and students of social and political theory, critical international relations and globalization studies.

Peter Lenco teaches Global Governance at Bielefeld University, Germany.

Routledge innovations in political theory

1. **A Radical Green Political Theory**
   Alan Carter

2. **Rational Woman**
   A feminist critique of dualism
   Raia Prokhovnik

3. **Rethinking State Theory**
   Mark J. Smith

4. **Gramsci and Contemporary Politics**
   Beyond pessimism of the intellect
   Anne Showstack Sassoon

5. **Post-Ecologist Politics**
   Social theory and the abdication of the ecologist paradigm
   Ingolfur Blühdorn

6. **Ecological Relations**
   Susan Board

7. **The Political Theory of Global Citizenship**
   April Carter

8. **Democracy and National Pluralism**
   Edited by Ferran Requejo

9. **Civil Society and Democratic Theory**
   Alternative voices
   Gideon Baker

10. **Ethics and Politics in Contemporary Theory**
    Between critical theory and post-marxism
    Mark Devenney

11. **Citizenship and Identity**
    Towards a new republic
    John Schwarzmantel

12. **Multiculturalism, Identity and Rights**
    Edited by Bruce Haddock and Peter Sutch

13. **Political Theory of Global Justice**
    A cosmopolitan case for the World State
    Luis Cabrera

14. **Democracy, Nationalism and Multiculturalism**
    Edited by Ramón Maiz and Ferran Requejo

15. **Political Reconciliation**
    Andrew Schaap

16 **National Cultural Autonomy and Its Contemporary Critics**
Edited by Ephraim Nimni

17 **Power and Politics in Poststructuralist Thought**
New theories of the political
Saul Newman

18 **Capabilities Equality**
Basic issues and problems
Edited by Alexander Kaufman

19 **Morality and Nationalism**
Catherine Frost

20 **Principles and Political Order**
The challenge of diversity
Edited by Bruce Haddock, Peri Roberts and Peter Sutch

21 **European Integration and the Nationalities Question**
Edited by John McGarry and Michael Keating

22 **Deliberation, Social Choice and Absolutist Democracy**
David van Mill

23 **Sexual Justice/Cultural Justice**
Critical perspectives in political theory and practice
Edited by Barbara Arneil, Monique Deveaux, Rita Dhamoon and Avigail Eisenberg

24 **The International Political Thought of Carl Schmitt**
Terror, liberal war and the crisis of global order
Edited by Louiza Odysseos and Fabio Petito

25 **In Defense of Human Rights**
A non-religious grounding in a pluralistic world
Ari Kohen

26 **Logics of Critical Explanation in Social and Political Theory**
Jason Glynos and David Howarth

27 **Political Constructivism**
Peri Roberts

28 **The New Politics of Masculinity**
Men, power and resistance
Fidelma Ashe

29 **Citizens and the State**
Attitudes in Western Europe and East and Southeast Asia
Takashi Inoguchi and Jean Blondel

30 **Political Language and Metaphor**
Interpreting *and* changing the world
Edited by Terrell Carver and Jernej Pikalo

31 **Political Pluralism and the State**
Beyond sovereignty
Marcel Wissenburg

32 **Political Evil in a Global Age**
Hannah Arendt and international theory
Patrick Hayden

33 **Gramsci and Global Politics**
Hegemony and resistance
Mark McNally and John Schwarzmantel

34 **Democracy and Pluralism**
The political thought of
William E. Connolly
Edited by Alan Finlayson

35 **Multiculturalism and Moral Conflict**
Edited by Maria Dimova-Cookson and Peter Stirk

36 **John Stuart Mill – Thought and Influence**
The saint of rationalism
Edited by Georgios Varouxakis and Paul Kelly

37 **Rethinking Gramsci**
Edited by Marcus E. Green

38 **Autonomy and Identity**
The politics of who we are.
Ros Hague

39 **Dialectics and Contemporary Politics**
Critique and transformation from Hegel through Post-Marxism
John Grant

40 **Liberal Democracy as the End of History**
Fukuyama and postmodern challenges
Chris Hughes

41 **Deleuze and World Politics**
Alter-globalizations and nomad science
Peter Lenco

Deleuze and World Politics
Alter-globalizations and nomad science

Peter Lenco

LONDON AND NEW YORK

First published 2012
by Routledge
2 Park Square, Milton Park, Abingdon, Oxon OX14 4RN

Simultaneously published in the USA and Canada
by Routledge
711 Third Avenue, New York, NY 10017

Routledge is an imprint of the Taylor & Francis Group, an informa business

First issued in paperback 2013

© 2012 Peter Lenco

The right of Peter Lenco to be identified as author of this work has been asserted by him in accordance with the Copyright, Designs and Patent Act 1988.

All rights reserved. No part of this book may be reprinted or reproduced or utilized in any form or by any electronic, mechanical, or other means, now known or hereafter invented, including photocopying and recording, or in any information storage or retrieval system, without permission in writing from the publishers.

Trademark notice: Product or corporate names may be trademarks or registered trademarks, and are used only for identification and explanation without intent to infringe.

British Library Cataloguing in Publication Data
A catalogue record for this book is available from the British Library

Library of Congress Cataloging in Publication Data
Lenco, Peter.
Deleuze and world politics : alter-globalizations and nomad science / Peter Lenco.
　p. cm. – (Routledge innovations in political theory ; 40)
　Includes bibliographical references and index.
　1. Globalization. 2. International relations–Philosophy. 3. World politics–Philosophy. 4. Deleuze, Gilles, 1925–1995–Political and social views. I. Title.
　JZ1318.L45 2011
　327.101–dc22   2011014396

ISBN: 978-0-415-59008-2 (hbk)
ISBN: 978-0-415-71361-0 (pbk)
ISBN: 978-0-203-80205-2 (ebk)

Typeset in Times
By Wearset Ltd, Boldon, Tyne and Wear

Contents

Preface ix
List of abbreviations xi

Introduction 1

1 **World politics and the AGM** 8
 A challenge to theory 8
 The arrival of the AGM on the global stage 12
 Definitions and conceptualizations 19
 Theoretical perspectives 27
 Theoretical directions 39

2 **Deleuze and politics as becoming** 42
 Points of entry 42
 Difference and univocity 52
 Representation 60
 Immanence 68
 Counteractualization 85
 The philosophy of becoming 89

3 **Deleuze and world politics** 95
 New directions 95
 Space 98
 Time 115
 Neo-medievalism and the postmodern 118
 Emergence 120
 Nomad science 134
 The AGM as an emergent political form 138

4 Subjectivity and political agency 144
Politics and the individual 144
The subject 146
A brief genealogy of subjectivity 148
The fold 155
Deleuzian subjects 162
Post-Marxism 165
Deleuze and consequences 169
Globalization/alter-globalization 177
The 'catch' 183

Conclusion: world politics as nomad science 188

Notes 194
References 204
Index 217

Preface

The research behind this book began as an attempt to understand various subjectivities of resistance using Deleuze, but during the course of the initial research I became overwhelmed by an ever-increasing field of questions about Deleuze's philosophy which seemed more and more to destabilize the integrity of the argument. In searching for answers to these questions I came to see that something much more general and perhaps practical could be said about Deleuze and world politics; in other words, I realized that Deleuze's philosophy was much more comprehensive than 'just' a philosophy of minoritarian resistances. This insight began to steer the direction of the work towards the social sciences where it was clear that such an approach to Deleuze was sorely needed and yet sadly lacking. As a result of this process, the book is very much interdisciplinary, and walks a fine line between sociology, politics, International Relations and philosophy. Such a broad scope, however, not only reflects that virtuosic range of subjects dealt with in the more familiar *A Thousand Plateaus*, but perhaps more importantly signals the super-theoretical nature of Deleuze's thought. In effect Deleuze, like all good philosophers, offers no philosophy of world politics, only philosophy *tout court*. Amid this therefore necessary wide scope, I hope that likeminded readers will find a resonance with their own research paths.

Since putting down the pen on this book (early in 2009) there has been an exponential increase in the number of books on Deleuze in areas as diverse as law and architecture. And although the present work does not directly address these texts it is hoped that it will connect with them in various, wondrous ways in what will surely be seen as an interesting decade of Deleuze studies and Deleuze interventions, in the social sciences in particular. Also, although the majority of the research and writing of this book was done between 2005 and 2008, as the final touches were being applied, many polities in the world began to voice their dissatisfaction and challenge the status quo of seemingly intractable regimes. Regardless of their significance and direction, it is precisely these kinds of well-grounded yet complex, singular yet related, wholly unpredictable yet seemingly inevitable lines of political activity that this books seeks to address.

This book would never have been possible without the enormous input and assistance of others. Of tremendous support in terms of encouragement and suggestions was the political science graduate research team at Bielefeld University. Of these fine colleagues I would like to single out Suna Aydemir, Jan Helmig, Eva Herschinger, Oliver Kessler, Martin Koch, Tobias Kohl, Stephan Stetter, and Jochen Walter for their patient open-mindedness in discussing early drafts of chapters. I want to especially and sincerely thank Mathias Albert for his continuous scholarly support and professional advice. Bielefeld University as a whole was extremely good to me and I thank the Bielefeld Graduate School in History and Sociology and the Institute for World Society Studies for their generous financial and material support.

Special thanks also goes to the people at Routledge: first of all to the anonymous referees who read various stages of the manuscript for their criticisms and suggestions, and who not only shielded the manuscript against a number of errors, but acted as a sounding board in the difficult process of introducing Deleuze's philosophy to the study of world politics. Craig Fowlie deserves acknowledgement for deftly steering the manuscript through the review process, and Nicola Parkin did an exemplary job bringing the author through the practical stages of publication.

Finally I would like to thank my family, in particular the unknowing contribution of Arun and Ilya, and now Hanan. The book is irrevocably intertwined with these beautiful people.

My deepest thanks go to my wife, Daniela Kempkens, who in uncountable ways saw me through the research, writing, and publishing phases of this project with patience and good humour. This book is dedicated to her.

Bielefeld
May 2011

Abbreviations

Texts by Deleuze

AO	Anti-Oedipus
ATP	A Thousand Plateaus
B	Bergsonism
C1	Cinema 1; The Movement Image
D	Dialogues II
DR	Difference and Repetition
DP	'Desire and Pleasure'
EP	Expressionism in Philosophy: Spinoza
ES	Empiricism and Subjectivity: An Essay on Hume's Theory of Human Nature
F	Foucault
LB	The Fold; Leibniz and the Baroque
LS	The Logic of Sense
N	Negotiations 1972–1990
NP	Nietzsche and Philosophy
WP	What is Philosophy?

Bodies and networks

AGM	Alter-globalization movement
ATTAC	Association pour une Taxation des Transactions Financières pour l'Aide aux Citoyens (Association for the Taxation of Financial Transactions for the Aid of Citizens)
EZLN	Ejército Zapatista de Liberación Nacional (Zapatista Army of National Liberation)
GONGO	Government-organized non-governmental organization
IGO	Intergovernmental organization
IMC	Independent Media Centres
IMF	International Monetary Fund
(I)NGO	(International) Non-governmental organization
MST	Movimento dos Trabalhadores Rurais Sem Terra (Landless Workers Movement)

PGA	People's Global Action
TNC	Transnational Corporation
TSMO	Transnational social movement organization
WEF	World Economic Forum
WSF	World Social Forum
WTO	World Trade Organization

Introduction

As the world settled into the post-Cold War era, one of the most often heard refrains in the study of world politics was that theorists lacked the concepts, methods, conceptual tools, or vocabulary to understand or account for global affairs. Such sentiments continue to be found across a broad spectrum of disciplines. Looking broadly at the socio-political literature, it seems as if the building blocks, the independent variables, of the study of world politics are increasingly under challenge, unsettling the research agendas of those fields concerned with this area of study. We are told by scholars that the political world today, and certainly increasingly over the past decades (and in every likelihood increasingly into the future) is characterized by fluidity over stability, change over fixity, ambiguous forces over clear processes, ignorance over knowledge, and paradox over clear logic. Nothing seems to stand still and analyses of elements and actors tend to be less clear than they once seemed, especially in the mainstream of various academic pursuits including but not limited to sociology, political science, and international relations (IR). The actual forces cited as contributing to this confusion and disorder include glocalization, integration and disintegration, the periphery coming to the centre, and both the apparent loss and strengthening of identity.

Within this context one of the most striking developments in recent years that challenges a great many of the received categories of social science inquiry is the so-called anti- or alter-globalization movement (or simply 'AGM'). Generally, it has been extremely challenging to employ traditional modes of inquiry to the speed and ephemeral nature of the AGM, as if theory in general has not kept pace with empirical findings. And although innovations in complexity, network, systems, and transnational studies, as well as the influences of postmodernist and post-structuralist theory have met some of the challenges, a firm understanding of the AGM remains elusive. This is not only due to its breadth and complexity, but the way it in which it morphs, changes, and develops, sometimes in many seemingly contrary directions at once. The starting point for this book is that the AGM is not just an isolated aspect of contemporary affairs, but rather is indicative of world politics in general. The central argument of this book is that the univocal ontology and corresponding immanent metaphysics of the French philosopher Gilles Deleuze (1925–1995) can go considerable distance towards providing a theoretical perspective capable of accounting for the complex nature of world politics as exemplified by the AGM.

Coming out of the first decade of the twentieth century, marked by terrorism, war, as well as financial and economic failure, one might reasonably question the theoretical and political relevance of the AGM. This is particularly the case given that the esteem of the institutions of neoliberalism – the putative Other of the AGM during the 1990s – has dropped significantly in the eyes of mainstream government policy makers and the global public in general. However, the apparent demise of the Washington Consensus which, as many have pointed out, was more indicative of classical American imperialism rather than the smooth space of Empire, has once more pushed the nature of world politics towards more ambiguous, diffuse, and open-ended processes. And once again so-called 'movements from below' are gaining prominence in the political discourse, and not only through mass protest. This persists in the wide and varied transnational social movements, but perhaps more significantly, it is nowhere more striking than in the 'emerging economies', whose polities now have an enhanced and more direct connection to the world order due to enhanced political and economic capabilities and through such institutions as the G20. But even if the AGM proper were a thing of the past, there has never been an acceptable postmortem. In fact, there has been little agreement on what the AGM is or was, with some arguing as fervently as ever about its theoretical and analytical importance, and others having dismissed it out of hand long ago. The fact is, as this book and especially the first chapter will try to show, that the apparent novelty and impenetrability of the AGM has never been acceptably clarified, nor has there been any rigorous analysis of it that would please even an acceptable minority of commentators, supporters, and critics. On top of all this, engagements with the AGM, whether in the media or academia, have been rife with ideological and normative posturing, clouding any analytical insights that might be gained. In another sense, understanding the AGM is urgent in the context of this book since it is taken to be indicative of world politics – but only as one aspect of many. Others would include all manner of transnational ties, be they global epistemic communities, lines of technical transfer, or financial flows and regimes of (de-)regulation, as well as various associations of violence, such as terrorist networks, the arms trade, and additionally irregular forces and clandestine intelligence operations. In other words, given the thrust of the overall argument, one could write a different book using these other exemplary aspects of world politics. In this sense the book pays homage to what I take to be the tenor of Deleuze and Guattari's *A Thousand Plateaus* (1987), namely, treating different cases (war, psychoanalysis, linguistics, etc.) with Deleuze's unique theoretical and analytical lens. To be sure, some domains such as demographics and public opinion polling have less to gain from the nomad science presented here, but a nomad science of other 'hard realities' such as nuclear weapons, for example, would make an interesting study. Thus the AGM presents an excellent laboratory for developing novel approaches to these complex and often ambiguous phenomena.

The central argument of this book rests on the notion of difference. The act of distinguishing between two or more entities is integral to the philosophical tradition of the West, and is one of the fundamentals of scientific investigation. We say that one country is different from another in such and such a respect; that one person is different from another in so many ways. And yet such a notion of difference is highly unstable. As Deleuze argues, and as explored in this book, such difference only functions with entities locatable midway between Being and individuals. Distinguishing between large categories such as animals and minerals is not very effective with such a notion of difference; likewise distinguishing between small differences. How does one meaningfully differentiate between two individuals, say, Noam Chomsky and Michel Foucault? There is no way, in a general sense, to distinguish them as members of a large set, for there is nothing general that makes one belong more to that set ('human', for example) than the other. Risking the propagation of another neologism, one might say that Western science suffers from 'a crisis of difference'. But is any alternative available? Deleuze thinks there is and that it is found not in difference within the concept (animal A is different from animal B through difference x and y), but in the notion of difference as a concept in itself. He calls this true difference or real difference, wherein entities need not rely on other entities for their difference. Such difference differentiates itself, thus providing the foundation for a compelling and ultimately elegant theory of both stability and emergence.

The methodology proposed by this book – as emphasized in the title – hinges on the notion of science.[1] What Deleuze refers to as nomad science, as will become clear in the following chapters, is an approach that is empiricist without being positivist, post-structuralist but materialist. It is a science insofar that it has clear methodological principles, an unrelenting adherence to the dictates of logic, is parsimonious and comprehensive, and has a distinct notion of the thinker and what thinking is. On pages 361–2 of *A Thousand Plateaus* Deleuze and Guattari lay out what is involved in such a science. It is one that favours the hydraulic model over the solid, becoming over the eternal, 'curvilinear declination' over straight lines, and the problematic over the theorematic. 'Favours' here must be understood in such a way that the second term in the couplet is not rejected altogether, but that the first of the couplet is taken to be primary and ultimately determines the second. In this book I refer to this as the two-poled approach. I argue that precisely this kind of thinking – this nomad science – is particularly well suited to understanding the complexities and flows which are characteristic of world politics as exemplified by the AGM, and it does this without recourse to essence, categories of Being, or hylomorphism. With such bold claims it becomes obvious that this is no easy task, but when applied comprehensively, a nomad science addresses many of the challenges confronting contemporary social and political theory. Properly employed it amounts to no less than a challenge to some notions that form the basis of scientific investigation in the broad Western tradition. With a consistent notion of difference it dismantles the edifice of social science research, though the goal is not the latter's total destruction. What nomad science does highlight is that what is generally thought of as Western science precludes a rigorous and consistent account of contemporary world politics. From this perspective the science of Rousseau, Marx, Durkheim, or Bordieu is not, in itself, sufficient for understanding the complexity of contemporary global affairs.

The analysis in this book is admittedly theory driven. That is to say rather than focusing predominantly on protests, social fora, and indigenous movements it devotes most of its energy to the analysis of the various theoretical approaches to such phenomena and subsequently a great deal of time to Deleuze. In other words, those seeking a sociological account of the AGM derived from field research will not find it here. Instead, this book uses the AGM rather as an analytic signifier, engaging in a theory of politics rather than political theory. Any attention the AGM receives is primarily to investigate in sufficient detail the shortcomings and difficulties of contemporary socio-political theory. The reason for such theoretical depth lies in the pay-off: a deployment of Deleuze's philosophy that goes considerable distance in addressing – and perhaps overcoming – the weaknesses inherent in current scientific investigations of contemporary global affairs. But there are challenges. First, it is exceedingly difficult to unpack Deleuze in a way meaningful to a social science investigation, and there is great divergence amongst the variety of Deleuzian 'approaches' to date. Because of this, when encountering Deleuze, readers, unarmed against such theoretical variance, can often be overwhelmed by the philosophical jargon and left feeling merely inspired or worse, put off. Second, those who have indeed been introduced to Deleuze's philosophy need a certain amount of background to understand my particular reading and how I wish to employ it for the question of the AGM and world politics. This investigation will not treat Deleuze as an artefact – unchanging, originary – but rather as a living player in an unfolding drama of theory. Thus, while great attention will be paid to the works of Deleuze, some time will be spent considering his reception and the various influences from commentators such as Paul Patton, Manuel Delanda, and Constantin Boundas.

One initial question for the reader might be, why Gilles Deleuze? The answer is that he devoted most of his career which spanned more than four decades dealing with questions of change, difference, and even politics. However, despite a handful of publications addressing themes that might be of interest to researchers of social movements, IR, or international political sociology, there has been as yet no systematic study of his thought which delivers a detailed analysis of his philosophical positions pertaining to the study of world politics. Moreover there is certainly room to decouple Deleuze somewhat from general post-structuralist critique – and certainly postmodern experiments – and to apply his thought more as anti-representationalist or as in the tradition of process philosophy to the analytical problems of world politics.[2] Although this book does not put forward the thesis that the only worthwhile analytical lens through which to study the AGM is the Deleuzian one, based on the investigation of Deleuze's political ontology it will argue that Deleuze provides a comprehensive and compelling analysis of such a broad spectrum of activity such as the AGM which can offset, complement, or guide other research perspectives.

Having said all this, it is worth acknowledging the considerable amount of hesitation or inertia when making dramatic shifts in theoretical starting points. This may go some distance in explaining why a comprehensive study of this kind has not been forthcoming. It may be objected that Deleuze is too distant to be applicable, or that his critique of Western metaphysics is too radical to be of use. After all, why should one abandon the tradition of transcendence which has predominated in the West since early Christian times? Immanence is too much trouble. Why should one tolerate the complete revision of basic principles such as the subject, difference, identity, and even thinking itself? The response is quite simple: Why not immanence? Why do researchers automatically begin with transcendence, as the default mode, as it were? When we think about it, in the mode of Henri Bergson, for example, there is a strong case for beginning with immanence. The beauty of Bergson is that in very simple language he dismantles fundamental principles such as the act of perception, or the notion of number, thereby turning assumptions into prejudices. Bergson's point could be summarized thus: it is ultimately more difficult and complicated to believe in fixed entities, essences, distinct subject and objects, and transcendent principles. It is much simpler and in fact reflects human experience quite well to hold that everything subsists, becomes, changes, evolves, and fades away on an immanent field, without mediation or external organizing principle.

This book is laid out in four chapters. Chapter 1 provides a brief history of the AGM and overviews some of its manifestations, though this does not pretend to be an exhaustive empirical folder. The findings of this survey suggest that the notion of *a* or *the* AGM is extremely complex and in fact quite unstable. What one encounters are hugely varying accounts, some focusing on protests in Western capitals, others on its significance as a social movement, and still others from the perspective of a critical, emancipatory politics. Based on this discussion the chapter outlines three specific facets of world politics that are challenged by various aspects of the AGM, namely identity, hierarchy, and power. In doing so this chapter sets up the problem of trying to conceptualize much less operationalize a political phenomenon that sometimes seems to have little in the way of fixed or bounded identity, does not map easily onto institutional frameworks, and often does not aspire to traditional political goals. The chapter then analyses several approaches to social and political theory which deal explicitly with the AGM, namely global governance theory, international relations, social movement theory, Marxism, and post-Marxism. It examines the way that each approach has difficulty in accounting for power, identity, and hierarchy, and then outlines some general theoretical considerations that can be garnered from this discussion.

Chapter 2 consists of a thorough investigation of Deleuze's ontology and metaphysics as it pertains to questions of world politics. Due to the wide variety of interpretations and uses of Deleuze's thought, considerable time is spent at the beginning assessing various receptions and appropriations of his philosophy, outlining and ultimately arguing for the convergence of two main thrusts: the ascetic reading – where Deleuze is the exacting and politically indifferent philosopher – and the communitarian reading – where Deleuze is the resistance prophet of liberated minorities. Deleuze's philosophy as it pertains to the problem of the AGM in world politics is broached through Deleuze's understanding of the typical notion of difference as mentioned above. The chapter then shows how for Deleuze only a univocal ontology can support a workable notion of difference, but in order to account for the diversity of material expression a two-poled though non-dualistic metaphysics is necessary, called here the virtual and actual of the real. This allows for a general account of both continuity and change, as well as what one might call a sustainable notion of difference. Not only does this imply an innovative notion of space and time, but shifts the analytical focus from beings to what Deleuze and Guattari call assemblages (*agencements*).

From the discussion in Chapter 2, Chapters 3 and 4, in social science terms, argue against – or try to imagine a science *without* – methodological nationalism and methodological individualism, respectively. Chapter 3 investigates in some detail the major theoretical building blocks of world politics including space, time, territory, and the state. It shows how a Deleuzian reading of time and space problematize territoriality as a notion and the state as an analytic principle. But what is significant here is that the materialistic impulse of Deleuze's philosophy implies movement both towards stratified systems as well as open, ephemeral relations. The argument is that the AGM belongs, at least partially, to a politics that is spatially and temporally characterized by its relative movement towards the virtual, a general feature of contemporary global politics. The chapter then proceeds to show the extent to which Deleuze's political philosophy can combine with complexity theory in the formation of a general account of emergence, highlighting the way that Deleuze's two-poled approach offers the flexibility needed to account for complex phenomena that nevertheless often exhibit more stratified behaviour. After noting some principles, which, from both their post-structuralist and materialist credentials suggest some innovative approaches to social science research, the chapter ends by making a tentative assessment of what the AGM might be, or at least how we are to think of it in social-scientific terms.

The final chapter deals specifically with the political subject. It presents a genealogical account of the subject in the West and then proceeds to detail Deleuze's 'subjectless subjectivity'. The analysis makes particular use of Deleuze's notion of the fold and how this relates the Whole to the many, or the One to the multiple, an argument which draws on the analysis in Chapter 2. A useful comparison to post-Marxist theories of the subject is made to distinguish the two apparently similar, though in fact radically different, approaches to the subject. Finally, the consequences of such an approach are analysed and then applied to questions surrounding the AGM, noting the problematic nature of any anti-globalization political agenda. This chapter is particularly important because not only does it expose the inconsistencies of any theoretical approach that admits both systems and entities – that is, discrete entities acting within systems – but it illustrates the considerable costs involved in a rigorous reading of

Deleuze. In other words, if we are serious about adhering to the metaphysical implications of his univocal ontology, then we must jettison any baggage in the form of the autonomous self of European modernity as an unassailable assumption.

I mentioned that the analysis of this book is theory driven and perhaps overall neglects the specifics of the AGM. A comprehensive examination of the AGM would be a long study indeed, and is beyond the scope of this book. On offer here is a compelling, parsimonious (though no less dense for it), and effective approach for dealing with the AGM as an object of study. For more detail, what could be called an assemblage theory analysis of particular aspects of the AGM would be required. I leave this to future research. Additionally, although Chapter 4 does deal with political strategy in terms of the subject, there is little in this book on the normative aspects of the AGM, nor of the damaging effects of the processes of neoliberal globalization against which it putatively struggles. Indeed, one of the points of this book is that a nomad science precludes any moral considerations, though as we shall see this does not mean that it is value free.

This book is for people interested in Deleuze in social science research, especially in empirically-grounded analysis. More specifically it is written for those who would like to use Deleuze in IR, or who deal with theoretical and methodological issues for which Deleuze as laid out here might be of some help. It would be of interest to those social science scholars – especially in politics and IR – interested in Deleuze, systems, and complexity, and to the burgeoning Deleuze readership. It is particularly suited for those researchers who have a genuine curiosity about Deleuze (especially those interested in empirical questions or research methodologies) but are put off by the way in which so much written on Deleuze does more to 'fascinate' and 'mystify' than to deliver theoretical and analytical insights. Indeed, one of the main aspirations of this book is to normalize or 'deradicalize' Deleuze's thought. Deleuze's philosophy is admittedly complicated and technical but it can actually 'feel' natural because of – and not despite – his fundamental commitment to a univocal ontology. With this in mind the following investigation marks but one step towards a more comprehensive understanding of world politics. Finally – and this is part of the charm of Deleuze's philosophy – although it levels a bold challenge to 2,500 years of Western philosophy, it does not necessarily rubbish or dismiss the latter. It is, rather, a form of supertheory that can be useful in mapping the role of other theories for the study of world politics, as well the lines of flight of which world politics consists.

1 World politics and the AGM

A challenge to theory

The study of political theory during the early part of the post-Cold War period was steeped in anticipation about what the new world order would look like in the absence of a bipolar system of power. From a variety of theoretical backgrounds, offerings were put forward about how best to understand this new era, ranging from the clash of civilizations (Huntington 1993), to the end of history (Fukuyama 1992), to globalization (Robertson 1992), to postmodernism (for example Der Derian and Shapiro 1989), which seemed to find a new lease on life. None of these perspectives, predictably, turned out to be without problems, and it seemed that each had difficulty capturing a political field that now included a whole host of increasingly important non-state actors such as non-governmental organizations (NGOs), transnational corporations (TNCs), and institutions such as the World Trade Organization (WTO). To be sure such actors had always played a role in world politics in one way or another, but now they seemed to take on enormous relevance. To address this hyper-expansion of the number and role of political agents by the middle of the 1990s, further advances were made in the application and development of such approaches as network theory (Castells 1996), complexity studies (Eve *et al.* 1997), and global governance (Held 1995) in the social sciences in general and the study of world politics in particular.

Towards the end of the 1990s, however, a still more novel phenomenon appeared in the form of new socio-political experiments and massive and often worldwide protests against some of these global institutions and corporations or the countries which supported their policies. Taken collectively, these came to be known as the anti- or alter-globalization movement (AGM). Since that time there has been an enormous amount of literature on the subject, and some innovative and promising attempts to tie the nature of these political expressions and events to a plausible theoretical vision of world politics, such as Hardt and Negri's *Empire* (2000). But by and large – as this chapter will argue – the main theoretical approaches which deal with the AGM have proven problematic in a number of ways. Just as Huntington's clash of civilizations theory was of little use when addressing the nature of local conditions which turned out to be crucial if not determining factors in world politics, it seems that to date theories of world politics are poorly suited to addressing what for now we will call the new forms of political activity, subjectivity, and organization as expressed by the AGM.

This can be linked to two general observations about global political action today, shared over a very wide field of literature and also among many disciplines. The first is the formation of regimes of political power that operate outside traditional, twentieth century, Western models of national politics. This has been roughly encapsulated in concepts such as transnationalism, Appadurai's different 'scapes' (1990), global governance, neo-medievalism, and is considered to be tightly linked to processes of globalization. Criticisms that the actual nature of globalization is unclear and its value as an analytical tool uncertain (see Rosenberg 2005) notwithstanding, the upshot of these observations is that political subjects (individuals and groups) find themselves in a patchwork or web of political connections rather than stable, bounded political containers such as the state. The second related observation is the emphasis on the individual, both as a political unit and an analytical starting point, which finds some of its strongest expression in the work of Giddens (1991) and Beck and Beck-Gernheim (2002). The implication here is that rather than relying on representatives to negotiate their way through political processes of ever-increasing complexity, political subjects or, rather, individuals, rely increasingly on direct action and participation. This results in a surge of social movement participation (Rucht 1999: 215), for example. In terms of the AGM, this has meant some rather new features. One is a sense of power which goes beyond traditional conceptions, tending to ignore and thereby defuse or fracture state power, and indeed a distinct sense that many facets of the AGM are explicitly anti-power, forgoing political platforms and manifestos. Furthermore this double process of global power diffusion and individuation has been accompanied by a rejection of identity politics and the introduction of new notions of difference and diversity. Finally, new organizational or, perhaps better, disorganizational forms are a crucial part of the AGM. Beyond just network connections, aspects of the AGM strive for a completely horizontal politics, that is, one without hierarchy or leadership. Now, all three of these aspects must be understood as theoretical directions which, in different ways and to different extents, are being experimented with by various participants in the AGM. As such they are ideal components or characteristics of a putatively new kind of politics. Despite the fact that they may not be expressed in any pure form (although as we will see in Chapter 3, it is very difficult to find any political patterns in pure form) they nevertheless must be addressed by any competent theory of world politics.

Without making any overall epistemological or ontological claims at this point, the position of this book is that any attempt to understand world politics today must come to terms with these aspects of the AGM: power, identity, and organization. This chapter will consider a broad range of such attempts, but there are a number of research fields that through an extensive body of literature seem particularly pertinent to the examination of the AGM. These include global governance, international relations (IR), social movement theory, Marxism, and post-Marxism. The aim of the second half of this chapter will be to distil the problems and challenges these approaches to world politics face in their account of the AGM. But first, what can be said of the AGM? What is it?

The first thing of note is that the AGM has been, until relatively recently, a largely unexplored phenomenon. What slowly began to draw attention in the mid-1990s became a more urgent field of inquiry after mainstream media in the West took interest in events of the late 1990s, such as the well-known and somewhat iconic 'Battle of Seattle'. As the twenty-first century began, researchers, both affiliated and independent, including journalists, academics, and activists, took to examining the AGM with increasingly rigorous scrutiny, moving beyond broad claims to specific analyses of more familiar socio-political aspects. In other words the AGM as an object of inquiry became integrated into mainstream scientific discourse. Of course conclusions have been by no means universally positive nor optimistic; in fact many are dismissive. There are many good reasons for this, including a healthy dose of cynicism towards the AGM's political significance and novelty. And yet another reason, as this chapter will show, results from a number of analytical problems that researchers encounter when looking at the AGM. The elephant and the blind man analogy so frequently rolled out to describe various approaches to globalization would also seem to apply to anti- and alter-globalizations: any given analysis or assessment is always dependent on the approach taken by the researcher as well as on the criteria for 'measuring it'.

There are a number of factors that make the AGM an important as well as interesting object of academic study. First, it represents an important component of contemporary global politics. It is certainly possible to raise or lower this relevance based on one's particular perspective or means of assessment, but it would be difficult to deny that the AGM has decisively affected global political events, one of the classic examples being the decision to cancel the G8 meeting in Seattle in 1999 and the resulting trend towards making subsequent meetings inaccessible to everyday citizens (Tyler 2003). Looked at from a broader perspective, the effects of the AGM globally have been significant. As reckoned by Bruce Podobnik, as of 2005 the effects of the AGM include the following:

> at least eight governments have been overthrown due entirely or in part to pressures exerted by grassroots campaigns. In 70 other instances, moderate to severe political crises have been created by these protests – and many government officials have been forced to resign their offices. Meanwhile, in over 50 cases IMF [International Monetary Fund] austerity programmes and World Bank projects have been cancelled, delayed, or revised because of mobilizations. And at least 24 global summits/trade meetings have been significantly disrupted.
>
> (cited in Mac Sheoin 2007: 108)

Although arguably G8 disruptions have little effect on the general political trends within global regimes of capital, power, and knowledge, the symbolic effects have done much to underscore the difference between the decision makers and those who must abide by their decisions, as well as to unify and focus the movement. In any case the goal at the outset of this chapter is not to define the AGM; it does not fundamentally matter at this point whether it is a political space, a media device, an inspiration, or a laboratory where new practices can be worked out. The question here is to overview some of the key aspects and events in the history of the AGM and to delineate some observations about how it functions, and perhaps some of the directions it might be going in terms of political participation and action. For now, this book is not primarily interested in what it does, in terms of effects, or how successful it is (how much power/significance it has). It suffices that it does effect political change to some extent; in other words it qualifies as what is traditionally known as 'an actor'. Rather than wondering about success, efficacy or even its practical significance for global politics, the question for this book is rather different: what does the AGM tell us about contemporary world politics and especially what demands does it make on theorizations of the political?

The second important aspect that makes the AGM a worthwhile object of study is that it is a new phenomenon. This is not to diminish the significance of social movements over the last centuries, and especially during the last 40 years, but saying that the AGM is a new phenomenon highlights not only its global connectivity but also new patterns of organization and communication which will be discussed below. The mere fact that something called the AGM *is* an object of inquiry makes it novel. Third, the AGM is important because it is part of what is known more generally as global civil society. This is one of the most topical objects of interest among those who argue for change to the current global system. Such change comes in various forms, from global development (both in theory and practice) to the reinjection of accountability into politics through some as-of-yet undetermined new global political regime. Thus the AGM becomes increasingly relevant to researchers across a variety of fields and raises a number of questions. Does it in fact represent new forms of political organization? Can we find in the AGM any political principles or lessons that might illuminate contemporary political practice? Is it possible to distil any conceptual, analytical, or organizational models from it?

Finally, in addition to these questions the main reason for studying the AGM is sheer academic interest. As yet there is no theoretical approach which puts global activism in the context of world politics (Olesen 2005: 110), and as Martin Weber argues: 'the analytical lenses deployed in the globalization literature for dealing with non-state actors' – such as "alter-globalists" – role in changing world order fail to adequately grasp the qualitative difference of the politics of the "alter-globalization"' (2005: 191). In another one of many examples, Peter Waterman describes this kind of activity as having 'a growing political presence and impact as the twentieth century draws to a close, but has been subject to little strategic reflection and has as yet little or no theoretical status' (1998: 4). If we are to understand the political practice of the future, the AGM surely stands out as an excellent research laboratory.

The arrival of the AGM on the global stage

In the broadest sense, the AGM is the result of the perception that the project of economic liberalization, applied globally with increasing zeal since the 1980s, has not delivered on its supposed promise of benefit for all, and the seeming inability of any governing body, whether local (municipalities), regional, national, supranational (EU), or international (UN), to remedy or even to mitigate to any meaningful extent the detriments that this liberalization has caused. When considering sites of resistance or contention, many in the media and academia point to the often high-profile protest events that tend to follow global finance and trade talks. However, a nuanced approach reveals that the AGM is much more than this and includes various kinds of meetings, direct action, social fora, and a multitude of other activities that generally escape the attention of all but the most committed activists.

One of the key events in the emergence of the AGM cited in the literature is the International Encounter for Humanity and Against Neoliberalism which took place in Chiapas, Mexico in August 1996. People from over 50 countries developed the Second Declaration of La Realidad, a vision for an 'intercontinental network of resistance'. One of its statements was: 'This intercontinental network of alternative communication is not an organizing structure, nor has a central head or decision maker, nor does it have a central command or hierarchies. We are the network, all of us who speak and listen.' (1996). Although encounters such as this did not garner the attention of mainstream media outlets nor globalization theorists, Naomi Klein notes

> many who attended the first *encuentros* went on to play key roles in the protests against the World Trade Organization in Seattle and the World Bank and IMF in Washington, DC, arriving with a new taste for direct action, for collective decision-making and decentralized organizing.
>
> (2002a: 96)

Such encounters certainly influenced the Ya Basta! movements in Europe in the late 1990s. Also significant was the formation of the People's Global Action (PGA) in Geneva in February, 1998. This is an explicitly non-reformist, anti-neoliberal worldwide network of 'all those who fight the destruction of humanity and the planet by capitalism and build local alternatives to globalisation' (2001). It was attended by trade unions, an Indian farmers' league (the KRSS), Maori representatives, the Brazilian Landless Workers Movement (MST), various anarchist groups and, the only North American showing, the Canadian Postal Workers Union. What is remarkable here is that the PGA 'is not an organisation and has no members' (People's Global Action 2001).

Some also see the precursors of the AGM in the mobilizations in the mid-1990s in countries such as France and South Korea against neoliberal reforms carried out by those governments. What marks these protests as different from, for example, labour unrest of the past was the recognition that although the targets were nations, the problems and structures were very much seen as global, and moreover, that the solidarity between varied and geographically distant protests was significantly high. As many point out, this global consciousness or awareness is what marks the AGM as a new phenomenon: not just against imperialism or global working conditions, but as against a specific form of global political ordering. This is dramatically different from former struggles which tended to be incommunicable. The latter were localized and issue specific,[1] and as few groups recognized the relevance of other groups, desires and needs could not be translated into different contexts, and thus no global network of revolt was effected (see Dirlik 1994: 83; Hardt and Negri 2000: 54). Gareth Dale illustrates this difference nicely: 'Imagine if, a generation ago, the Campaign for Nuclear Disarmament, Solidarność, the Sandinistas, the Kwangju Uprising and the German Greens had all been widely perceived as belonging to a single movement family' (2001: 369).

More familiar to academics and especially journalists are the number of globally coordinated protests that began towards the end of the 1990s. These were largely targeted at global financial and trade institutions and organizations, and in terms of numbers were mostly attended by what has come to be known as 'summit hoppers' – white, middle-class twenty-somethings (Day 2004: 728). J18 (18 June 1999) was one of the first major globally coordinated protests. This took place mainly in European and North American cities in response to the G7 economic summit in Cologne, Germany. However, perhaps most well known is the (so-called) 'Battle of Seattle' in November–December 1999 where approximately 50,000 people played a role – there were other, inherent problems with the talks themselves – in the disruption of many high-profile and key aspects of WTO ministerial meetings. As a direct result of the protests, opening ceremonies were cancelled and ultimately no joint communiqué was released at the end of the talks. Many commentators were impressed by the spontaneity (Chesters and Welsh 2005: 201) and newness (Brown and Szeman 2002: 185) that characterized the organization of the diverse groups of demonstrators. In February of the following year the World Economic Forum (WEF) gained notoriety when thousands protested in sometimes violent clashes with seemingly unprepared Swiss police in Davos. Following these were the protests against the IMF in Washington, the Asian Development Bank in Chiang Mai, the WEF in Melbourne, and then in the autumn of 2000 the IMF and World Bank in Prague. The protest in Genoa gained notoriety for the death of one activist, but it should be noted that despite more recent interest in protest-related deaths (Myanmar in 2007, for example), the deaths of protesters in non-Western countries go largely unnoticed, particularly by mainstream media.

But more recently the cycle of mass protests has slowed considerably, at least in Western democracies. There are several possible reasons for this. First, the movement's relative lack of enthusiasm may be due to 'protest fatigue' or a clear agenda, as is charged by some. Most proponents, however, argue that ever-heightened security, especially after the attacks on the US on 11 September 2001, has made access to global meetings all but impossible. Moreover, one gets the impression that many protesters exhibit self-restraint, either through solidarity with the victims of terrorist bombings in Western capitals or through fear of a crackdown by those governments. Additionally, a certain amount of 'media fatigue' may have contributed to the movement's lower profile. Finally, a significant shift to anti-war/anti-imperialism seemed to cast doubt on the significance and meaning of a more general anti-globalism position. The heady days of the coincidence of the publication of Hardt and Negri's *Empire* (2000) with a multitude of protests gave way to the second Iraq war and charges that classical imperialism in the form of American hegemony, rather than smooth globalism with its neoliberal face, best describes the opponent of the Left.[2]

Many argue that the movement is far from dead, though that it has broadened its scope somewhat, and in general there is a perception that the AGM has moved on from the first, formative phase and is now in the process of developing a means of moving forward. One can read this as evidence that the AGM has moved away from more conflictual, spontaneous gatherings (anti-) to more productive, positive gatherings (alter-), and that this latter represents some sort of 'organizational' phase. This brings us to another significant stage in the development of the AGM, the World Social Forum (WSF). It is interesting to note in the literature a distinction between those who focus on (often exclusively) direct action protest and those who also include more creative, productive encounters such as social fora – and this seems not to be determined by any degree of radicality or political view. From the perspective of this book, however, it does signal a need for a political ontology that can accommodate both protest/resistance *and* alternative practices and everyday politics.

Coinciding with the World Economic Forum meeting in New York, the first WSF took place in 2001 in Porto Alegre, Brazil, a city already known for its progressive community initiatives such as participatory budget assemblies. Although the first WSFs were initially characterized by the participation of groups and individuals from South America and Europe, the moves to Mumbai in 2004 and Nairobi in 2007 represent attempts to make these encounters more globally representative. There is even the notion that the WSF is a further step in a sort of progressive development of the AGM, the middle step in a spontaneous protest–organization–democratization series. This would entail coming up with an increasingly political platform – or declarations of demands – rather than merely a space in which to experiment with alternative forms of expression and collaboration. For some, this means essentially devolving into a species of global political party and is for this reason rejected by many participants on theoretical grounds (see Robinson and Tormey 2005: 225). Apart from this it might be said that social fora have to date had little mass impact in terms of political, cultural, social, and economic life. However, at present this activity is generally seen as an exploration of and experimentation with new forms of life and relations, and has more to do with critical mass than raw political impact.

At a fundamental level theorists have had difficulty defining the AGM because it encompasses so many diverse elements with seemingly different aims. These elements include, but are not limited to, feminists, women's groups, anarchists, labour activists and trade unions, farmers, mothers, local ecologists, hunters, consumer advocacy groups, charitable foundations, relief organizations, and doctors. Moreover, the geographical, cultural and linguistic field over which it is spread complicates matters even further.[3] In attempting to describe the nature of these elements there is, again, considerable difficulty: in general all are part of what is loosely called global civil society, that is, a loose body of NGOs, informal transnational networks, and social movements. Although such a general view is seen as promising in a progressive political sense (He and Murphy 2007), many see it as problematic (Etzioni 2004: 343). Whatever its merit in this sense, the term global civil society must be reserved as a much broader term than the AGM, as civil society – that is, non-state, non-market actors – include all manner of private groups such as corporate lobbyists, community groups with no particular political agenda (for example, model aeroplane enthusiasts), as well as criminal organizations which tend to have narrow or non-commutable interests defined in financial terms. Jan Aarte Scholte, in his 'Cautionary Reflections on Seattle', offers a compelling argument that in general global civil society favours the status quo (2000: 119). However, more than highlighting the lack of effectiveness of the AGM, this only underlines a weakness of the notion of global civil society in general. Moreover, it is important to note that although NGOs are an important component of the AGM in the sense of a global network, and as a distinct part of global civil society feature prominently in global governance research, to the extent that they are hierarchical, externally funded organizations they represent a more liberal, ossified, and reformist aspect of the AGM. Indeed, they are often seen, especially at the WSF or by grassroots activists, as getting in the way of progressive politics due to their top-down nature and often Western-backed financial structure.

In addition to some of the more high-profile groups that could readily be considered part of the AGM such as Direct Action Network, Reclaim the Streets, and ATTAC (Association pour une Taxation des Transactions Financières pour l'Aide aux Citoyens), the everyday nature of the AGM must also be acknowledged. What this means is that much of the actual activism, interest, and critical mass is added not by groups or semi-organized networks but by mobilized individuals who participate on an ad hoc or issue-centred basis. These individuals act out their political beliefs through social centres, squatting, the creation of independent media organizations such as Indymedia, and unaffiliated yet conjoined protests across a range of issues from animal rights to welfare reform to the protection of immigrants and asylum seekers (Scholte 2000: 346). As Anita Lacey notes, 'The protest spaces generated by global anti-capital activists are fluid and open; signed-up, paid-up membership is not required to participate' (2005a: 415). Thus, with at least this freely associative aspect of the AGM, there is no description or criteria of who these concerned individuals are. They can be peasants, students, workers, professionals, indeed anyone who lends their support and voice, in however small a manner. In its contrast to identity-based politics (see Klein 2000: 109), this important aspect of the AGM overlaps with more traditional community-based concerns and forms of peaceful protest.

Since there is no central organization of the AGM as such, there are no definable strategic objectives or tactics. However, one can make a few general observations. In doing so it is useful to distinguish between the anti- (protest) and alter- aspects of the AGM. In the former case perhaps the first general strategy is visibility. In a struggle that is at least partly dependent on publicity, the activities of the AGM must be attention-grabbing and newsworthy (Indymedia 2005). Of course there is a certain amount of cynicism in appealing to mainstream media which are often heavily criticized by AGM activists, but nevertheless, despite George Monbiot's somewhat ironic remark (given that he is often denounced as a liberal 'inroader') that the movement no longer needs mainstream media since it has its own (2003), it is the urgency of global public awareness which is often the deciding factor in pressuring or shaming governments and corporations into action. Indeed, a great deal of activity on this front is in the form of consumer activism, viewed by some as a legitimate and effective political strategy in attaining social justice (see Micheletti 2003). A second tactic, which can also be viewed as a principle, is non-violence. Although most groups and alliances involved in protests condemn violence and the destruction of property as the actions of fringe and particularly conservative groups, and invest considerable effort in ensuring peaceful action, a number of key protests have been marked by violence of one sort or another. Although the debates surrounding the nature of the violence and who is typically involved is beyond the scope of this brief overview, it should be noted that despite the real anger and animosity many participants feel towards police and security forces, generally the mantra of peaceful protest is universally adopted.

One of the ways this expresses itself is through the tactic of subversion. In order to destabilize, de-centre, or disrupt typical roles, relationships, and interpretations, protesters and activists sometimes rely on irony and humour. This could involve, for example, costumed 'counter-police' meeting a line of riot shields with garlands of flowers. And of course perhaps one of the most general campaigns is that of the Media Foundation[4] which uses humour and satire to subvert media messages and corporate advertising ('culture jamming'). Another tactic involves performative attempts to redefine space. In terms of protest this can be seen as a new language of civil disobedience involving street theatre ('guerrilla theatre') and parody. This explains why AGM activities often have what observers describe as a carnival atmosphere wherein what are normally antagonistic spaces of resistance become dynamic spaces of expression. The goal of these spaces tends to be creation and openness as opposed to confrontation via fixed messages and demands. The question remains open as to whether this is merely media attention grabbing or the dismantling of hegemonic discourses, but despite criticisms of the ineffectualness of such tactics (and how it in fact plays directly into existing power structures), the aims remain significant. Lacey describes the two key characteristics of the AGM over the last two decades as such: 'On-going experimentation with rhizomatic, or open-ended and non-hierarchical, forms of organization and with self-production and distribution of media' (2005a: 408). In using terms like 'rhizomatic' this certainly prefigures the discussion of Deleuze and complexity in the chapters to come, but for now we can note strategies which differ considerably from tactics of past moments of peaceful protest and political resistance.

Turning to the more 'alter-' aspects of the AGM, participants tend to stress the themes of openness and non-hierarchical structures or free association. This includes deliberative democratic methods (isocracy, consensus building), the rejection of leadership, as well as inclusiveness or the celebration of diversity. At a local level such kinds of activity can be found at social centres: spaces kept free, generally in urban areas, for any number of activities or social and housing programmes (see Chatterton and Hodkinson 2006), they are distinct from 'community centres' run by government as well as from those organized by NGOs. Although it is difficult to generalize on their purposes and aims, one can roughly characterize them as being not-for-profit, strictly autonomous, without organized leadership, and sustained through voluntary work. Also significant is the fact that through meetings, exchange and support, social centres – along with zines and info shops – furnish the possibility of AGM networking activities that do not rely on the Internet (see Lacey 2005b). But perhaps one of the most interesting developments, from the view of world politics, is the WSF. From its Charter of Principles (WSF 2001) we can note the following points:

- The move from a moment in time and space to a world process.
- Brings together and interlinks, does not represent.
- No 'decisions' are taken as a body, thus
- No one can claim to express the views of the participants.
- Non-hierarchical; interrelates organizations.
- Upholds participatory democracy, equality, solidarity; condemns domination and subjugation.
- Values exchange among participants.
- Non-violent resistance.

Naturally the reality of these tactics and principles remains hotly debated, with some critical of de facto power structures. Additionally, the effectiveness of decision-making through consensus remains problematic,[5] with some arguing that such an overly cumbersome process only actually works when outcomes are decided during behind-the-scenes negotiation by what amounts to a ruling elite (Callinicos 2003: 100).

In terms of technology, the Internet and mobile communications obviously offer considerable networking possibilities. They also allow for real-time mobilization in the case of street protests, without formal hierarchies, central command, or cumbersome bureaucracies. Perhaps most importantly, information dissemination on the Internet raises the awareness of issues and the sophistication of understanding as well as heightening solidarity. In other words, a wide range of potential participants can cheaply and easily access general information that can awaken, enhance or justify political positions, feelings, and intuitions. One must no longer devote one's life to the research of obscure, inaccessible, and difficult texts to arrive at a more or less theoretically rigorous ideological or ethical position.

Media coverage has played a large role in the development of the AGM with continuing debates regarding mainstream outlets' role in and portrayal of mass protests and their almost universal lack of interest in world or regional social fora. An important stage in this development was the emergence of Independent Media Centres (IMCs).

> IMCs aim to combat corporate concentration in media ownership through the creation of alternative sources of information, and in so doing to participate directly in the negation and reconstruction of mass-mediated realities. Not only is each centre independent from the corporate world, it is also independent from the other centres – there is no hub that disseminates a particular editorial line, and on some parts of some sites, there is no editorial line at all. Each centre tends to be driven by the interests and resources of the local communities it serves, thus building a high degree of differentiation into the system at its most basic level.
>
> (Day 2004: 731)

Despite counterclaims of isomorphism amongst these supposedly autonomous centres, such technological possibilities highlight the novelty of the AGM. Also important from an early date were cyber-protests. For example, during J18 there were more than 10,000 cyber attacks against the computer systems of large corporations (Steger 2005: 128).

In general the literature on the technical aspects of the AGM tends towards two extremes. On the one hand there are those who focus on the technological aspects, basically treating global public protest as a technological phenomenon. There seems to be some justification for this, as the current state of coordinated and/or networked global political resistance operates or functions largely through technological media such as IMCs, email lists, as well as networking sites such as Facebook and more recently Twitter. On the other hand there is a sense in which the AGM is not entirely dependent on technology for existence. Many commentators and researchers of the AGM emphasize the importance of face-to-face encounters in sustaining the AGM. Just as in business or formal, organized politics, there seems to be no substitute for showing up, sitting in a room with someone, and exchanging ideas. Thus, generally speaking one should assume that an abundance of digital media technology is the sufficient, but not necessary, cause of the AGM. Additionally it is worth remembering that the AGM's over-reliance on technological means – especially in terms of protest – need not translate into effectiveness since potential adversaries (largely state security apparatuses) also deploy technologies to their advantage in the form of data sharing, video surveillance, e-monitoring and astroturfing.

But what are the putative aims of the AGM? It is naturally difficult to get a clear impression of the aims of such a heterogeneous movement such as the AGM. At the global organization level, the aims are presented typically as manifestos. The goals of the high-profile network ATTAC are to safeguard democratic control from the Right by seizing power from financial institutions. Generally this means 'to re-conquer space lost by democracy to the sphere of finance, to oppose any new abandonment of national sovereignty on the pretext of the "rights" of investors and merchants', and 'to create a democratic space at the global level' (ATTAC 1998). The WSF, as noted above, is currently going through some growing pains since the publication of nine general objectives for WSF 2007 (2006). This publication can be read in contradiction to the *World Social Forum Charter of Principles*, specifically article five which reads: 'The World Social Forum brings together and interlinks only organizations and movements of civil society from all the countries in the world, but it does not intend to be a body representing world civil society' (WSF 2001). The question then for activists and organizers/facilitators is this: Should the WSF remain strictly as a space for encounters or should it be 'allowed' to evolve into some sort of a political organization (see for example Patomäki and Teivainen 2004: 146)? What is striking is that the debate is not about what the principles of the WSF should be, but rather if it should have any principles at all.

What this points to is a critical difference between the aims and the means of the AGM. Many argue that its methods are its goal: horizontal organization resulting in more democratic forms of political, social, cultural, and economic coexistence (see for example Holloway 1998; Marcos 2001; Eschle and Stammers 2004; Tormey 2005a). It 'is less about seizing state power than about exposing, delegitimizing and dismantling mechanisms of rule while winning ever-larger spaces of autonomy from it.' (Gaerber 2002: 68). According to Naomi Klein, the participants in the AGM do not want to take over the state, 'they want less state power over their lives ... their goal is not to win control, but to seize and build autonomous spaces where democracy, liberty, and justice can thrive.' Sweeping generalizations aside, this, for Klein, constitutes a revolution that makes revolution possible (2002a: 98), one that plays out especially well on the global stage as 'a network of very local initiatives, each built on direct democracy' (202–3). Of course this points to the crucial question: What does it mean to retake spaces of autonomy, to live, as much as possible, outside traditional forms of power? Moreover, how can we approach such a process theoretically?

Definitions and conceptualizations

The AGM has proven almost impossible to define or to conceptualize – and this may be, as was suggested earlier, what makes it so intellectually interesting and challenging. Although it may be difficult, as Richard Day argues, 'we need some way to talk about the resurgence of struggle that has coincided with the intensification of the global reach of capitalism and its electronic systems of exchange and surveillance' (2004: 728). Perhaps a good starting point is to briefly sketch a number of ambiguities surrounding the AGM with which one can further build some theoretical questions. First, unlike the modern territorial state with its narrow criteria and accepted institutional forms, the AGM as yet has no firm boundaries. Indeed, there is no distinct body of literature on the AGM because it scarcely has a name (unlike the term 'social movements' which neatly suggests a field of study), though suggestions include global social movement, movement of movements, global justice movement, global civil society, and globalization from below. Naturally because the phenomenon that one is trying to capture is referred to by different names, this makes for a very messy field with different overlaps and considerable non-correspondence or contradiction. For example, in addressing the transformative nature of a new global politics in an empirical sense, Eschle and Stammers, who never use the term anti-/alter-globalization movement, refer to Transnational Social Movement Organizations, or TSMOs. This at first seem promising, but then they merge these with NGOs (2004: 335, 339), a problem that overlooks many of the nuances in AGM activity as discussed in this chapter. Della Porta and Kriesi are also somewhat loose with definitions such as social movement, social movement organizations, and NGOs, listing Greenpeace, Amnesty International, and Friends of the Earth as 'transnational social movement organisations' (1999: 18). Moreover the objects of analysis or components of the AGM are very difficult to identify and locate. Although finding out what Greenpeace is or what ATTAC is striving for may not prove difficult, the proliferation of 'submerged networks' (Melucci 1985: 812) that lack a clearly defined organizational structure and thus a presence in media or academia often foil attempts to take stock of the field.

Additionally, it is important to remember that many activists themselves reject various designations. Most do not like the term anti-globalization in particular, as they feel they are not anti-globalization, in the sense of being against a global intensification of all kinds of connections, at all. In fact, finding activists who oppose transnational exchange and interaction would be difficult. On the other hand, although the subtitle to a book derived from the first World Social Forum in 2001 reads *Popular Alternatives to Globalization at the World Social Forum* (Fisher and Ponniah 2003), the authors in this volume are almost universally anti-globalization. They explicitly treat globalization itself as a neoliberal process that has gone wrong and to which they juxtapose their own views and prescriptions as a diverse field of remedies. Thus it seems that the debate on the anti-globalization aspect of the contemporary phenomenon is far from over. Another ambiguity concerns capitalism. On the one hand inscribing the global political phenomena described here as anti-capitalist makes considerable sense, as many of the sites of resistance concern issues directly related to the control of global capital. The problem with this, of course, is that views on capitalism expressed by various aspects of the AGM – in Seattle, at any number of World Social Fora or other gatherings, for example – are rather blurred: in addition to an uncompromising anti-capitalist stance, they include more explicitly reformist perspectives such as expressed by various Green parties. Such distinctions go from practice to theory. Richard Falk argues that globalization-from-below advocates want good globalization – which, as he specifically points out, means good capitalism (2005: 127). This would seem to suggest that the AGM is, in principle, in favour of capitalism as a way of ordering global relations. Thus how to account for and include this aspect of the AGM which is not anti-capitalist per se is a much debated topic,[6] and such claims are further complicated by more traditional Marxist perspectives that see capital relations as the key battleground in global resistance. Within this latter perspective alone Alex Callinicos, showing characteristic analytical clarity, distinguishes between six kinds of anti-capitalism: reactionary (romance/traditionalist); bourgeois; localist (decentralized market economy/fair trade); reformist (state regulators); autonomist (Hardt and Negri adherents, Zapatistas, Klein-ites); and socialists (Trotskyists, etc.) (2003: 53). On the other hand, these arguments obscure the fact that for many, the issues involved go beyond economic disparities: they have to do with culture, identity, ideology, and democracy in general. What this shows above all is the incredible diversity within the AGM in terms of political-philosophical positions, historical and cultural backgrounds, as well as the broad spectrum of political perspectives, from the far right through to liberals, leftists, socialists, and finally anarchists. Such labelling problems pose challenges for coherent theorizing, revealing the need for a broader (and deeper) theoretical conception rather than just a heteronomy of categorical characteristics.

One major distinction that cuts across many fields is that between the Global North and the Global South. As Day points out, when the AGM is seen as 'nothing more than a violent clash between protesters and police, the only thing special about Seattle was that it happened where it did' (Day 2005: 3). The point here is that such clashes in the Global South go largely unnoticed by Western academics and media. If, as Klein suggests, globalization as it is known today is merely a continuation of a much longer process (500 years) of 'colonisation, centralisation, and a loss of self-determination' (2002b: 200), then resistance to such a process did not start with Western student activism in the 1960s. As many have noted, international solidarity in the past has been characterized by the exporting of Western models or organization to other parts of the world. Significant here is that many believe the opposite is now taking place. As Gaerber notes, 'Many, perhaps most, of the movement's signature techniques – including mass nonviolent civil disobedience itself – were first developed in the global South. In the long run, this may well prove the single most radical thing about it' (2002: 65–6).

Additionally, by some definitions it would be possible to include right- wing and terrorist networks within the AGM,[7] and indeed, separating right-wing movements out of the AGM is somewhat difficult for there are certainly right-wing movements that share common characteristics such as individual participation, limited hierarchy, anti-power, and greater calls for democracy. The network connections of far right groups in Europe as well as the recent Tea Party movement in the US are examples of this. More interesting still is the fact that some commentators slide or blur the Left into the Right, posing considerable conceptual problems. For example, most activists would not want to be associated with an organization such as Le Front National; just as most activists would probably resist placing Hugo Chávez on the Right, or at least object to such pigeon-holing

– but Steger, for example, does so very decisively (2005: 106ff.). This forces the dialogue to the question of whether one needs to draw a line and *not* include within the AGM nationalists and supporters of localizing alternatives such as Walden Bello, the director of Focus on the Global South. Furthermore there is the question of indigenous and secessionist movements: could or should First Nations organizations in North America or ETA (Euskadi Ta Askatasuna or '*Basque Homeland and Freedom*') be considered in some way part of the AGM?

Meghnad Desai and Yahia Said clearly distinguish between an isolationist and alternative stance to anti-capitalism[8] but this complicates matters considerably (apart from the fact that they assume the anti-capitalist aspect). According to them, the former (isolationists), the only openly anti-globalization civil society response, include groups like Friends of the Earth (an environmental group), Focus on the Global South (a think tank), Global Exchange (an advocacy network), the MST, individuals such as Bello and Noam Chomsky, as well as publications such as *Le Monde Diplomatique*. The latter (alternative) includes all the various forms of street protest, Zapatistas (the indigenous movement of the Chiapas region in Mexico), Adbusters (an alternative culture network), and 'submerged networks which come to the fore only around certain campaigns or exercise resistance through a particular lifestyle' (2001: 65). Such distinctions, however, overlook an important aspect of global political action as they fail to take into account the effects of individualization to any extent – which in terms of everyday politics or 'ephemeral tribes' is an important part of the AGM in particular and contemporary politics in general. The activities of the vast majority of the 'supporters' of these groups (excepting of course Chomsky and Bello, although in a sense they have become 'groups' in themselves) are occasional and sporadic, whereas Desai and Said take these more or less well-defined groups to be made up of card-carrying members. On the contrary, an individual's sometime support of Friends of the Earth (whether through volunteering, giving money, or just showing up), for example, in the context of the AGM, must be seen as a significant political act, not to mention attending an anti-war rally. As this brief overview shows, although to be sure there are substantial differences amongst all these aspects of the AGM, there is reason to remain hesitant about such binaries. First, looking at the writings of the groups themselves there is no reason to conclude that such conceptual distinctions exists – for example, following various definitions, many of the Zapatistas' work must be seen as isolationist in addition to alternative (indeed, this movement is sometimes criticized precisely for this reason). Second, they share much in common, for example, the identification of the status quo as the biggest obstacle to human and environmental betterment. Third, the background, motivation, and position of many of the 'isolationist' groups is too complex for one simple label. Finally, many of the shades of isolationism can easily be merged with, or simply be called, alternative. Alberto Melucci goes some distance to addressing this problem by focussing on means, maintaining that collective action phenomena can entail both conflict (demonstration) and consensus (a peaceful march of football enthusiasts after the match) (1989: 28). In terms of the present research this highlights both the anti- and the alter-; both the reactive and creative. It remains an open question – the question this book poses – as to a theory capable of accounting for this double aspect.

Returning briefly to violence, placing violent protest and sabotage/terrorism as one of the activities of anti-/alter- globalization is surely problematic as most who participate in, support, or have an affinity for the AGM distance themselves from such strategies. Nevertheless violent activities are not part of the AGM only to the extent to which they are denounced by other participants. This in itself is problematic, for although it excludes certain forms of non-state violence, there are many examples which serve to associate the AGM with violence such as The Battle of Seattle, eco-terrorism, as well as the Zapatista uprising. Looking to the long history of political revolution, ideology, and violence it is no surprise that some in the AGM see violence as inevitable and its renunciation as playing into the asymmetrical power relationship of neoliberal organizations whose own use of 'legitimate' violence is based on what are seen as highly contestable premises. On the other hand, planned, targeted, systemic violence is seen as being on the margins or excluded from the AGM, but as with any basic definition of the AGM, there is no easy categories and certainly little consensus.

In the face of this confusion a pertinent question is why retain the term AGM at all? As has been mentioned, there are several other possibilities such as the 'global justice movement' or 'the movement of movements'. The danger with the former term, as will be discussed at greater length in Chapter 4, is that this drives the discussion towards an articulated concept of social justice. Such concepts, however beneficial in an ideational or normative sense, suffer, as we shall see later, from considerably theoretical deficits, namely that there already are many codified forms of social justice such as human rights regimes, the implementation and enforceability of which are extremely problematic as well as controversial. At the same time such moves for social justice suggest a totalizing form, which in itself runs intellectually contrary to many participants in the AGM. As a term, 'the movement of movements' is more neutral, but suffers first from its ambiguous and apolitical overtones, and second through its commitment to a specific form of socio-political enquiry, namely social movement theory. This branch of theory is informative in many ways but the accompanying restrictions that go along with social movements research, as will be shown below, fail to encompass the AGM as a global phenomenon. The term anti-globalization retains both the political rejection of neoliberal globalization and highlights the notion of struggle and contention, but suffers from the suggestion of reform or localization, or that politically the only question is how to reshape the processes of global capitalism. Combining 'anti-' with the 'alter-' (the terribly cumbersome 'anti-/alter-globalization movement') has too binary an overtone: as if any given group or individual must be either anti *or* alter; or as if there are two separate groups under the umbrella. Simply 'Alter-globalization Movement' is perhaps the most useful alternative as it captures (a) the global sense of the phenomenon, (b) shows its positive or productive aspect, and (c) evokes a reference, not least through its anagram (AGM), with the more militant anti-globalization, which retains the charged political nature of the phenomenon. A final good reason for using the term 'alter-globalization movement' is that it is one that almost everyone – participants, supporters, critics, opponents, detractors, apathetic public – recognizes and at least purports to understand. So, though far from perfect, especially for a political phenomenon which defies labels, for these reasons 'AGM' derived from its 'alter-' orientation will be retained in the pages to come.

At least some aspects of the AGM as described so far in this chapter pose a challenge to mainstream socio-political theory. They can be summarized as the non-pursuit of power, the subordination of identity to difference, and the express lack of leadership and hierarchy. As was noted above, this does not describe the AGM in its entirety. Indeed, it would be difficult to find any expression of the AGM which exhibited all three characteristics to any degree of depth or consistency. Nevertheless, if we are seeking a theory of world politics that captures the supposedly new character of the AGM, these remain the benchmarks by which any such theory should be measured. First, in considering the long history of global movements of resistance, many have affinities with the AGM in that their target can be framed as a species of economic ideology. These would include all kinds of Marxist–Leninist parties and related resistance movements, as well as more mainstream socialist parties and more recently, the Greens. Challenges to global political regimes can also be found in the feminist, civil rights, and international workers' movements such as the International Workers Association. However, we can immediately distinguish between these movements and the AGM in that the latter were by and large party and state oriented. Although it is an overstatement to say that these movements had no non-state-oriented component – to see the global feminist movement purely in relation to the state is to overlook its impact on other political sites such as the family or the human body – in many ways their political efforts and ultimately their effects were expressed directly or indirectly in party politics. Although the AGM has affinity with some political parties in some parts of the world, and some of its 'members' are members and supporters of political parties, a distance from mainstream political organization is one of the key features of the AGM.

Thus what marks the AGM as unique and innovative is the apparent rejection of any aspirations towards seizing, and at least in some cases, challenging state power. One of the drives from within the movement has been to avoid powers associated with representation, or, in other words, a leadership representing a people or a group. 'Unlike the formal political struggle for representation, the "struggle" of global civil society from below is for autonomy, held to be a self-constituting goal or end point' (Chandler 2004: 323). This is particularly significant since from the perspective of globalization theory the reduced power of states means that a struggle from below may be more effective than seizing institutional power (Burbach 2001: 79). When we look at groups which tend towards the alter- side of the AGM, this becomes even more pronounced. For example, although Mexican authorities and many media outlets presented the EZLN (Ejército Zapatista de Liberación Nacional) or Zapatistas as another

Marxist-Leninist guerrilla group, it is 'precisely the fact that they are not an orthodox group of revolutionaries that makes them theoretically and practically the most exciting development in oppositional politics in the world for many a long year' (Holloway 1998: 161).[9] Indeed one of the developments of the last couple of decades in both theoretical and practical terms is the entire problematization of power. For many, power is no longer seen as the goal but rather the problem in the first place, leading some theorists to make the distinction between 'power to' and 'power over'. The latter involves the powerful objectifying the activity of the less powerful and is inherently antagonistic; the former is a creative relationship of mutual benefit.[10] One can easily see how Foucault's work can be instrumental in forming the basis of such a position. He famously said that power should not be viewed as a sort of zero-sum domination between those that have it and those that do not, but rather as something that circulates (1994a: 36). As such, seizing power is not possible; one can only seek to interrupt its flow. The People's Global Action (PGA) for example, does not put forth a set of demands over which to negotiate with the neoliberal powers that be. It is uncompromising and non-reformist. In terms of control – as was suggested in the discussion of tactics above – many expressions of the AGM use irony and imagery to challenge media messaging and capitalist ideology. They do not seek control, only to challenge the perceptions and perspectives of the observers and participants. As Lacey notes, 'Taking to the street ... is a vital form of political discourse and dissent that is not reliant on formal access to power' (Lacey 2005a: 411–12).

Second, one of the most important 'new' aspects to the AGM is the promotion of inclusion at the expense of identity. Over the past decades we can see a double movement of identity. On the one hand it has never been so important for social struggles on all levels in the form of multiculturalism, affirmative action, and 'identity politics' in general. At the same time, however, identity appears to have been eroded by contemporary social forces. However one wishes to explain this phenomenon (material changes, globalization, postmodernity, reflexive modernity, individualization) the result is essentially the same. As Melucci writes, '[t]he pace of social change, the plurality of memberships, and the abundance of possibilities and messages thrust upon the individual all serve to weaken the traditional points of reference (church, party, race, class) on which identity is based' (1989: 109). As was noted above, unlike in previous eras when groups felt bound and somewhat isolated by the particulars of their identity (granted the notable exceptions of Marxist accounts), the activities of the AGM in the last decade and a half have been marked by a commonality which seems to transcend and even reject identity and especially a politics of identity. This has not been to undermine or sweep aside the very real regional and local concerns as well as the challenges facing minority groups everywhere, but rather to recognize a commonality amongst them. It is for this reason that regional actions, global protests, as well as World Social Fora and experiments with social centres have included such a wide spectrum of people and groups. Rather than an experience of identity, these activities purport to be an expression of difference: of collectivity and solidarity. As Holloway puts it, the simple statement 'here we are' is a struggle against definitions, against barriers (1998: 170). Indeed, there is the strong sense that identity is a result of power, that it is power that forces, shapes, and moulds people into certain identities (Marcos 2001: 169). In some respects the most innovative and perhaps radical aspect of the AGM is a common sense of solidarity, connection, and purpose built simply on otherness, on being different.

A third way that the distance from mainstream political participation is maintained is the creative and experimental ways that activity normally considered political is carried out. For example, although the PGA has a minimal organization, they favour decentralized mobilization. This highlights the fact that many groups associated with the AGM are often purposefully disorganized and have no membership per se. In the words of Subcomandante Marcos, 'This intercontinental network of resistance is not an organizing structure; it has no central head or decision maker; it has no central command or hierarchies. We are the network, all of us who resist' (2001: 117). In this sense the AGM can be seen as a kind of network of organizations and individuals, but what kind of network this might be, or, more importantly, what relationship this has to its political objectives, remains far from clear.[11] Eschle and Stammers point out the proliferation of network forms of organization which involves

> an apparent flattening of hierarchies so that authority and legitimacy flows more horizontally and interactively, rather than vertically in a pyramidal command structure. Further, it is suggested that networks are 'lighter,' less bureaucratic, more flexible and mobile than traditional organisational forms. There are also strong hints that the network form is inherently more egalitarian and democratic.
>
> (2004: 350)

The cogency of these claims will be investigated in some detail in Chapter 4, but for now it is important to note this apparent lack of organizational form. Finally, many see the importance of the AGM in its bottom-up nature making it a 'grassroots' movement rather than one resting on ideological or party grounds and methods of organization. This is precisely the weakness that many participants of the AGM see in traditional Marxism and for this technical/theoretical reason the latter is often rejected out of hand. (Burbach *et al.* 1997: 4).

We can thus present a rough sketch of the AGM (shown in Table 1.1). It is important to re-emphasize that such a summary description is not a definition of the AGM, rather it reflects the direction of certain elements which make up the

Table 1.1 AGM (potential)

Power	Identity	Organization
Renounced; 'power to'	Broad, open, inclusive	None, anti-

AGM. As Halliday notes, 'to posit it as a straightforward, or unequivocal, global trend is to simplify.' (2000: 126). In other words at least some participants of the AGM view power, identity and organization/hierarchy in the manner just described and act accordingly. And thus we can now state clearly that at least some aspects of the AGM operate against power itself, on the basis of inclusiveness through difference, and with purposefully and explicitly non-hierarchical organizational practices. The next question is to what extent is contemporary theory capable of accounting for and understanding these aspects of the AGM.

Theoretical perspectives

This section sketches out how the various developments of the AGM over the last decade have been approached by different theoretical perspectives in order to justify the need for Deleuze's ontological position and political metaphysics to be introduced in Chapter 2. The purpose is to show how each of these perspectives falls short, in one way or another, of accounting for the variation, discrepancies and apparent contradictory character of the AGM and so fails to provide a coherent and complete picture of it. It must be noted that the following consists of broad sketches and is not intended to offer a full engagement with the different theoretical perspectives, but rather seeks to highlight their analytical strengths and weaknesses. It seeks to assess the mainstream literature in each approach and freely assumes that there will always be exception and innovation within each field, some of which will be taken up later in the book. In any case, from the general analysis of the AGM presented so far we can say that the theoretical challenges come from two distinct directions. On the one hand, the majority of theoretical perspectives to be discussed below cannot account for the special patterns of power, hierarchy, and identity expressed by certain elements (the alter- part) of AGM as just described. On the other hand, theories which do show some promise – for example, the work of Graeme Chesters and Ian Welsh as well as John Urry – tend to oversimplify, focussing on complex network connections at the expense of more mainstream forms of resistance that nevertheless form part of the AGM through more grounded, established networks, organizations such as NGOs, and directed mainstream political activity. It cannot be stressed enough that the novelty of the AGM comes – at least in part – from the mixed and overlapping nature of variably coordinated and networked groups (including, among others, reformist, isolationist, alternative, and localizing aspects), as well as more or less spontaneous forms of individual action or everyday politics. Any competent theory of world politics must be able to account for this diverse and variable mixture, and this will be assessed in greater detail in Chapter 3. But beginning with the problems of power, hierarchy, and identity, the theories dealt with presently, selected on the basis of their sustained engagement with the phenomenon of the AGM in one form or another, are global governance approaches (neo-Kantianism, liberalism), IR (particularly the ubiquitous state-centric approaches), social movement literature, and Marxist (world proletariat), and post-Marxist (the problem of hegemony) approaches.

Global governance pertains to a rather broad body of literature interested in transnational space and its governance, one that analyses 'the role of various national and multilateral responses to the fragmentation of economic and political systems and the transnational flows permeating through national borders' (Steger 2005: 35). One of the most often cited areas which justifies a global governance approach is in business, where firms interact with each other more or less directly on the basis of legal regimes. Cutler *et al.*, for example, describe seemingly endless ways and reasons for firms to cooperate (1999: 5ff.). A baseline assumption in global governance literature is that the world has some sort of system of governance that goes beyond the view of a number of state actors acting out of self-interest. There are, it seems, an ever-increasing multitude of actors interacting in different ways on different levels making for a complex and overlapping system of global governance. This undermines the traditional distinction between the domestic and the foreign, shifting the study of world politics from geopolitics (trade, power, security) to social and ecological questions (Held 2004: 365–6). The question for researchers of global political action or policy is how to best analyse this complex global system, and then, hopefully, how to reform it for the better.

As an analytical approach, global governance is convincing in that is heavily tied to what are largely perceived as empirical realities since at least 1990. It argues that that any understanding of world politics must be sensitive to the mixture of actors and forces that shape the agendas, activities, and outcomes of world politics. One if the implications of this is that no one actor has any analytical priority, so for example, rather than using state interests or system demands as the alpha–omega of investigation, the concept of global governance draws on a great number of actors, from the global to the individual. These include supranational actors (EU), inter-governmental organizations (UN), states, all kinds of transnational organizations (religious and cultural groups, multinational corporations, trade unions, expert and professional associations), NGOs, financial markets, bond rating agencies, media, social movements, lobbyists, citizens and refugees, and many others. Although the state remains an important component of global governance it does so largely as an international legal entity which has, as Rosenau suggests, become more of a policy ratifier (2002: 220), or the strategic site of coordination and legitimacy (Held and McGrew 2002: 9). While analysing global governance or power structures through a more state-centric lens is appropriate in very specialized cases, the broad argument here is that most regimes are created in a diffuse, multi-layered environment permeated by lobbying, media, private, and other interests.

The strength of this approach is that by including such a range of groups it eschews, to a certain extent, the problem of level of analysis (see Buzan 1994). It includes by and large all segments of the social fabric (media, government, groups, individuals), reflecting the fact that all people in the world today putatively live within the complex web of connections and intensive relationships that are susceptible to the forces of what is generally known as globalization which transcend both unit and system accounts. Held stresses the multi-faceted nature of contemporary global governance, arguing that a 'thickening web of multilateral agreements, global and regional institutions and regimes, and transgovernmental policy networks and summits has evolved' (2005: 59).

Held himself is naturally aware of some of the problems with this position. He acknowledges that realists and Marxists are sceptical of the global governance perspective because it lacks explaining power: it describes phenomena well enough but fails 'to penetrate beyond the dynamics of global politics to the underlying structures of power' (Held and McGrew 2002: 13). Although perhaps more nuanced than other approaches which remain bound to nation states as the principle actors, from the perspective of the forgoing analysis global governance approaches in general lack the theoretical tools to account for some of the contemporary phenomena such as street carnival, social centres, and the WSF which seek to subvert power or are anti-power. Furthermore, the problem here is not the failure to penetrate global systems, but the lack of a conceptual apparatus to deal with the inclusive and disorganized aspects of the AGM. To be sure, world politics according to global governance approaches can be characterized as a multi-range, multi-level, often highly asymmetrical power/influence struggle, but nevertheless these are struggles amongst essentially identifiable, bounded agents with interests. It cannot explain nor account for the loose network associations, everyday, taking-to-the-street politics, or political 'entities' whose formation is not contingent upon easily describable identities. One can find this problem in books such as *Contesting Global Governance* (O'Brien 2000), which tend to view what here are called the expressions of the AGM as the activities of discrete social movements clearly defined as actors (with interests) in juxtaposition to global institutions such as the IMF, WTO, and World Bank. The nature of these actors in terms of formation, constitution, and identity, however, remains underproblematized.

When global governance theory addresses the loose coordination of something like the AGM, it most often moves into the terrain of classic civil society theory, drawing on the notion of global civil society. As Martin Weber convincingly argues, this is the fall-back position for those looking to capture the 'informal agency' of the AGM (2005: 192). The AGM can be seen as belonging to global civil society in the latter's classical definition – that is, those activities outside the sphere of the market or the state. As Cox points out, ' "civil society" has become the comprehensive term for various ways in which people express collective wills independently of (and often in opposition to) established power, both economic and political.' (2005: 108). In general, the civil society literature forms a well-documented map of political change over the past two decades. The main problem with such an approach is that the vast majority of analysis of global civil society is of a distinctly normative character (see for example Demirovic 2000: 139–40; Falk 2005: 125–6), pitting a (good) globalization from below against a (bad) neoliberal globalization from above, and thus remains essentially reformist. Although there is nothing inherently wrong with examining the normative aspects of the AGM, there is a conceptual problem here in that such a reformist position cannot capture the non-reformist nature of some aspects of the AGM such as the PGA or social centres. A related problem concerns exactly what to include in global civil society. As noted above, following the classical roots of civil society theory (Hobbes, Hegel), one must include all non-state and non-market entities, many of which are at best ambivalent towards various aspects of the AGM. In other words, global civil society as broadly conceived in the literature is not inherently an antidote to what many view as the detrimental effects of neoliberal globalization.

Another problem is that the designation global civil society seems to be rather regional or class specific. Jan Aarte Scholte highlights a common observation when he writes, 'In general global governance agencies have tended to reach mainly Northern, urban, elite, English-speaking civil society professionals, failing to engage wider (and often more marginalized) constituencies' (2004: 216). Of course this is changing as more and more diverse groups converge and, moreover, participants in the AGM in its more specific organizational forms (the WSF, for example) become aware of this deficiency and make efforts to address this problem. Nevertheless the point here is that the AGM and the environment in which it operates are far too diverse and complex to allow for analytic generalizations about the class or regional diversity of its participants such as implied, empirically at least, by the notion of global civil society.

Global civil society also has the further problem of its association with NGOs. Although some NGOs are formed directly from social movements and maintain a level of autonomy, through cooperation with government or intergovernmental organizations (IGOs) and private individuals and interests (the Bill Gates Foundation, for example), many brand name NGOs come to resemble – sometimes merely through engagement – the governmental structures they are usually understood to be mitigating or taking over from (Weber 2005: 192). In this context this means that perhaps they do not so much belong to a pristine, politically neutral global civil society environment, but perhaps to something less socially productive and more in tune with global capitalist interests (Eschle and Stammers 2004: 349). Furthermore NGOs, it is often observed, tend to go through processes of bureaucratization, oligarchy, and assimilation (Hudock 1999: 2–4; Scholte 2004: 24). The trend towards professionalization and bureaucratization

> is a serious constraint upon the democratic potential of INGOs/TSMOs. Indeed, it ought to be considered whether the incorporation of formal democratic procedures within INGOs/TSMOs, officially required as a precondition of being granted consultative status at the United Nations, actually functions to legitimate oligarchy and to help it work more effectively.

The oligopoly of NGOs creates market leaders, the procedures of which all others must adopt thereby stifling diversity. 'In sum, there seems to be a strong likelihood that INGOs and TSMOs will become increasingly integrated into elite structures of power over time, detached from the control of their memberships and from potentially broader movement constituencies' (Eschle and Stammers 2004: 349–50). Thus it is tenuous to proclaim the new profound role of NGOs in global governance as a utopian transformation of social, cultural, and political activity. More importantly in the present discussion, we can see how the global civil society–NGO nexus runs counter to the general observations regarding the anti-power and pro-diversity nature of some aspects of the AGM. If one attempted to summarize the global governance perspective along the lines of the analysis of this chapter, it could be generally characterized as seeing power as the point of struggle, identity as bounded (unproblematic), and organization as diffuse, though perhaps tending towards structure.

Called 'the dominant view' of the AGM by Eschle and Stammers (2004: 335), IR is one that, as the name suggests, has been struggling with a legacy of state-centrist approaches that have little concern for non-state actors. Mainstream IR, almost universally, at an analytical level understands world politics through exchanges of power on the international level amongst distinct states.[12] Here we can follow Rob Walker's assertion that in traditional terms society is usually viewed to be somehow separate from politics. Indeed, it is the political, state system which makes society (as in civil society) possible; social movements or non-state forms of political activity are usually viewed as being subordinate to or outside the state system. Thus viewing political action through the lens of the state system in IR becomes a sort of habit – Walker calls it 'the inbred common sense of modern political discourse' wherein contingencies are treated as ontological absolutes when there is no reason a priori for doing so (2005: 136). In so far as this is the case it seems difficult for IR to shake its Eurocentric ahistoricism[13] whereby little attention is paid to non-Modernist (or non-Western) conceptions of political association and action. Consequently researchers tend to view even non-state (note the negative formation of the word itself) political action as a function of the state system thereby understanding specific movements in terms of altering state behaviour (reform) or seizing state power (revolution), strategies that are incommensurable with at least some aspects of the AGM. Of course there is far more variety, subtlety and complexity in IR than is given in this brief assessment, but the larger point in terms of the present discussion is that a coherent notion of the AGM must admit exchanges amongst elements from the broadest levels of analysis, the understanding of which relies on different categories and points of analysis than mainstream IR theory provides. In other words, in the context of this chapter, the challenge is to find a way of viewing the AGM beyond the frame of the state system, without using the state as either an alpha or omega. In so far as it is admitted into IR theory, more useful are perhaps concepts such as neo-medievalism,[14] wherein political subjects are located in a dense web of non-territorial, overlapping jurisdictions. This, however, leads to similar problems as in global governance approaches, including understanding power as being exchanged amongst unitary actors over an asymmetric terrain of struggle.

As already noted, identity in the last decades has paradoxically become more diffuse or weakened yet at the same time plays an increasingly important role in politics. As evidence of the latter we can witness the many indigenous peoples' projects as well as the general cultural policies of some countries aimed at preserving and supporting local cultures and identities, as well as those of more recent arrivals. Whatever the case, from an IR perspective the functioning of identity in politics is clearly the realm of the state (Buzan and Little 2001: 21), concerned most often with territoriality and limits and thus inclusions and exclusions. The problem here is that there are so many aspects of the AGM with seemingly different identities and aims: 'Whatever it might come to mean to establish a politics of connections ... it is unlikely to look like the politics of inclusions and exclusions, of the reconciliation of identities and differences, expressed by the modern territorial state' (Walker 2005: 147). State structures tend to be, or at least are largely understood to be, some of the most stable and enduring, whereas the AGM appears as the pre-eminent example of an actor capable of transcending such limits and boundaries. In short there is no reason to believe that social and political movements 'down there' or 'over there' are contained by the state. From this short description it comes as no surprise that IR, with its focus on territory (or at least boundaries) and agents would have some difficulty accounting for forms of political participation such as the AGM, which not only are very transnational but lack institutional structure, organization, and leadership.

These difficulties are intimately related to implicit, foundational, and underproblematized notions of space and time whereby IR has cast world politics in terms of billiard table and cobweb analogies, defecting prisoners, in short, rational, bounded (albeit often inter-connected) agents on a quantifiable geographical terrain moving through a time which serves as an independent variable. Again, citing Walker,

> a large proportion of research in the field of international relations remains content to draw attention to contemporary innovations while simply taking a modernist's framing of all spatiotemporal options as an unquestionable given. While it is not surprising that a discipline largely constituted through categories of spatial extension should experience difficulties coming to terms with problems of historical transformation and temporal acceleration, the implications of these difficulties have remained rather elusive.
>
> (1993: 7)

These themes of space and time will be returned to in considerable detail in Chapter 3. But for now the basic position of IR approaches to the AGM and world politics in general can be characterized as being organized primarily at the international level around state power, where identity often functions to differentiate territorial fields.

Normally social movement theory offers little in the way of an explicit picture of world politics in the sense that IR or global governance does, and in its sociological concerns tends to be bound to specificity or locality,[15] rarely attempting to theorize an ongoing global movement.[16] However, a considerable amount of the literature dealing with forms of alter-globalization is couched in terms of social movements, and recent research that treats transnational social movements in the context of a world of state and non-state actors makes social movement theory a contender for understanding the AGM as part of world politics. But although the approaches of most social movement theory capture the flexible and more horizontal nature of the AGM (see for example Rucht 1999: 208–9), perhaps social movement theory's biggest challenge lies in coming to terms with the AGM through its traditionally central concept of collective identity. The problem is that most of the literature on social movements highlights the importance of shared identity (Eschle and Stammers 2004: 342) whereas the AGM seems often to lack any such cohesiveness.

Francesca Poletta and James Jasper offer the following critique: that the concept of collective identity has merely served to 'fill the gaps in structuralist, rational-actor, and state-centred models' (2001: 285). In terms of the AGM it can only go so far in describing some contemporary mobilizations. Recent analyses 'suggest that it is the increasingly problematic status of individual experience in network society, and not the mechanisms involved in mobilizing collective identity in relation to the political system, that needs to be at the centre of analysis of contemporary conflict and power' (McDonald 2002: 114). Such a view highlights the need for theories that can deal with the fluid nature of the AGM, and yet there remains little in the way of serious innovation, resulting in essentially the re-emphasizing of old categories, often in ever more baroque and elaborate forms. McDonald draws attention to the lack of a grammar of social action and conflicts, asserting that social movement theory is, rather, stuck with the 'instrumental mobilization of collective identity' (2002: 124). In other words social movement theory has difficulty accounting for action without collectivity and subjectivity without identity.

In more general terms, a pertinent question is, how can one theorize about identity if identity itself is being eroded? If contemporary society in much of the world (especially the industrialized or 'cosmopolitan world') is one of shifting, temporary, serial identities seemingly incapable of all but the shortest term commitment as many sociologists would suggest,[17] there can be little analytic value in any even fleeting collective identity based on a common belief or membership in some group. Of course one could argue that today collective struggle is precisely against social forces such as globalization or capitalism, but then again, in terms of contention, the diversity of demands of something like the AGM remain so broad – not to mention anti-power 'non-demands' – as to make the idea of collective identity nonsensical, as Fred Halliday argues (2000: 127). This would strongly imply a need to move beyond conceptions of collective identity that have become integral to social movement analysis and to seek an account of coordinated diversity. The challenge is to move away, for example, from what McDonald calls a new orthodoxy of social movement theory such as expressed by Della Porta and Diani: 'Collective action cannot occur in the absence of a 'we' characterized by common traits and specific solidarity. ... A collective actor cannot exist without reference to experience, symbols and myths which form the basis of its individuality' (Della Porta and Kriesi 1999: 87, 92). Such orthodoxy systematically ignores the increasingly bountiful evidence of the AGM that remains inconveniently oblivious to this 'we' in the form of global action, spontaneous protest, and global coordinations like the WSF. McDonald presents data on affinity groups where there is no leadership, no representation, no banners or sound bites, media policy, etc. Even the names of the groups themselves move from identity (identifying with a problem or concept) to actual movement. As an example one can juxtapose Mothers Against Driving Drunk (MADD – founded in the US in 1980) and Reclaim the Streets, a nebulous action–movement which has no central 'official website' or organizational history at all. Thus it has nothing to do with collective action around a common identity, leading McDonald to conclude: 'Increasingly the concept of "collective identity" is a conceptual liability, an obstacle to exploring the relationship between individual and collective experience in contemporary social movements and conflicts' (2002: 124).

One of the main restrictions of a social movement theory based on identity is that, like many approaches in international relations, struggles are typically seen to be played out at the national level. Although Tarrow argues that such struggles are (only) often very power-based and anti-state (1998: 3), writers such as Della Porta and Kriesi remain explicitly state-centric (1999: 4), while Thomas Olesen, for example, cannot but be fixed on the exercise of state power, even when studying social movements that might transcend it (2005). State power thus retains its central role providing the measure of all other expressions of power. Even when investigating recent social fora Peter Marcuse argues that '[w]hile it is true that all problems are globally linked and neither accounted for nor confined to national borders, the effective vehicle for democratic public action remains at the national level' (2005: 420). He adds that social fora are impotent for the simple reason that only government can achieve shifts in power, and moreover that the former suffer from a deficit of political representation. His solution is to conclude that social fora cannot be understood as social movements at all, depriving them of their political potential. Although perhaps bold and simple, this approach highlights an overall problem in thinking about alter-globalizations today where phenomena that do not fit existing theories must be made to do so, or excluded altogether. Marcuse's approach, which is by no means unique, fails analytically by ossifying the concept of a social movement at the expense of being able to theorize contemporary conditions.

In terms of action itself, orthodox theory sees social movements as essentially a form of protest based on contention where resisting a dominating power is the sine qua non (see for example McAdam *et al.* 2001). This results in misleading characterizations about new forms of political activity as aimed 'to produce a counterhegemonic discourse that challenges the dominant deterministic claims of globalism' (Steger 2005: 121). Although the notion of counterhegemonic struggle is no doubt useful, it is complicated by the uncertainty as to what the dominant force might be, how it operates, and most importantly where it is located, the question being, of course, whether ultimate power rests in the state or in the representatives and activities of transnational institutions. Perhaps more importantly, however, it is difficult to operationalize the concept of contention when for various groups political activity is less about seizing state power than striving to create autonomous spaces from it, as the Gaerber quote above shows. Following Day, the sociology of contention represents a politics of demand that is 'oriented to improving existing institutions and everyday experiences by appealing to the benevolence of hegemonic forces and/or by altering the relations between these forces' (2005: 80–1). However, contemporary global political action as expressed by the AGM has arisen, at least partially, from the perception that historically in the West what seemed like emancipation through liberal and especially neoliberal programmes has merely been the relative displacement of domination – either on the individual or global level. To take another example, according to Oommen, in order to understand social movements, one must understand what he calls the property of the situation in which they emerge and crystallize. Three elements of the property of the situation are 'the core institutional order of the society, the vanguard and the chief adversary of the movement' (2004: 196). The AGM does not fit this framework as – at least some of the time – the order is variable, there is little in the way of vanguard, and sometimes no clear adversary.

So although it is probably an exaggeration to say that we have recently experienced a 'misguided decade of thinking global and acting local' (Chesters and Welsh 2006: 4), sensitivity to the emerging challenges of theorizing political action at the global level should be of the utmost importance, and yet it is something that social movement theory, with its general adherence to collective identity, contention, and the central role of the state has not adequately addressed. In short, despite the potential of social movement theory to shed light on these forms of political activity and therefore to clarify our understanding of the AGM in world politics, 'the attention given to transnational social movements across several different academic disciplines has failed to generate the intellectual and disciplinary synthesis needed to understand their potential' (Eschle and Stammers 2004: 333).

Marxian accounts of new or newest social movements and transnational activism are appealing in that perhaps more than any other perspective here – even global governance – they have a built-in reliance on the global dimensions of oppression and struggle. Moreover, a Marxian position on capitalism perhaps rings truer in the last decade than at any other time in the last century (see Harvey 2000: 7), and unlike other approaches overviewed here, it is, almost by definition, non-reformist. Having said that, Marxian approaches face a number of difficulties in dealing with the aspects of the AGM that have been highlighted here. The most important difficulty is organization. The traditional or orthodox Marxist account of any political practice which does not organize into a party ready to seize state power is that this practice does nothing to confront the domination of the capitalist class. A simplified account – admittedly grossly simplified here – would insist on the need to convince the (globally) exploited classes of their position with an emphasis on organizational structures built around a party leadership or vanguard, or at least some sort of unified political movement. All but the most unorthodox Marxists would insist on a global organizational structure.

Thus in addition to various forms of economic determinism and base–superstructure analysis, the obvious characteristic of this kind of approach is that it tends to read everything – even micro-temporalities – as parts of more or less huge unitary agents and historical structures, for example seeing the Battle of Seattle as essentially a labour movement. So although in the context of the AGM one could legitimately rank the Marxian critique of neoliberal economics as the most effective and productive, especially when delivered by authors such as Brenner (2002), Harvey (1999), and Callinicos (2001), because their goal is not the investigation of emerging socio-political phenomena, analytically they tend to favour big structures at the expense of the individual. Thus Callinicos has no problem fitting the 'movement against capitalist globalization' into a much larger historical structure (2002: 263), and despite many innovations over orthodox Marxist approaches, Waterman's analysis at the outset reverts to something called 'the new internationalisms': 'the wave of international solidarity activity associated with the new alternative social movements (ASMs)' (1998: 4). However, such a view is irreconcilable with the apparent lack of any over-arching identity or solidarity amongst alter-globalizations, and moreover the way in which some participants explicitly pursue their goals. Additionally, although it could be argued that the solidarity or 'merging rivulets' of the AGM has its roots in Marxism, the renunciation of power and the absence of any class antagonism (or class, for that matter) means that Marxian approaches cannot cover the AGM in its entirety.

Adding to its long tradition as a cornerstone of literary theory and cultural studies, post-Marxism in recent years has become a prominent avenue of political theorizing. Perhaps denuded of its political sting and agenda, it has nevertheless moved to the foreground of progressive thought about power, security, borders, and organization. It is not difficult to see its applications to phenomena such as the AGM, and in general it makes a good showing in the literature, tending to understand events such as the Battle of Seattle (Gill 2003: 214) or the first World Social Forum at Porto Alegre (Ponniah and Fisher 2003: 12–13) as counterhegemonic. In terms of identity in the AGM, post-Marxism does very well, where, tending to draw on Althusser (see 1971: 162ff.), the acting political subjectivity (the subject) is interpellated by the hegemon (the Subject). This means that ideologically formed subjectivities are essentially created through the mutual action of being identified within a system, and through the acceptance of this identification. In the present discussion the neoliberal forces of globalization interpellate or create subjects by confining or restricting their identities. Thus in most post-Marxist approaches identities are certainly not fixed but nonetheless are indeed crucial in creating a chain of equivalences. It is in this sense that identity is transcended, which maps quite nicely on the contemporary AGM as outlined above. However, if we take Laclau and Mouffe's seminal work, *Hegemony and Socialist Strategy*, to be in any sense indicative of the post-Marxist approach, then we run into conceptual difficulty. Their main argument is that

> [i]n the face of the project for the reconstruction of a hierarchic society, the alternative of the Left should consist of locating itself fully in the field of

the democratic revolution and expanding the chains of equivalents between different struggles against oppression. The task of the Left therefore cannot be to renounce liberal-democratic ideology, but on the contrary, to deepen and expand it in the direction of a radical and plural democracy.

(1985: 176)

The problem for the purposes of the discussion here is that such an approach affords no place for affinity groups, direct action, and experiments in consensus decision making. For Day, it is

> difficult to apply Laclau and Mouffe's theory of hegemony to the analysis of many contemporary forms of activism. In the case of certain elements of the anti-globalization movement, for example, the goal is not to create a new power around a hegemonic centre, but to challenge, disrupt and disorient the processes of global hegemony, to refuse, rather than rearticulate those forces that are tending towards the universalization of the liberal-capitalist ecumene.

(2004: 730)

In order to meet the theoretical demands of the AGM as described in this chapter we need an approach that takes us beyond reform and revolution to a politics of non-power, and moreover expresses disorganization and non-representation.

Stephen Gill further characterizes post-Marxism by drawing a firm distinction between counterhegemonic resistance and 'transformative resistance' (2003: xi), the latter being one of the most striking characteristics of the AGM. The fault line between these is perhaps the most volatile and venomous within the literature surrounding the AGM. On the one hand it is easy to understand the relative indifference and ultimately dismissiveness with which some post-Marxists tend to view the 'alter-' aspects of the AGM that have been highlighted in this chapter. But Simon Tormey argues that 'Marxist groups, radical democrats and fashionable neo-Leninists such as Slavoj Žižek offer scathing criticism of "summitism", "spontaneity", "movementism" and other crimes besides because they misunderstand what they are for' (2005a: 345). The charge here is that for all these so-called radicals political activism is about gaining power, marshalling forces, creating a Party that will give the masses back their due, but such a view overlooks the distinguishing characteristics of contemporary politics as exemplified by the AGM. Likewise Day reminds would-be critics, 'if anarchist-influenced groups look disorganized, this is perhaps because the ways in which they are organized cannot be understood from within the common sense maintained by the hegemony of hegemony' (2004: 471). Again we are faced with the problem of understanding solidarity, however diffuse, in the absence of an overarching front:

> A politics of connection is, I believe, absolutely crucial. Movements do connect, converse, learn from each other, and sometimes develop partial

solidarities. But a politics or connection is not necessarily a politics of a united front or a counterhegemonic strategy.

(Walker 2005: 147)

Thus political resistance need not only imply 'the extension of the field of democratic struggles to the whole of civil society and the state' (Laclau and Mouffe 1985: 176), but can consist in transforming political practice and thereby political space. Moreover, despite Gill's assertion that the AGM is 'often connected to the actions and conduct of leaders that exemplify and inspire collective action' such as Gramsci, Gandhi, and Mandela (2003: xi), many aspects of the AGM remain explicitly leaderless. In short, although the post-Marxist analysis is indeed illuminating and productive when considering those who wish to challenge hegemonic structures in order to achieve recognition of difference and autonomy, it fails to account for the structureless aspects of the AGM that do not seek to gain power.

We can summarize the above discussion (Table 1.2): Although each theoretical approach has its strengths in accounting for the AGM – global governance for its multi-perspectivism; IR for its relegation of identity; social movement theory for its diffuse organization; Marxist theory for its global aspect; and post-Marxism for its view of identity – from the above discussion we can see how each of the approaches falls short of delivering a comprehensive account of the AGM. For global governance theory, power is precisely the problem in a system without clear hierarchy. In the case of traditional IR, power is measured as capability in a system organized by more or less stable, structural entities (states). For social movement theory (as well as global governance theory) power is diffuse, though is expressed through the state, and while identity is obviously crucial, it is usually in the form of collective identity. For more classical Marxism both power and identity are key features of the system, and establishing the proper organizations is in fact the goal. Although the post-Marxist approach to identity does connect well with the new aspects of the AGM, power is hegemonic, and by and large the movement is understood to be organized around a sort of vanguard or elite.

Table 1.2 Summary of perspectives

	Power	*Identity*	*Organization*
Global governance	The problem	Bounded	Diffuse but structured
(Mainstream) IR	As capability	State based	State based
Social movement theory	Diffuse	Constitutive	Key
Marxism	Structural	Structural	Key
Post-Marxism	Hegemonic	Shifting	Vanguard
AGM (potential)	Renounced; 'power to'	Broad, open, inclusive	None, anti-

Difficulties accounting for 'global complexities' can also be related to positivism, in the sense that science – in particular the social sciences – must be based on measurement (Walker 1993: 11). To be sure there is plenty of thought about world politics that is far from the positivist sciences. Nevertheless, in almost all cases, epistemologically speaking, what is taken as a relevant fact or evidence is based on notions of linearity and measurement. What this suggests is that one of the reasons for the challenges faced by the theories overviewed here is that they tend to be fixed on measurable, bounded entities, and perhaps share in common an inability to account fully for the very fluid and complex nature of the AGM. What is required is a theory capable of capturing some of the speed and movement that seems characteristic of certain aspects of the AGM. At this point it must be stressed once more that a number of theories have been more successful in accounting for this special nature of the AGM, namely Chesters and Welsh's Deleuzian approach to social movements combined with complexity approaches (2006), as well as John Urry's work in complexity (2003). However, as was suggested above the biggest problem with these approaches to the AGM is that they tend to go too far and to oversimplify. As will be discussed in Chapter 3, they are particularly well suited to accounting for non-power, difference over identity, and dis-organization in the AGM, but have difficulty in seeing the AGM in any broad sense that would include the multitude of groups, organizations, and individuals with varying points of view, politics, and network connections that might show up at any given protest or attend a social forum. The important point is that the totality of diverse movements very often constitutes what normally is seen as a whole or actor – there's continuity, overlap, collaboration amongst its various aspects or expressions; indeed, this is what makes it so novel and interesting – but these aspects are at once pro- and anti-power; highly organized and expressly disorganized; promote identity and belonging or see these as restrictive. What we need is a theoretical approach that can explain this convergence and divergence, integration and disintegration, organization and dispersal.

Theoretical directions

In trying to make sense of contemporary political action such as to be found in the AGM, Walker evokes a politics of connection wherein movements have a certain amount of convergence and yet lack a united front or focussed (counterhegemonic) strategy. Although somewhat short on details, he does argue that a metaphysics of inclusion and exclusion with its categorical notions of the world and its contents is incapable of grasping this politics. Moreover, he argues that not only does modern political thought confine us to theoretical prejudices, but that an empirical reading of social movements can make clear the paucity of these theories in the first place (Walker 2005: 147). As Simon Tormey says, in theorizing contemporary politics

> we are daily surrounded by the limitations of 'traditional' politics, the 'death of the nation state', the 'end of ideology', 'liquid modernity', the crisis of

liberal democracy. Political theorists are of course aware of such issues; but many seem caught in the headlights, aware of the vanishing horizon of statist (and post-statist) presuppositions, while lacking the vocabularies to begin moving towards this weightless world of flight, speed, intensities and velocities.

(2005a: 427–8)

Moreover, one observation we can make is that these 'traditional' approaches share a common approach to the political subject entailing – with variation, to be sure – an autonomous and bounded entity endowed with a capacity for rational thought. In terms of politics, all of the theoretical perspectives discussed above posit that such a capacity allows this entity to choose amongst options, and thereby to improve (again, presumably) its position as it sees fit. In other words at these theories' deepest roots we have people making choices, though granted there is indeed considerable variation within the details, from a sense of free-will amongst the cosmopolitan democrats, to the notion of material conditions amongst Marxists, to interpellation amongst post-Marxists. Regarding the last, which has perhaps the most subtle understanding of the subject: although an individual in society may indeed be discursively formed in its entirety (see Laclau and Mouffe 1985: 101; Glynos and Howarth 2007: 109), it seems to me that this still implies a locus, some 'hard kernel' that is rarely questioned or probed to any extent in the literature. And as for the actions of this discursively formed entity, the means through which it chooses its action assumes it would be possible to distinguish the good (radical democratic space) from the bad (hegemonic chain of equivalences). Such questions regarding the subject and political identity will be addressed in Chapter 4.

In light of the discussion of this chapter, the criteria for a comprehensive theory of the AGM (as an example of contemporary political action) and thus world politics must include a plausible explanation of globalization; account for individual action, but also global coordination; account for group action without resorting to identity or framing; provide a model of (dis-)organization; show what a politics of non-power (and especially non-state power) might look like; and perhaps most importantly, account for the dual and sometime contradictory nature of the AGM wherein some aspects appear to dissolve notions of identity, organization and power, while other aspects remain understandable through classical definitions and techniques – and yet both are part of the same thing or movement.

The following chapters will show how Deleuze's philosophy can meet these challenges, thereby highlighting the contribution it can make to the study of world politics. There are several reasons for embarking upon an investigation of Deleuze's work and thought. First, Deleuze's conception of action and organization maps closely onto (or has arguably inspired if not informed) much of the available scholarship on the AGM. One need only look to the terminology, some already cited here, for evidence of this such as deterritorialization, flows, multiplicity, rhizome, nomads, and nomadism.[18] In short, a correspondence in the key points of interest between the AGM and Deleuze is already present. Second, there is a burgeoning literature surrounding the AGM and Deleuze, as well as in more general political theory. Indeed a great deal of the Deleuze scholarship in the fields of cinema or literary criticism has a deep political tinge, though a sustained critical engagement with the political concepts of Deleuze is only now taking shape. The following chapters aim to pick up on and develop this trend further. Finally, and most importantly, in response to the above quotes by Walker and Tormey, Deleuze's approach rejects classical approaches to political analysis that seem wholly inappropriate for understanding the fluid nature of the AGM while at the same time avoiding the extreme relativism of various 'post-all' approaches (which, erroneously and ironically from the perspective of this book, also usually include Deleuze). One of the arguments in the following chapters will be that Deleuze is important to this line of inquiry because he, unlike other thinkers who are often grouped into categories such as 'post-structuralism' (Derridaians, for example), is interested in talking about structures and systems as well as individuals, people, and things. In contrast to the typical post-structuralist thrust, Deleuze's approach is not a 'deconstructive, genealogical, interpretive-analytic' (Ashley 1996: 246). Many point out that Deleuze is the philosopher of movement and mobility (Wuthnow 2002: 184), but there is as yet little in the way of a systematic and thorough investigation of one of the most important philosophers of the last century in terms of how his work pertains to issues of world politics, in particular from a social science perspective.

2 Deleuze and politics as becoming

Points of entry

The purpose of this chapter is to investigate in some detail the political ontology of Gilles Deleuze and to bring the results of that investigation to the point where they can be applied to questions of social science such as the analysis of world politics and the AGM proposed in this book. Thus the bulk of the chapter will be a detailed inquiry into Deleuze's philosophy in so far as it relates to the specific research questions addressed in Chapter 1, wherein notions of space and time will be examined thoroughly at the expense of, for example, sense and logic. To provide a brief summary of the chapter at the outset, the inquiry starts with the problem of difference which can be approached through a discussion of the special role of univocity in Deleuze – the only position for him which is immediately related to difference and gives the latter its own concept. According to Deleuze, Western thought has had, with a few exceptions – notably Scotus and Spinoza – difficulty dealing with difference because of the way it seeks to address (and overcome) the initial problem of difference through the equivocal position of analogy. In Deleuze's view, since Aristotle, the problems associated with an equivocal position on Being have been negotiated or overcome by what Deleuze in *Difference and Repetition* sometimes refers to as the four collars of representation, which are ultimately guaranteed through a transcendent principle. It will be argued in Chapters 3 and 4 that the majority of sociology and political science perspectives – and certainly those dealt with in the first chapter – are not immune to what Deleuze holds to be such illusory – or at least secondary – constructs. Deleuze invokes in their place an immanent ontology without identity and transcendence as key operatives, but instead difference and its counterpart differentiation (differen*t*iation and differen*c*iation, to be more precise) and a two-poled, though non-dualistic ontic system which functions through the relationship between the actual and the virtual aspects of a material reality.

Another way of approaching Deleuze's political thought that will be discussed in this chapter has to do with the possible and the real. Because Deleuze cannot reconcile his immanent philosophy with the problem of the *possible*, he offers instead the rich spectrum of the real – that is, the virtual and the actual both as facets of a reality that admits no possibility in the ontological sense.

This, as will be shown, highlights the importance of Deleuze's research for the science of complexity and the notion of becoming. If ontology is the science of being and metaphysics the study of the fundamental nature of reality – a reality that persists beyond the realm of perception – then we can say that it is Deleuze's univocal ontology that leads him to discover his metaphysics of the virtual and the actual. In other words the former necessitates the latter. Some of the advantages of such an approach are that it accounts for both groups and individuals (though perhaps in an unfamiliar way), extension in space, a coherent account of time, a theory of emergence and change, as well as sensitivity to the modalities and expressions of human experience. The later sections of this chapter lay the groundwork to be able to deploy these advantages in the study of world politics. First, however, due to the number of texts and secondary sources, as well as the dense style and technical content, some time needs to be spent positioning Deleuze's thought in general as well as his reception in academia, including his initial impact in the humanities through to later social science deployments.

The philosophical project of Gilles Deleuze holds an interesting place in the twentieth century, especially in that brand of French thought known as post-structuralism. This latter term usually denotes a sort of breakage or rupture with what was seen as the prevailing methodological dogma of the 1950s and 1960s as influenced by Lacan and Lévi-Strauss, among others, and, in a general sense, this is a relatively accurate assessment. The following passages do not argue against any notion of post-structuralism itself as a commonality of assumptions and methodological practices, only that although Deleuze is generally seen as a post-structuralist thinker, in at least one important respect the shape and style of his thought differs from his contemporaries such as Foucault and especially Derrida. Whereas these latter two at some point in their careers became concerned with a razing or critique of a totalizing modernity, or at least a totalizing system of thought, Deleuze's philosophy tends from the outset to be more constructive and practical. As Daniel Smith reminds us, Deleuze did not want to overcome metaphysics, but to build a different one. He 'saw metaphysics itself as an open structure, which is far from having exhausted its "possibilities"' (2003: 50). This means that in addition to carefully assessing the development of Western metaphysics from the pre-Socratics to the twentieth century – something that many thinkers of the post-structuralist vein have also done – Deleuze, especially in *Difference and Repetition*, builds his own very different brand of metaphysics. In the tradition of Russell and Whitehead he maintains a detached admiration for metaphysical questions and so does not see metaphysics itself as inherently impoverished. On the contrary he constructs what might be called an alternate history of metaphysics, seeing a continuity stretching from the Stoics to Henri Bergson to Ilya Prigogine. In reference to phenomenology, with which Deleuze's philosophy is sometimes associated, his approach deals with the minimal difference of a given entity prior to the machinations of modern metaphysics.[1] But unlike phenomenology this does not lead to an ethics based on essence – that is, the minimal difference does not refer to things. Rather, the 'open structure' of Deleuze's metaphysics denies the possibility of essence, leading to some startling conclusions regarding difference, reality, as well as evolution and change.

It is from this perspective that Keith Ansell Pearson cautions that we should not be too quick to interpret Deleuze's work as the typically French philosophy of difference that emerged in the late 1960s (1999: 79).[2] Far from a co-reaction to seminal works by Derrida (1977) and Foucault (1969), Deleuze began his research on difference as a subject of philosophical inquiry in the mid-1950s and again, grouping Deleuze with the 'philosophers of difference' overlooks the extent to which his thought is indebted to Henri Bergson's biophysical concerns (Ansell Pearson 1999: 79) which sets him apart from his contemporaries. The result is that his philosophical trajectory differs dramatically from the one drawn by Heidegger, Levinas, and Derrida (Boundas 1996: 90); a difference which forms a dimension of the analysis to come in this and subsequent chapters. With this distinction in mind, at times I will distinguish the positions I probe here from other thinkers in order that the reader not be swayed by previously encountered terminology and theoretical positions. In other words, some of the notions I wish to develop here are quite specific and often opposed to the more familiar interpretations. This is justified particularly in light of the many rather unstable attempts to contain radically different approaches – Deleuze and Derrida, for example[3] – within the same theoretical categories.

In terms of Deleuze and his own philosophy of difference, there have been tentative (Tormey 2006) and more total (Chesters and Welsh 2006) deployments of Deleuze in the kind of social and political theory which this book addresses, namely how to understand world politics and account for something that might be called *global* political activity. Whatever their mode, all employ Deleuzian terms such as rhizome, multiplicity, immanence, plateau, among many others. However, more often than not, scant attention is paid to the specific productive potential of these terms or, moreover, to how they have been developed and used by Deleuze himself. Of course, a great deal of productive research has been carried out using the conceptual tools found in Deleuze, especially those found in works such as *A Thousand Plateaus*. Indeed, the productive aspects of these engagements mirror Deleuze's view that the task of philosophy is the creation of concepts (*WP*: 9), not a quest for truth or meaning. In other words, the production of new ideas and perspectives is of greater value than representation or interpretation. However, despite profound assertions of novelty and productive potential – and I am not necessarily thinking specifically about Tormey and Chesters and Welsh here – these terms and concepts, taken at a considerable distance from their positioning within Deleuze's philosophical system, risk becoming mere metaphors. As George Marcus and Erkan Saka point out,

> Few in the social sciences who have found the modernist sensibilities embedded in the concepts that Deleuze and Guattari deploy for their purposes to be attractive have appreciated, understood or incorporated those purposes in their own. Rather, it has been the power and often beguiling attraction of Deleuze and Guattari's language that has encouraged the

piecemeal appropriation of certain concepts for the remaking of middle-range theorizing that informs contemporary research projects.

(2006: 103)

To be sure, metaphors can be useful in analysis, but besides the fact that Deleuze does not understand his own philosophy in terms of metaphors – indeed, it is adamantly materialist – the use of these highly ambiguous and usually quite cryptic terms, as productive and provocative as they might appear, often struggle in the final analysis to illuminate the subject to which they are applied. Instead, they become a sort of professional Deleuzian code, or form part of a hidden premise.[4] Orphaned from their ontological framework, it is fair to wonder how useful a single notion[5] of Deleuze's might be in explaining with any rigour a socio-political phenomenon. In short there seems to be a great deal taken for granted, and it often feels as though one must already be somewhat of a Deleuzian expert in order to understand works that draw on Deleuze. But rather than propagating various Deleuzeisms, it seems to me that such ambiguous and cryptic terms must serve as signs of something more fundamental and offer more possibilities than mere inspiration. For instance, in the face of Deleuzian deployments, all kinds of questions present themselves, such as how might any given term relate to others and other fields of analysis and thought? That is, is the term field-specific or more universal, and if the latter, then how? How is such a system possible? What criteria might it satisfy and what purpose does it serve? What positions does it preclude?

One of the goals of this chapter is to address such questions. Deleuze commands us to experiment, never interpret (*N*: 87), but experimentation can also include experimentation with Deleuze's work itself, and doing so is not the same as asserting that when Deleuze says 'line of flight' he definitely means x. The experimentation towards which Deleuze incites us certainly can involve an engagement with his basic ontological position. This is exactly what this chapter and this book seek to accomplish. However, to be clear: what I am interested in establishing with this chapter is a minimum ontological and metaphysical position from which it would be possible to derive epistemological, methodological, and even ethical and aesthetic principles. In other words I do not seek immediately to seize on an interpretation of a Deleuzian methodology or politics, for example.

Within this context it is important not to present Deleuze's ontological position as the product of philosophical whimsy. Rather, mirroring somewhat a Deleuzian epistemology here, his ontological position can been seen as a solution to a problem. Such an observation can serve as a guide in exploring Deleuze by allowing us to follow the logical, if not exactly chronological, flow of his thought. Accordingly, this chapter seeks to sketch out in some detail what kinds of problems Deleuze was interested in and how they drove him to come up with the solutions that he did. One of the difficulties found in a great deal of Deleuze scholarship, especially that which directly addresses political or sociological questions, is the lack of this vector of development. Although it is possible to talk about differentiation in the abstract, and perhaps Deleuze himself actually did have an innate predilection towards things like rhizomes and multiplicities, I think it is much more convincing, significant, and ultimately productive to demonstrate how such notions are the result of his careful thought regarding (and ultimate dissatisfaction with) the philosophical positions with which he had come in contact through his self-professed classical – and hence often rather awkward and dated (*N*: 5) – philosophical training.

One aspect of the literature surrounding Deleuze that often distorts any deployment of his philosophy is the fact that from the perspective of his work since the early 1970s, Deleuze is perhaps best known as the philosopher of Desire, which opened his work to the field of literary criticism as well as postmodern approaches in general. This view of Deleuze was launched through his association with the politics of the student movement of 1968 and was secured through the works he co-authored with Félix Guattari, especially the first volume of *Capitalism and Schizophrenia*. Such a reading sees him as 'liberating the anarchic multiple of desires and errant drifts' (Badiou 1997: 11) and became strongly associated with various political ambitions and social movements of the late 1960s and early 1970s. In *Anti-Oedipus* Deleuze and Guattari posit Desire as the autoproduction of the unconscious. 'Desire does not lack anything; it does not lack its object. It is, rather, the subject that is missing in desire, or the desire that lacks a fixed subject.' (26). Moreover, they argue, there is no mediation between Desire and the social field: 'There is only desire and the social, and nothing else.' (29).[6] This marks a very broad and perhaps ambitious intellectual pursuit, for as Paul Veyne puts it, Desire is the answer to the question 'why?' (1997: 163). However, as Jérémie Valentin points out, it is possible to enter into a discussion of politics à la Deleuze from outside the perennially dominant perspective of Desire (2006: 185). To give an example, Goodchild's excellent and critical book, the subtitle of which is *An Introduction to the Politics of Desire* (1996), uses Desire as a point of reference and orientation quite productively and informatively. And yet Goodchild tantalizes the reader with the suggestion that Desire, desiring machines, and the desire-repression couplet were all dropped in *A Thousand Plateaus* due in no small part to the veiled criticism of the 'philosopher of desires' by Foucault (1996: 132–3).[7] The move away from reading Deleuze through his deployment of Desire can be seen as a move to rehabilitate Deleuze away from the height of 1970s French intellectual fashion and its subsequent assimilation into Anglo-American academia into a more refined, serious figure in the history of philosophy – not just post-war French philosophy but philosophy in general. It is this effort which propels the renewed interest in his work over the last few years.

This leads to the next question before embarking on a detailed analysis of Deleuze's philosophy as it pertains to the study of world politics. Namely, whether he is the populist, emancipating philosopher of minorities and resistance, or whether he is fundamentally clinical, ascetic, and elitist. This is not merely idle speculation, as the consequences of such a distinction are enough to prod Paul Patton, a leading Deleuze scholar and author of the highly influential

Deleuze and the Political, into arguing against any reading which sees Deleuze as 'anti-political' (2000: 105). Presumably one of Patton's antagonists here is Alain Badiou, who writes that 'contrary to all egalitarian or "communitarian" norms, Deleuze's conception of thought is profoundly aristocratic', insisting that those, 'who believe that Deleuze's remarks may be seen to encourage autonomy or the anarchizing ideal of the sovereign individual populating the Earth with the productions of his/her desires' are mistaken in their reading (1997: 11–12). The antagonism of Badiou's position is echoed by Slavoj Žižek who asserts that none of Deleuze's own texts (meaning those not written with Guattari, nor the one with Claire Parnet) is 'in any way directly political' and that Deleuze himself is a 'highly elitist author, indifferent towards politics.' (2003: 20). This clinical reading of Deleuze is by no means limited to such controversial views as Badiou's or Žižek's.

What seems to be playing out here is a battle for Deleuze between two main positions or readings, both of which, from the perspective of applying Deleuze's political philosophy to the question of the AGM, have advantages and disadvantages. On the one hand we have authors such as Paul Patton and Philip Goodchild who belong to a tradition which deploys the philosophy of Deleuze in the analysis of an emancipatory politics – either in tandem or against Marx.[8] We might call this the communitarian or populist group. On the other hand there are writers such as Keith Ansell Pearson, Daniel Smith, and Manuel Delanda who, despite important differences in their work generally, see in Deleuze a somewhat clinical and yet dynamic philosophy that lends itself toward a comparatively dispassionate view of various systems – political or otherwise – and whom we might call the elitist or ascetic group. The difference between the positions is considerable. Members of the former tend towards cultural studies, post-all theory, critique, radical politics, and aesthetics. The principle works employed in this pursuit are both volumes of *Capital and Schizophrenia*, but particularly *A Thousand Plateaus*. Although such forays are evocative, challenging, and productive, when it comes to specific theoretical applications or empirical studies they risk using Deleuze's philosophy in a self-referential manner, deploying – sometimes in a rather ad hoc fashion – terms such as rhizome, nomad, or desiring machines rather evocatively.

The latter group tends towards metaphysics, systems, complexity, and the physical sciences. The main advantage to their approach is that they are generally more philosophically rigorous (and metaphysically more consistent), tending to draw on Deleuze's work as a whole including especially the central, early masterwork *Difference and Repetition* (first published in 1968). Perhaps most importantly, they go to some lengths to clarify how Deleuzian terminology specifically fits the topic at hand. In general the works of this group can often be more challenging for the author as well as engaging for the reader, and open up more possibilities or avenues of investigation, including emergence and evolution, time–space analysis, and systems theory. Having said this it is also worth mentioning that perhaps some from this group go too far in their 'Deleuzism', presenting his thought as entirely biophysical (Ansell Pearson 1999) or writing as if Deleuze were a self-professed complexity theorist (Protevi 2001, Bonta and Protevi 2004), sometimes missing the political and aesthetic significance of the work. To be sure, the more sterile or ascetic themes obviously interest Deleuze immensely, but it is equally true that questions of the human condition, revolution, and even Marxism play an important role in his work from the very beginning. One need only survey the seminal 1962 *Nietzsche and Philosophy* to see how concerned Deleuze is with topics such as value and ethics. Moreover, because Deleuze is an anti-representationalist philosopher and as such always disdainful of interpretation as mentioned above, it is dangerous to try to contain his terminology. Thus there is a danger of giving too clinical a reading to Deleuze. He is an extremely exacting philosopher, philosophy for him being the only endeavour capable of pointing to the virtual or the Idea (*WP*: 135ff.). But such philosophy remains somewhat impotent if it does not take into account human life in the world – its forces, movements, changes, resistances, and revolutions. It is precisely for this reason that Deleuze has lent himself to the contemporary investigations of political resistance or alter-globalizations.

Ultimately both positions are valid and accurate in their own way. What seems to be needed, and what this chapter attempts to do, is to apply the rigour of the ascetic reading to the object – that is, what is at stake in the study of world politics – of the communitarian reading. The question of whether Deleuze's ontological position supports a liberating populist politics or rather something far more cool, clinical, and elitist is a question that will be addressed in some detail in Chapter 4. For now, however, one final question is what sorts of things should we be keeping in mind as we unpack Deleuze's political ontology?

The first consideration is how precisely to introduce Deleuze's ontology of difference and its associated terms and figures into an investigation of world politics such as this one. As a rather unknown and bewildering figure in continental philosophy, or more specifically French post-structuralist theory, Deleuze's philosophy has infiltrated the fields of literary criticism and cultural studies in a rather piecemeal fashion. In what could be called a third form as distinct from the populist and the elitist versions discussed above, this is most often found not in scholars or academics who deploy Deleuze in a general sense, but theorists and activists in whose work various aspects of Deleuze's thought play a direct or indirect role. The results are mixed. Richard Day, for example, appropriates the Deleuzo–Guattarian figure of the Smith (see *ATP*: 410) with considerable mettle (2005: 17), and at the same time is harshly critical of the notion of the rhizome (262). Hardt and Negri's immensely popular *Empire* (2000) draws on Deleuze and Guattari extensively, not only in its technical terms (deterritorialization, the multitude as multiplicity or at least as a Body without Organs,[9] and also the itinerant Smith), but arguably in its ontological background and as a source of broader political objectives. It is debatable, however, whether these ideational artefacts are sufficiently understood in the literature in general so as to warrant such straightforward treatment. I am not arguing that Day and Hardt and Negri are wrong in their reading, only that they are negligent in importing Deleuzian, and in this case, Guattarian figures.[10] In Deleuze and Guattari the notion of the

Smith as an itinerant figure of central importance in terms of its capacity for emancipatory and perhaps truly democratic politics depends on crucial distinctions that require a clear understanding of neighbouring notions such as smooth space and becoming, how they function, and their significance in political thought more generally. There are certainly signs of promise and limited success, but the work done on Deleuze to date suggests the need for a further, more rigorous exploration of the relationship between some of the key terms and notions.

Far more common is the abrupt insertion of a Deleuzian notion which serves more as an allusion or touchstone. This kind of 'inspirational Deleuze' has lent support to a considerable number of effective research programmes such as Appadurai's (see for example 1990), but has at the same time resulted in Deleuzian terms being completely orphaned from their source and relative meaning therein. This is the case with 'rhizome' in Pieterse (2004) and Bauman (1992), 'nomad' in Ashley (1996), or 'line of flight' in Urry (2005a) and Agamben (1998), to cite only a few examples. There is, moreover, the other possibility of borrowing a given term but deploying it with another sense. A common example is using 'multiplicity' to mean 'a great number' or 'very complex' (see for example Wagner 1999: 70). Such terms, although certainly suggestive, in themselves do little to illuminate political and social phenomena, thereby reinforcing Villani's argument that we must take Deleuze's 'entire work' into account in order to understand the concepts within it (2006: 239).

Perhaps understanding, processing, and deploying Deleuze's complete opus is beyond the interests and time restraints of most political philosophers – let alone social science researchers – but what this does suggest at the very least is that a certain amount of comprehensiveness when using Deleuze's terminology might lead to as yet undiscovered territory in the investigation of social phenomena. Furthermore, a lack of comprehensiveness often proves tedious and off-putting. As David Rabouin rather scathingly remarks, '[O]ne may repeat endlessly a few well-coined formulas – brandishing everywhere the expressions "desiring machines", "plane of consistency", and "lines of flight" – one will not prevent the deplorable alchemy that makes today these formulas as heavy as lead' (cited in Valentin 2006: 188). Put in these terms anyone interested in Deleuze's work is faced with a serious terminological problem wherein there is a danger of focussing on how terms and jargon 'fascinate' and 'mystify' (Valentin 2006: 186) without appreciating their potential rigour or productive value, or, perhaps more importantly, without showing how these terms relate to each other in a comprehensive analysis of phenomena, in this case social and political ones.[11] It is possible that more superficial formulations may be very attractive for some fields of inquiry and yet cause considerable problems when applied directly to questions such as those of the present work, namely dealing with world politics and society.

In short, the use of Deleuze – and not only in the Anglo-American world – suffers from a lack of profundity and productivity when it comes to Deleuze's terminological system (if one can call it that) as a whole and how political questions can be mapped upon it. Scholars such as Didier Bigo and Rob Walker might draw on Deleuze, but they only suggest that he incites us to be topologists of a different kind (2007: 723), and not how he conceives of this project or what his theories fundamentally say about such a methodology. The result is that there is a creeping dissatisfaction with Deleuze deployment to date, with Tormey characterizing the work on Deleuze in general as, 'one that despite the many efforts of sympathetic commentators remains at best suggestive and at worst opaque' (2006: 140). In light of all this one of the general arguments of this book and the main points of this chapter is that the innovations which one might garner from Deleuze's philosophy are at their most powerful only against the background of his philosophy as a whole. Here I side with Williams in his assertion that in order to do justice to the demanding ideas that are found in *Difference and Repetition*, care must be taken to understand the arguments on which they are based (2003: 2).

There is a further sense in which a comprehensive appropriation is necessary. Because Deleuze's ontology necessitates the rejection or at least the rethinking of a vast array of elements of thought upon which the bulk of political research is conducted (including difference, identity, actor, method, structure, change and force), there is a tendency, especially during the process of making Deleuze real or relevant, to normalize, integrate, or (re-)habilitate single aspects of his system of thought, often thereby depriving the latter of not only its cohesion and accuracy, but also of its novelty and productive potential. Examples include adopting 'line of flight' but retaining a traditional modernist form of political agency; operationalizing multiplicity but relying on the possible; and perhaps most significantly for the purposes of this chapter: exploring difference but ignoring repetition. In light of such criticisms and cautions it is nevertheless true that Deleuze's terminology is loose to the extent that it is sometimes difficult to say for certain, especially in works which are co-authored, what Deleuze is arguing for or to systematically structure his thought. For example, during a crucial discussion about line of flight – a key concept of his philosophy in general and intimately related to the virtual, counteractualization, and hence change – Deleuze confides that sometimes he presents there being three varieties, sometimes two, sometimes one and admits that this is rather 'muddled' (*D*: 102). He does, of course, provide a reason for this, but such ambiguity extends to at least half a dozen of his key political terms. Another problem is that Deleuze routinely changes his terminology from one book to another. For example, sometimes he refers to a virtual field, or a plane of immanence, or a body without organs to mean more or less the same thing. Delanda suggests that

> the point of this terminological exuberance is not merely to give the impression of difference through the use of synonyms, but rather to develop a set of *different* theories on the *same* subject, theories which are slightly displaced relative to one another but retain enough overlaps that they can be meshed together as a heterogeneous assemblage. Thus, the different names which a given concept gets are not exact synonyms but near synonyms, or sometimes non-synonymous terms defining closely related concepts.
>
> (2002: 157)

However, I think it is more appropriate to reverse the formulation: Deleuze's terminological exuberance is the result of the treatment of different subjects with the same theory (strictly based on his ontological principles) and the use of different terms for these subjects. Such an assessment is consistent, for example, with Deleuze and Guattari's comparison of philosophy, science, and art at the end of *What is Philosophy?* (216) where they have multiple names for the same operating principle (in this case conceptual personae, aesthetic figures, and partial observers), depending on the field of subject in which it lies (that is, philosophy, art, and science, respectively). This has, of course, led to a number of problems. Different commentators often use the same term to mean different things, or different terms to mean the same thing. Moreover, different authors tend to take different 'slants' on Deleuze depending on which terms or notions in Deleuze they take to be primary. A prime example of such a notion that receives a wide interpretation is counteractualization, variously understood as vice-diction, line of flight (simply), absolute deterritorialization, and even actualization.[12] The list could continue with other notions and figures such as rhizome, milieu, duration and vice-diction.

The present exploration is of course not exempt from this confusion and so may not readily map onto other Deleuzian investigations or perhaps even be recognizable to other readers or scholars of Deleuze. Nevertheless every effort has been taken to find the location of closely related terms and to be forthcoming where ambiguities lie both in the source and, where relevant, secondary literature. With this in mind this book will, when exploring Deleuze's political ontology, draw on earlier terminologies such as those found in *Difference and Repetition* and *The Logic of Sense*, and then from there branch out into variations, such as those found in *Capital and Schizophrenia* that specifically address political notions such as change, emergence and resistance. It should be remembered that this is by no means an attempt at a definitive overview of Deleuze. It is rather a comprehensive analysis of the parts of Deleuze pertinent to understanding world politics with attention to philosophical and logical continuity.

Finally, the renewed interest in Deleuze over the last decade or so, especially in the social sciences and in politics in particular, has led to a general curiosity and perhaps even a normalization of Deleuze – something worthy of pursuit and which may ultimately result in the 'Deleuzian century' as Foucault famously prophesied.[13] However, this popularity may mean that his philosophy will be denuded of its originality, rigour, totality, and, ultimately, its political significance. Patton's favourable comparison of Deleuze with Rawlsian liberal theory (2005: 410) can be read as a prime example of such a denuding.[14] There is a potential bifurcation here in Deleuze deployments and scholarship. Either the fascinating and mystifying language will become further integrated into broader research fields, as did various aspects of postmodernism or the methodology of deconstruction; or the current curiosity will lead to a serious reconsideration of Deleuze's philosophy and how it might be significant to social science investigations. The task set by this book and this chapter in particular is to aid in the latter possibility. A careful analysis of Deleuze's work is worthwhile as it avoids or offers potential solutions to many of the shortcomings in social science and political research outlined in Chapter 1. At the same time it represents a constructive departure from a theory of total, radical exteriority such as offered by Baudrillard (1983a) on the one hand and, on the other, a politics which operates solely within hegemonic discursive systems (Laclau and Mouffe 1985) or the production of the Other (Said 1995, Spivak 1999). Though this is not to say that with Deleuze we are bound to talk about signification and interpretation – although these nevertheless can remain important variables. Jeffrey Nealon puts it thus:

> Deleuze and Guattari's work represents a golden opportunity for theoretical work in the humanities finally to free itself from its long apprenticeship to the paradigms of literary criticism, and simultaneously to free itself from the charge that cultural studies or political theory merely produce more or less 'literary' readings of 'cultural' phenomena.
>
> (2003: 161)

A divergence towards Deleuze's political philosophy is quite timely as it allows us to talk about things. It is a radical materialism, and, crucially for political investigations, arguably a kind of realism.

What this all seems to demand is a more schematic or at least long-sighted and consistent investigation of Deleuze's thought as it might apply to the social sciences and the study of world politics in particular. And although there are a growing number of more or less philosophical volumes devoted to Deleuze including those by Colebrook (2002), Williams (2003), Schaub (2003), and a few general surveys such as those by Massumi (1992), Goodchild (1996), Hallward (2006), and May (2005), none fits this requirement.[15] One must be wary of providing a systematic reading, as Williams proposes to do (2003: 1) since as I have noted earlier, Deleuze's philosophy demands production, not interpretation. Nevertheless it seems that a clear, comprehensive, and interrelated view of Deleuze's political philosophy and how it relates to the questions of this book is sorely needed. What follows attempts to address this deficiency.

Difference and univocity

In so far as difference and its relationship to the universal has been a key issue confronting social theory in recent decades (see Calhoun 1995: xii), the importance of the arguments and challenges surrounding Western metaphysics has come to the fore. But whereas some like Heidegger (1984: 109ff.) and Derrida (1983) saw metaphysics itself to be the problem, Deleuze did not want to do away with metaphysics, as pointed out in the introduction to this chapter, but rather to develop a different or alternate metaphysics. The closed nature of metaphysics is due, according to Deleuze, to its fundamental misapprehension of the concept of difference. In this misapprehension, rather than having a distinct concept of difference, difference is rather inscribed within concepts in general (*DR*: 40). In this way, difference becomes the predicate in the comprehension of the object. In other words we know things are different, that humans are different from birds, for example (in Aristotelian terms this is difference in the genus 'animal'), but this does not tell us what difference *is*. What we need, according to Deleuze, is a concept of difference itself.

Deleuze argues in *Difference and Repetition* that we need such a concept of difference because the Aristotelian notion of difference that came to dominate Western thought – as difference within an underdetermined concept – leads inexorably to a fundamental flaw that continues to exert its influence today. Deleuze reminds us here that the *greatest* difference in Aristotle is expressed in contrariety in the genus, namely 'the capacity of a subject to bear opposites while remaining substantially the same (in matter or genus)' (39). Thus such difference is contingent upon an identity within the concept itself. A human and a bird are different in that one has arms and one is winged, but this difference depends on them both being animals.[16] Because of this such an analysis breaks down as we move farther from the perfect or greatest difference at the level of genus–species, and becomes untenable when talking about very large or very small differences. We see one side of this when we look at difference at the level of the individual.[17] For although the differences between two individuals – Aristotle and Deleuze, for example – are manifest in any number of categories, ultimately what distinguishes an individual is an indivisible *thisness*[18] which is not determined on the basis of any difference capable of dividing a higher category. That is, we cannot imagine a difference (such as 'winged' or 'warm blooded') that could distinguish between two individuals. The latter are, in themselves, indivisible objects (*DR*: 39). Their differences are what makes them individuals – it does not divide them into species. This, Widder points out (2001: 440), is why Aristotle in Book VII Chapter 10 of the *Metaphysics* claims that we can have knowledge only of species. There is no knowable definition of individuals as such because *as matter* they are unknowable (1984a: 1635); we relate to them only through perception.[19]

Deleuze also shows how contrariety in the genus does not function at the level of the very large, either. In contrast to specific difference (that is, amongst species) which relies on the identity of an undetermined concept (genus), the difference between the genera themselves as determinable categories (just like a species is determinable) are large because they lack an over-arching identical concept or common genus. The reason for this is clear, if not readily apparent: Aristotle is very specific about the fact that Being cannot function as a genus (*DR*: 41). He forms his argument thus:

> Being is predicated of differences themselves.
> Genera are not predicated of differences themselves (that is, genera cannot be predicated of differences because it is they which divide the genera).
> Therefore Being is not a genus.

Thus (see Figure 2.1), at the level of species, although we do say that armed *is*, we cannot say that armed is *an animal* because it is the difference 'armed' that

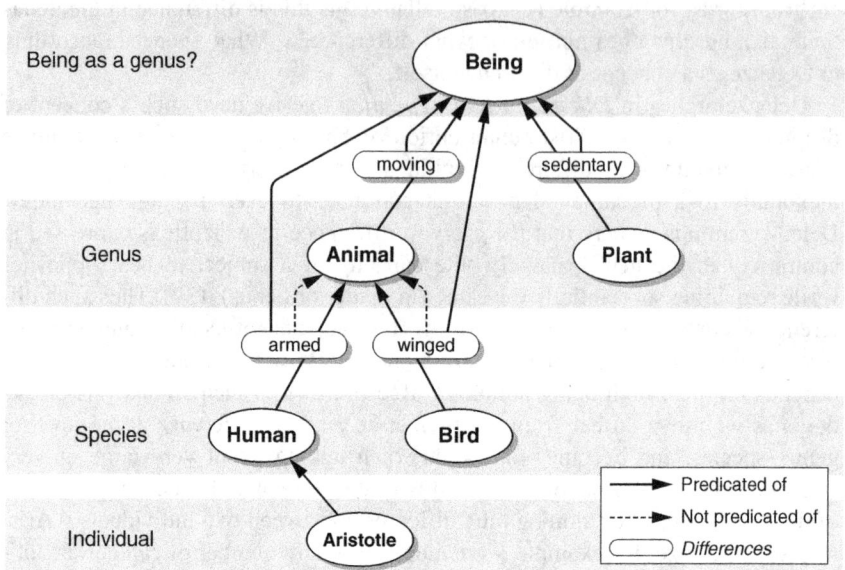

Figure 2.1 Difference in Aristotle.

divides the genus 'animal' in the first place. However, at the level of genera we do say that 'animal' *is*, but also that 'moving' (the difference that might discriminate animal) 'is'. But here we have that which divides the category 'Being' (i.e. 'moving') functioning not only as a difference but also as members of the category itself (just as '*animal is*'). But differences cannot be a member of the category they divide, just as we cannot say that armed *is* animal. Deleuze puts it thus: 'genus is determinable only by specific difference from without' (*DR*: 43) and saying in this example that 'moving' *is*, is tantamount to dividing the species from within (by dividing it with one of its members). Again: at the level of species we say that armed *is*, but not that armed is animal because it is not attributable to that which it divides. However, we say that moving *is* (as all differences *are*), but that now means that our difference is a member of its genus or category, namely Being. In other words, the closer we get to Being the more the notion of difference within the concept breaks down.

In short, 'only in relation to the supposed identity of a concept is specific difference the greatest.' (*DR*: 40). Put another way, the only thing that holds this notion of difference together is the supposed unity of the concept. Moreover 'it is in relation to the form of identity in the generic concept that difference goes as far as opposition, that is pushes as far as contrariety.' So the fact that we say things are contrary – winged/non-winged, bipedal/non-bipedal – also relies on this supposed unity of the concept. In short

> Specific difference [difference amongst species], therefore, in no way represents a universal concept (that is to say, an Idea) encompassing all the singularities and turning of difference, but rather refers to a particular moment in which difference is merely reconciled with the concept in general.
>
> (*DR*: 40)

What this leads to, according to Deleuze, is in effect two kinds of difference, one concerning generic and the other concerning specific differences (*DR*: 41). Since for Deleuze the history of philosophy is the invention of concepts and the discovery of their applications, the positing of two kinds of difference – one generic and the other specific – represents a key turning point or 'propitious moment' in this history. Such a moment should signal an opportunity to investigate the nature of difference and hopefully develop a new and consistent way of thinking. In other words Aristotle's reasoning on difference should have sparked an investigation into the problems surrounding difference. However, this is far from the case. Aristotle and his inheritors rather bring in an elaborate ontological construct, a 'sleight of hand' (*DR*: 38) to maintain this 'fracture of thought', namely a transcendent principle brought about through the equivocity of being. In a brief but crucial passage in *Difference and Repetition* (42) Deleuze shows how this came about: Aristotle, rather than seeking a way to reconcile the problems of difference of the very large, treats Being not as a collective – like a genus in relation to species – but rather as a distributive and hierarchical function. It is as if there are two kinds of '*logos*': one univocal for specific difference and one equivocal for generic differences. In the latter, Being in itself has no content like a proper genus would have, but rather content only in relation to the subcategories of which it is predicated. These subcategories 'need not have an equal relation to being: it is enough that each has an *internal* relation to being' (42). It is distributive in the sense that it partitions concepts, what Deleuze calls common sense. 'A distribution of this type proceeds by mixed and proportional determinations which may be assimilated to "properties" or limited territories within representation' (45). It is hierarchical in that it measures the subject, what Deleuze calls good sense or first sense. What Deleuze means here is that since Being is not a category we must use other means to relate it to what would normally – again, in the case of a genus – be its members. We are obliged to rely on common sense to divide up concepts in the first place, and then good sense to determine where they might fall or be located in relation to other concepts (are they categories or rather are they more like species, or again closer to individuals?). The phrase Deleuze uses to describe this 'dragging in' of identity of the concept to the real of Being is the analogy of judgement. Thus, double armed with common sense and good sense 'the analogy of judgement allows the identity of a concept to subsist, either in implicit and confused form or in virtual form' (42). It is in fact something akin to a logical leap of faith that allows one to treat this relation between Being and its categories in the same manner as the greatest difference in the species. It is, according to Deleuze, an illusion (146).[20]

The analogy Deleuze is referring to is, of course, the means of relating Being to beings by relying on the difficult-to-maintain ontological position of equivocity wherein Being is said differently of different things *tout court*. Such a position would hold, for example, that 'humans are' in a completely different way than 'God is'. The analogous argument states that although any two modes of being are not equal, they are related through analogy, which brings us back to judgement being capable of upholding such analogy. It should be no surprise at this point in the discussion that such a position of analogy – the one which found its first expression in Aristotle and was then amplified in the Christian world most notably by Thomas Aquinas – is not sufficient for handling in any rigorous or consistent way any encounter with the world without some external guarantor of the relationship between Being and beings. This is the transcendent principle and will be discussed shortly, but for now what this means for understanding difference is clear: true difference cannot come from the partitioning of the concept nor, more importantly, through an analogy within judgement itself – both mediating principles. Difference therefore must be located somewhere else. It must be something that relates Being to individual difference that is neither specific nor generic. For when we get to the level of the individual we cannot, as Aristotle (and later Aquinas) says, rely on material and form to account for differences between individuals, for in conforming to the general one can only list accidents and not individuating factors: 'what makes Socrates this particular man does not make him more of a man than Plato' (Widder 2001: 443).

So how to extricate ourselves from this problem? For Deleuze this is the fundamental ontological question, and his choice for the only ontology that addresses this problem is univocity (*DR*: 44). The requirements this places on difference are significant:

> Univocity of Being, in so far as it is immediately related to difference, demands that we show how individuating difference precedes generic, specific, and even individual differences within being; how a prior field of individuation within being conditions at once the determination of the specification of forms, the determination of parts, and their individual variations.[21]
>
> (*DR*: 48)

To illustrate just how high the stakes are we need only look back to the medieval debates on which the current discussion rests. As both Widder (2001: 441) and Smith (2003: 53ff.) remind us, univocity – such as that promoted by Duns Scotus – challenges the assertion that God's existence is of another order from the created universe, and thus ultimately unknowable through human experience. Such a heterodox and even heretical opinion opens the door, of course, to pantheism (*DR*: 49), or perhaps worse, from a medieval Christian perspective, atheism (Smith 2003: 54). The consequences, however, reach well into the twentieth century because, of course, there was another option to preserve the transcendent nature of God without resorting to analogy, namely negative theology.

This states that since God transcends all empirical properties or predicates, we have access to Him only through their negation. And it is this, argues Smith (2003: 56, 59) which ultimately forms the basis of Derrida's reliance on the principles of transcendentalism with his emphasis on the impossibility of the possible, measureless measure (Derrida 1992: 29–30), or, in a more general sense, aporias.

It is here that it is possible to detect two great branches of Western thought on which it is possible to locate the various players in this ontological game: Parmenedes–Scotus–Spinoza–Heidegger[22]–Deleuze relying on a univocal ontology on the one hand; and Aristotle–Kant–Freud–Levinas–Derrida with transcendence/negative-theology on the other. To be sure this quite crude division obscures many connections, relays, overlaps, and interesting and productive comparisons. However, it is nevertheless important, especially in so central an aspect as univocity and hence difference, to draw such distinctions. At the very least it exposes the dangers of misleading categories such as 'post-structuralism'. This term, merely on the basis of its tendency to adopt a position of critique towards certain nineteenth and twentieth century epistemological assumptions located within metanarratives and in particular notions of progress (dialectical materialism) and later inclusive systems (language for Saussure, mental life for Lacan, social/political life for Lévi-Strauss; see May 1993: 3), tends to encompass both Deleuze and Derrida. Yet the fundamental differences in their thought are incommensurable, and it seems to me the whole notion of a 'post-structuralist position' which would include Deleuze and Derrida has delayed Deleuze scholarship in the Anglo-Saxon, cultural–political field by at least a decade. In this sense Paul Patton's general thoughts on 'French philosophers of difference' or 'Deleuze's deconstructive reading of Plato' (2000: 46, 34) need serious re-consideration.

Whereas Deleuze treats Aristotle with obvious respect and sometimes admiration, his critique of Plato is particularly venomous because for Deleuze, Plato's game is the most dangerous of all. There is an aspect of irony here, for Plato's approach operates on the basis of a selection, a process parallel to Deleuze's view that the epistemological task is not to separate the true from the false or to establish the truth, but rather to select what is relevant from a distribution (*DR*: 238). Thus it is possible that the particular ire Deleuze shows for Plato is due, in part, to their similarities. In any case their differences in terms of selection rest on the criteria. Whereas in Deleuze the selection of elements must be the task of philosophy operating through a transcendental empiricism,[23] in Plato selection is accomplished by the *friend of philosophy* who acts as judge or authenticator. Here 'selection is not a question of dividing a determinate genus into different species, but of dividing a confused species into pure lines of descent' (*DR*: 72). Such a lineage is in the form of model, copy, and simulacrum as in 'Justice, the quality of being just, and just men.' (*LS*: 293). Again, Plato is close to Deleuze in that he does not adopt the *greatest*, middle difference as Aristotle does. On the other hand according to Deleuze, Plato's crime – and again we sense a hostility akin to Nietzsche's loathing of Socrates, and in this sense also a critique of neo-Platonic Christian theology – when the moment of selection finally comes to a head, is of directly and immediately inserting transcendence, this time as myth, as in the shepherd God in *The Statesman* or the circulation of souls in *The Phaedrus* (*DR*: 73). Plato's trick here is to have mediation without mediation per se. 'The introduction of myth appears, however, to confirm all Aristotle's objections: in the absence of any mediation, division lacks probative force; it has to be relayed by a myth which provides an imaginary equivalent of mediation' (74).

It could be argued that the short treatment I have given Plato here compared with the substantial exposition on Aristotle distorts Deleuze's intention. After all, in his early works it is an overturning of Platonism, a strategy borrowed from Nietzsche, that is his primary goal. However, when his writing is considered as a whole, it is representation pure and simple that is his greatest target and which characterizes if not defines Deleuze's work. And as such, Western philosophy is not best dismantled through overturning the model–copy–phantasm system of Plato and promoting a philosophy of simulacra in its place. In fact, Deleuze more or less gives up on simulacra as a productive notion in his later work.[24] In any event, the Aristotelian model of difference best serves to illustrate Deleuze's critique of Western metaphysics and provides the clearest perspective from which to approach Deleuze's own brand of immanent ontology. It is in Aristotle, as Deleuze writes, that representation is most truly deployed, and where it forgets 'its moral origin and presuppositions' (*DR*: 334). Delanda picks up on this point, writing that the best form of taxonomic essentialism can be traced back to Aristotle. His argument is that few would adhere to a sort of Platonic idealist essentialism, but that 'taxonomists *reify* the general categories produced by their classifications' (2006: 26–7). In other words, one ends up treating entities as having essential properties despite claims of non-essentialism. This illustrates the reinforcement of representation in scientific thought in general and hence why Aristotle serves as the best counter example to Deleuze.

Deleuze is careful in the remainder of the first chapter of *Difference and Repetition* to show in some detail the various attempts at reconciling difference with representation. This begins with a rather long discussion of two attempts at infinite representation (as distinct from Aristotle's finite representation), of the very large (with Hegel) and the very small (with Leibniz), which can, in one sense at least, be read as attempts to overcome the difficulty above and below the middle, perfect difference (genus–species) as described above. Deleuze concludes that 'infinite representation does not free itself from the principle of identity as a presupposition of representation'[25] because it 'invokes a foundation. While this foundation is not the identical itself, it is nevertheless a way of taking the principle of identity particularly seriously, giving it an infinite value and rendering it coextensive with the whole, and in this manner allowing it to reign over existence itself' (*DR*: 60). And furthermore it

> suffers from the same defect as finite representation: that of confusing the concept of difference in itself with the inscription of difference in the

identity of the concept in general (even though it treats identity as a pure infinite principle instead of treating it as a genus, and extends the rights of the concept in general to the whole instead of fixing their limits.)

(61)

Thus, perhaps it is more relevant to take infinite representation as the proper target of Deleuze's criticism as a progression beyond Aristotle. After all, it is to Hegel and Leibniz which he turns to in the conclusion in *Difference and Repetition,* not Aristotle. Yet for the purposes of this chapter the fourfold yoke or four 'iron collars' of representation – namely, identity of the concept, analogy of judgement, opposition of predicates, and resemblance of perception – will be dealt with in their finite form. The reason for this is that it suffices to explain the characteristics of representation as understood as the actual as opposed to the virtual. As Deleuze says, the purpose of Hegel and Leibniz's programmes are only to extend representation to infinity (*DR*: 331). As we shall see below, neither approach does anything to uncover the nature of the virtual.

What seems implicit in Deleuze's argumentation at this point is that all methods of inquiry, every 'philosophy of categories' (*DR*: 42), whether of the very large or the very small, borrows their concept of difference from this middle-range Aristotelian *greatest* difference. Whether in common parlance or exacting sociological theory, difference is taken to be as inscribed within the concept, thus leading to problems of groups/individuals as well as identity and singularity. This problem with difference likewise extends to IR, social movement theory, and post-Marxist theory in the form of structure–agency and level of analysis.[26] The basic tenor is evident, for example, in Craig Calhoun: 'There is no simple sameness unmarked by difference, but likewise no distinction not dependent on some background of common recognition' (1995: 193). It is in a sense of opposition to this basic assumption with which Deleuze critiques and ultimately rejects what in more contemporary terms might be called hierarchical or representational thought. The distinction between these two modes of thought is perhaps more well known in *A Thousand Plateaus*. Here Deleuze and Guattari offer rhizomatic thought in contrast to arborescent thought and the method of rhizomatics or nomadic science. In Platonic terms what Deleuze is arguing for is the denial of the very existence of pretenders: A world of simulacrum that precludes the very difference between model and copy.

How far does this go towards an understanding of political phenomena? At this very early stage we can say two things: First, in social science research difference is vastly underproblematized. It cannot simply be what determines an undetermined concept because, as we saw from the discussion of Aristotle, such a formulation only works in mid-range determinations. Differentiating the very large depends on analogy and differentiating the very small requires direct perception or apprehension which representation cannot offer. In order for these two forms of differentiation to function, a transcendent principle must be evoked which can serve as a measure of Being. Second, in Deleuze, Being is said of all things in the same way (univocity). Widder again: 'univocity is hardly concerned with establishing a unity among differences, but rather with linking differences through their differences' (2001: 439). If this is not a unity among differences or identity, what would it mean to think difference without identity? This is precisely the metaphysics that Derrida seeks to go beyond, one which Deleuze seeks to remedy or rebuild through a stringent but constructive logical critique covering the history of Western philosophy. Here he sides with Nietzsche: 'In its essence, difference is the object of affirmation or affirmation itself. In essence, affirmation is itself difference.' (*DR*: 63). Or as Delanda puts it, 'Deleuze conceives difference not negatively, as lack of resemblance, but positively or productively, as that which drives a dynamical process.' (2002: 63). The negative for him is an illusion, most damagingly bastardized by Hegel. This will be discussed later on in the chapter, but for now we can say that difference is pure positiveness, or what we will later call pure becoming. The two human beings Aristotle and Deleuze are different, but not in terms of negation, of what they are not in relation to each other – thus this has nothing to do with lack or the perennial Other – but in terms of their individual, positive singularity, in effect, their excess. Thus thinking difference in terms of such singularity means seeing beyond mere resemblance, or a lack of sameness. The apple is different from the orange in that it has a group of generally accepted traits or characteristics, which are, to be sure, different from the orange. Deleuze does not deny that objects can resemble one another, 'it is just that resemblances and identities must be treated as *mere results* of deeper ... processes, and not as fundamental categories on which to base an ontology' (Delanda 2002: 42). In terms of these processes the apple does not require the orange for its difference. The orange is not the Other of the apple. The process by which these apparent differences are produced will be discussed below, but in short 'Deleuze's aim ... is to show that ontology itself is constituted immanently by a principle of difference (and is thus a "concept", in the Deleuzian sense of the term)' (Smith 2003: 51).[27] This involves what seems at first to be a rather complex ontological configuration but ultimately reveals its metaphysical simplicity and logical parsimony. But before getting to that, its counterpart, representation, or what Deleuze sometimes refers to as 'dogmatic' thought, will be explored.

Representation

Many refer to Deleuze's critique of 'the image of thought' or what is generally termed representation thought. An understanding of this critique further illustrates how Deleuze arrives at his ontological position of immanence. With such a critique he unravels (Derrida might say 'deconstruct'; Foucault 'uncover the knowledge–power structures thereof') several centuries, or indeed millennia in Deleuze's case, of Western thought. However, this initial unravelling in turn drives a philosophical position that goes deeper than, for example, Derridaian or Foucauldian critique.[28] Such a position eventually leads back to critique, though this time not as a dismantling but with the full power of creation. In other words Deleuze does not displace or defer in an epistemological sense, but provides in detail an alternative to this 'image of thought'.

Deleuze expands his ontological critique of difference in the concept and the analogy of judgement into a general critique of the 'reflexive aspects' of representation. A suitable starting point is the form of representation in general that determines thought as the exercise of an innate faculty endowed with an affinity with the true (innate ideas, a priori nature of concepts), under the aspect of a thinker who wants and loves the truth – a *cogito natura universalis* (*DR*: 166; *NP*: 96). Deleuze's point here is that based on this image of what it means to think, it makes no difference where thought begins – subject or object, Being or beings – because everyone already *knows* what thinking is. This is not an idle observation: Deleuze here is describing two radically different notions of thought, one innate and internal, the other a 'thought from the outside', to which we will return in Chapter 4.[29] The intricate structure or texture of representation is a result of the four elements or principle aspects of representation, namely identity of the concept or the form of the Same in general, analogy of judgement, opposition of predicates, and resemblance of perception. Without going into too much detail – Deleuze himself only explains these briefly, almost in passing – a short overview seems appropriate here.

The first two aspects of representation we have already seen in dealing with difference – a concept holding a stable identity in order that it may *contain* contrariety in the species, and analogy which draws the relation between the category of Being and its genera. Opposition refers to the process by which possible predicates and their opposites are compared, something Deleuze calls 'memorial imaginative reproduction' (*DR*: 174). Resemblance of the object within the concept ensures perceptual continuity. For Deleuze, the most general principle of representation is the 'I think'. It is as if the 'I conceive', 'I judge', 'I imagine', 'I perceive' were the four branches of the *cogito* and, according to Deleuze, it is on these branches that difference is 'crucified'.

> They form quadripartite fetters under which only that which is identical, similar, analogous or opposed can be considered different: *difference becomes an object of representation always in relation to a conceived identity, a judged analogy, an imagined opposition or a perceived similitude.*
>
> (174)

The implication here is that the affirmed 'I' of the 'I think' is bound to the world of representation and unable to think real difference. So long as thought is subordinated in this way, argues Deleuze, difference cannot be one of individual difference, but rather 'remains only a general difference though it is borne by the individual' (*DR*: 309). In fact the status of the true individual that supports the fourfold 'I' is rather more complicated, as we shall see later in this chapter and particularly in Chapter 4. It is important to remember here that Deleuze emphasizes representation in terms of *Darstellung*; in fact, he rarely addresses *Vertretung* in any of his works.[30] This has deep political implications in that it is bound to his ontological premise of univocity and his metaphysical system, which in turn precludes certain theoretical political statements and empirical methodologies such as those considered in Chapter 1.

What Deleuze offers here is a reversal of the standard approach to thinking and difference, or perhaps more accurately to *thinking difference*. Rather than the representation–thought–difference sequences (for Descartes we can simply add *cogito* to the front of the series; for Kant it is rather more complicated but the model holds), Deleuze asserts difference–thought–representation. This places primacy on difference itself which in turn gives rise to thought and varying degrees of representation. Sometimes Deleuze calls this 'sub-representative' (*DR*: 68, 83). In any case, for Deleuze the four facets of representational thought are '*only effects produced by these presentations of difference*, rather than being conditions which subordinate difference and make it something represented' (*DR*: 182). In short, according to Deleuze, true difference comes first.

For Deleuze the development of occidental philosophy is intrinsically tied to transcendence. The latter, which refers to what is beyond the limits of possible experience, acts as the guarantor of representational thought by locating 'determinable singularities' inside 'a supreme self or superior I' (*LS*: 121).[31] This is accomplished, according to Deleuze, by the imposition of a false alternative corresponding to infinite or finite representation as described above: either an undifferentiated *ground* without differences or properties, or a supreme Being/Form, both of which serve as a bulwark to chaos. What this means, in effect, is that every singularity – whether the object of experience or not – is always already located in relation to or within the transcendent principle. And as, according to Deleuze, occidental philosophers have tended in general toward the transcendent, the history of philosophy becomes the discovery of a metaphysics capable of supporting such an equivocal position. A simple way of explaining the significance of this is to say that this movement to the transcendent always pushes both thought and thinker to some relative location: an undetermined object (object = x) always in relation to a bounded thinker (man–God), a transcendent guarantor (God), or an aporetic figure (lack). Because of Deleuze's commitment to univocity, that is, Being said of all things in the same sense, he is bound to an immanent metaphysics wherein no singularity is maintained through a proportionate hierarchy supported by a transcendent principle or unity. There must be another principle for relating series and elements to each other. But immediately a problem springs up, namely, if Being is univocal how can we differentiate between anything? How can we overcome the burdening sense of oneness, especially when Deleuze is precisely interested in talking about singularities and things called multiplicities? This is the starting point for Badiou's critique of the Deleuzian project in *Deleuze: The Clamour of Being* (1997). Badiou characterises Deleuze's metaphysics as arraying singularities in the universe via formal numerical difference and modal individuating difference wherein difference has no real status, and draws the negative conclusion that 'the world of beings is the theatre of the simulacra of the Being' (26). From this reading he classifies Deleuze's philosophy as an empty form of Platonism which, according to Badiou, must ultimately rely on a new formulation of the Platonic Good, corresponding in Deleuze's case to the Event.

We can find an analogous, and perhaps more familiar line of critique in many discussions of Michael Hardt and Antonio Negri's *Empire* (2000). In an example which serves as a good illustration, Timothy Brennan charges that Hardt and Negri cannot reconcile their theological monism (in this case, again, a conception of immanence borrowed from Spinoza) with 'heralding the rhizomatic decentring of the multitude' (2003: 359). At a certain level both Badiou and Brennan's argument share a common thrust: Anyone wishing to evoke any sort of One – univocity, the One-all, substance – needs to explain the connection between the one and the multiple (or perhaps more clearly expressed, the *many*). The counterclaim, however, is that such an objection misunderstands the relationship between univocal Being and beings.[32] There is a key phrase in *Difference and Repetition* that deals with this relationship:

> the essential in univocity is not that Being is said in a single and same sense, but that it is said, in a single and same sense, *of* all its individuating differences or intrinsic modalities. Being is the same for all of these modalities, but these modalities are not the same.
>
> (45)

So although Badiou is right to notice how Deleuze prioritizes the simulacrum, he wrongly characterizes 'being said of all things in the same sense' as pointing to a philosophy of simply 'the One'. That this cannot be attributed to Deleuze's ontological position is due to Deleuze's dynamic metaphysical framework of the virtual and the actual, which will be addressed presently. It is also worth noting that Deleuze is not a pluralist, and thus any theoretical appeal to pluralism (Liberalism would be the obvious example) cannot include Deleuze.[33] He is not speaking of numerality, but rather of the non-denumerable. In fact his ontological position demands this. As we will see again in Chapter 4 he is not interested in bounded and numerically distinct sets, but again, difference: 'Being is said in a single and same sense of everything of which it is said, but that of which it is said differs: it is said of difference itself' (*DR*: 45).

For Deleuze's metaphysics this means that if we hold to the univocity of Being, then we cannot even entertain the idea of the transcendent, because everything *is* in the same way. Thus, for example, whereas Derrida can draw a theory from the impossibility of the possible, Deleuze is unable even to entertain the thought of the possible, simply because everything already *is* in the same sense.[34] In fact, Derrida makes use of the transcendent in the form of the perfect gift and friendship (1997) *and* the immanent. As Smith shows, he retains the former as a sort of free-floater (free-rider, empty signifier, catalyst), and employs aporia in order to pry it apart (2003: 56). In light of this we can place Badiou in the same boat that Smith places Derrida, that is, as wanting more than one sense of Being. Deleuze on the other hand can only talk about the immanent and the experiential, and in this sense he is a committed empiricist. Objects, subjects, but also Events for Deleuze must relate to each other in a different way than through a representation via a transcendent principle. Before we develop this more later in the chapter, what we can say for now is that the principle that links Being and its singularities for Deleuze is multiplicity.

> 'Multiplicity', which replaces the one no less than the multiple, is the true substance, substance itself. The variable multiplicity is the how many, the how and each of the cases. Everything is a multiplicity in so far as it incarnates an Idea. Even the many is a multiplicity; even the one is a multiplicity. ... Instead of the enormous opposition between the one and the many, there is only the variety of multiplicity – in other words, difference.
>
> (*DR*: 230)

As will be shown in greater detail in Chapter 4, this means that both the Whole and the part, the one and the many are expressions of the same thing and implied in each other.

The most significant expression of the difference between immanence and transcendence is that ultimately we have access to the former. It still remains to investigate in some detail what Deleuze's immanent metaphysics – one capable of dealing with this question of the one and the many, and multiplicity – looks like, although at this point it is already clear what direction this is going in terms of the scientific investigation of social phenomena. Again, we need only to briefly compare Deleuze with two of the most general readings of what is known as 'continental philosophy' in the social sciences or political studies in particular, Derrida from whom we get text analysis and Foucault who has helped us to study power via discourse. I am not arguing that these are the main methodological tools or starting points of these two thinkers – on the contrary, the works of both are much more complicated, heterogeneous, and potentially productive than these general readings – only that this is how their work, in general, has been adopted into the empirical research of the social sciences. But rather than text and discourse, Deleuze offers us access of sorts to the empirical world in a style many have called his 'radical materialism'.[35] More will be said on such a project – what Deleuze calls his superior or transcendental empiricism – below, but for the moment it is important to state here the direction we are going. Deleuze is not going to talk about semiology, structuralism, textuality, or radical contingency. In short, in a world of transcendence we need to rely on an unknowable other, whereas the opposite is the case with immanence. The latter means no hierarchies, just one mixture that contains everything, and the task of the researcher is to figure out a way to see how that one mixture works in all its variation.

Now we can further see the significance of the two faculties of judgement, good sense and common sense, in how they relate to these four branches of the *cogito* and in turn reinforce and perpetuate the transcendental illusion. We have recognized above the role the *cogito* plays in underwriting representation, but for Deleuze it is not enough for representational thought to merely pose (or oppose) the *cogito* and its universal object. Rather there is a decisive middle step that binds the subject to this intermediary in mutual determination. What is necessary first is *good sense*. As has been noted above, good sense is the sense of measure, and it achieves this hierarchical measuring of subjects through its sense of direction. Good sense states that there is only one direction that moves from the most differentiated past to the least differentiated future, or in other terms from things to God (*LS*: 87). It gives the arrow of time its orientation, that is, *one*-directional; the 'right' direction (*DR*: 284). In doing so it grants a 'foreseeing' function (*LS*: 89) or a process of prediction to the present. This sense of direction provides the measure and distribution necessary for the establishment and functioning of the universal indeterminate object and the universal self (*DR*: 285). In other words it is not enough merely to posit a *cogito* – that is, the transcendental error of the universal self is, as an error, insufficient on its own. It requires good sense for its measure, distribution, and hence hierarchy to maintain its subjective identity and its relation to its indeterminate objects.

What this highlights is that for Deleuze we never encounter a universal indeterminate object or a universal self – which will obviously be important when we investigate the claims this makes on subjectivity in Chapter 4. Common sense, perhaps the more familiar in terms of a general critique of modern philosophy, is then the process of recognition which grants the identity of the self and in turn which provides unity and ground for the various faculties and for the identity of the object which is the focus of these faculties (*DR*: 284). Whereas good sense is the 'quantitative synthesis of difference', common sense is the 'qualitative synthesis of diversity' (285), taking so many diverse elements – selves in terms of the subject, instances in terms of the object – and giving them a qualitative unity. It contributes to the form of the Same in that it takes recognition as a 'subjective principle of collaboration of the faculties for "everybody"', implying that faculties must be the modality of a thinking subject (*DR*: 169). What this amounts to for Deleuze is the simple model of recognition defined by 'the harmonious exercise of all the faculties upon a supposed same object' (*DR*: 169) – like Descartes and his lump of wax: there is no doubt for Descartes that it is the same lump which he sees, touches, and pictures in his imagination (1960: 30). Likewise in Kant and beyond, as Smith points out (2003: 30), we have the object in general as the objective correlate of the subjective unity of consciousness. Although they are not self-constituting it is nevertheless clear that they are mutually reliant. They both transcend themselves toward the other and are thus mutually dependent. As Deleuze writes, 'In this complementarity of good sense and common sense the alliance between the self, the world and a God is sealed' (*LS*: 90).

Deleuze argues that such a conception of good sense and common sense is a hindrance to philosophy in that it only allows one particular, unassailable orthodoxy – stretching from Plato to Descartes to Kant, and by extension to the positivist sciences – namely, 'harmony of the faculties grounded in the supposedly universal thinking subject and exercised upon the unspecified object' (*DR*: 170). What this unspecified object highlights is the fact that this thinking subject is capable of exercising, in itself, its faculties upon the object in general – that is, any object. In Deleuze we will find that the object itself (or more specifically *difference* in itself) plays the fundamental role. Now, it could be argued here that for the purposes of this book this is beside the point, since, thanks to the healthy dose of postmodernism that social theory has ingested over the last decades, contemporary research approaches no longer have to deal with the problems of Kant. They are well able to integrate questions of subjectivity, diversity, and non-preferential systems in the form of objectivity by considering notions of identity, otherness, subjectification, discourse, and so on. My point here is not to argue that this is not the case, though without going into an in-depth analysis it certainly is arguable that few studies do actually get beyond these fundamental philosophical assumptions, most often sustaining at the basic level a bounded and mostly rational subject. For this reason we get charges of 'smuggling' mind or subject in through the back door (see for example Bains 2002: 103) and similar observations. Rather, I wish to illustrate here how Deleuze will not be content to warily avoid these distinctions of modern metaphysics inherited in their latest incarnation from Kant and proceed from there. Because of his commitment to an immanent philosophy Deleuze will instead seek to devise a system which accounts for such an orthodoxy and yet at the same time offers an alternative to it. Or more accurately, his refusal to accept the facts of judgement that are good sense and common sense leads him to his ontological position of immanence. In other words, rather than fighting or denouncing good sense and common sense, each of which constitutes one half of orthodoxy (*DR*: 284) or doxa (*DR*: 169–70), he is able to devise an alternative.[36]

From this last discussion we can see that in general Deleuze's critique of Western philosophy (thought, metaphysics) upon which the overwhelming majority of social investigations are built is understood through his analysis of difference (albeit loosely defined so far). However, an equally important and overlooked entry point can be his simple analysis and rejection of *the possible* as first detailed in *Bergsonism* (1988a). Deleuze's philosophy comes out in its starkest form, particularly when we come to look at emergence and complexity, when seen as a combination of two very powerful and mutually sustaining ontological fixtures: the drive for a concept of difference in itself and a rejection of the possible as having anything to do with reality or, more specifically, a theory of becoming. Indeed, as we will see below Deleuze will substitute repetition, the co-concept of difference, for this realization of the possible. Thus, like his problems with difference which ultimately necessitate univocity, Deleuze's rejection of the possible necessitates his metaphysical position of the virtual–actual couplet.

The possible normally functions as a field of potentiality and inheres in time when one possibility is realized over all the others.[37] In common parlance as well as in social research we say that there are a number of possibilities, possible reasons, or possible outcomes. The possible has no reality on its own, it is opposed to reality. Thus out of an array of possibilities one in particular comes to be or arises. In this sense Deleuze suggests that the real *resembles* the possible. However, Deleuze flatly rejects such a view, calling it 'the source of false problems' (*B*: 98) on the basis that it is ontologically unstable since the only difference between the possible and the real is existence: *the possible* as a notion merely has existence or reality added to it. Put another way, the possible resembles the real in every aspect save existence, it is 'ready-made, preformed, pre-existent to itself' (*B*: 98) and passes into existence on the basis of limitations which exclude certain 'possibles'. But if the only difference between the possible and the existent or the real *is* reality, then what is the point of using the notion of the possible at all? What function does it serve? Here we can see that if everything is already 'pre-made', then there is no way to account for becoming or the new. 'Hence, we need no longer understand anything either of the mechanism of difference or the mechanism of creation' (*B*: 98).

What is more logically and metaphysically insidious for Deleuze is the way in which the real 'projects backward' (*B*: 20) onto the possible. It is another 'sleight of hand' wherein the real comes about of its own accord (how else can we explain the emergence of the real?) but had nevertheless always remained possible, being possible at any time before it actually happened. 'In fact,' writes Deleuze, 'it is not the real that resembles the possible, it is the possible that resembles the real, because it had been abstracted from the real once made' (*B*: 98). In other words, once presented with an aspect of the real, we inevitably reverse the resemblance, and, extracting existence, devise a possible after the fact. Although we think in terms of existence being realized from amongst a field of possibles, in fact we merely model a possible based upon the real, implying that the real with which we are faced was realized from the possible. This is even more weighty when we consider the question of the mechanism for realization. Deleuze never tells us what the rule of limitation might entail, but we can guess that it would be no mean task to explain how this functions, how some possibles are limited whereas a single (are they infinite?) possible passes into the real. In short, this process of abstracting the possible from the real post facto does nothing to explain the coming to be of the real, and when pressed, it is not difficult to see how such a metaphysical principle becomes bogged down with problems of determinism: How is it exactly that one possible was realized when others were not? If it is a question of environmental condition, then is it the case that in fact the other 'possibles' that were not realized were, in fact, not possible at all?

In this discussion we can see many connections and parallels with Deleuze's metaphysics that we have dealt with so far. The possible–real couplet is intimately related to the mode–copy relationship in Plato: Courage, courageousness, and courageous individuals. For Deleuze, such a relationship is the first moral application of a metaphysics of resemblance in the Western world (*DR*: 155) wherein it becomes a moral duty to prefer the model over the copy, and identifying the model will always be the *métier* of the ever-illusive figure of the philosopher or lover of wisdom. Stronger still is the correlation between representation and the possible because the actualization of the possible relies on resemblance (as well as limitation) to function. In the face of this Deleuze eschews any theory of emergence based on essence as form or model. He 'replaces the false genesis implied by these pre-existing forms which remain *the same* for all time, with a theory of morphogenesis based on the notion of *the different*' (Delanda 2002: 4).

The question is, if the problem of genesis does not concern the realization of the possible through resemblance, then what? The fact is, according to Deleuze, we do not need the possible at all. In order to account for the possible–real problem we need the virtual, where true difference is located: difference in nature in the heterogeneous mixture (*B*: 20). As we will see below, we can say then that contemporary politics is not the realization of possible relations, but the actualization of virtual connections (differenciation). Thus we get rid of what Deleuze takes to be cumbersome aspects of Western thought such as representation (*Darstellung*), judgement (common and good sense), the thinking subject, and the universal object. But it is important to note that Deleuze's philosophy 'problematizes the field of the possible without ever articulating a plan in view of a telos' (Valentin 2006: 194). In other words, in jettisoning the possible he does not thereby invite the dead end of determinism. He will require a dynamic metaphysics that can account for emergence and change without falling into the paradox of the possible on the one hand, or determinism on the other.

Immanence

From the above discussion we can discern two main problems with representational thought. In the last section we showed how the possible is not ontologically stable. Before that we saw that in the analysis of difference and univocity and the problem of equivocal genera, a notion of difference dependent on the identity of the concept – and in this sense *representation* – is not ontologically sound in that it only functions at a middle level of categorical distinction; what Aristotle called perfect difference. Recall that such a formulation of difference breaks down when it tries to address the very small (individual difference) and the very large (generic difference), the latter relying on analogy to support an equivocal ontology. In terms of contemporary socio-political theory this means that the categories of differentiation which we use analytically function very poorly, unable to deal with individual difference and causing ontological problems when it comes to generic difference. For example, 'the State' as a species can be more or less precise, tending as it does towards 'perfect' difference. This will be of little help analytically, however, when we turn to, for example, Nigeria, or, on the other hand, when we seek to differentiate amongst various forms of human organization of which the state is but one sub-species. For Deleuze ontology can only be univocal (*DR*: 44) and, to look again at this crucial quote, he presents the criteria for a univocal ontology thus:

> Univocity of being, in so far as it is immediately related to difference, demands that we show how individuating difference precedes generic, specific, and even individual differences within being; how a prior field of individuation within being conditions at once the specification of forms, the determination of parts, and their individual variations.
>
> (*DR*: 48)[38]

This means that there can be no prior condition or essence which would determine and hence have a representational relationship with its object. So what would it mean to enact such a philosophical position? In general terms Deleuze could be recognized as a more or less familiar critique of socio-political thought with obvious overlaps with Foucault and Derrida, among others. Such a reading could come, as has been already mentioned, from Deleuze's general renunciation of an occidental metaphysics running from Aristotle to Aquinas and into the modern period with Kant and Hegel where it would subsequently solidify in the twentieth century through positivistic and rationalist methodologies, as well as in liberal thought endowed with good sense and common sense. But when we turn to how a metaphysics that can address how such individuating difference might actually work, we arrive at a take on the world that is quite interesting and sophisticated, and yet arresting in its ultimate simplicity, this time beginning with the univocity of Spinoza and drawing heavily on Henri Bergson.

Put succinctly, Deleuze, following Spinoza (1992: 31–5), posits one substance, and drawing on Bergson this substance has two aspects. On the one hand we have a whole or One; on the other its quantitative expression – what Spinoza calls attributes. In the Deleuzian terminology of which I want to make use here, this corresponds to the virtual and the actual, respectively. It cannot be stressed enough that this simple formula forms the basis of Deleuze's metaphysics and *all* of its subsequent applications and experimentations, including the works he co-authored with Guattari.[39] At the outset it might be useful to say what this formulation is not. It is not a form of actualizing the possible. It precisely the virtual–actual schema that allows Deleuze to skirt the problem of the possible and the real as presented above. Moreover, Žižek's assertion that Deleuze's formulation can be boiled down to the classical idealist–materialist duality (2003: 21ff.) must be rejected, as will become clear through the course of this chapter. By following Badiou's reading that Deleuze's metaphysical schema is a dualism disguised as monism, Žižek misses perhaps the most tantalizing aspect of Deleuze's work, namely that there is no ontological distinction between the virtual and the actual: they are both two aspects of the same thing or, more accurately, substance. It is somewhat ironic, then, that Badiou himself provides perhaps some of the most insightful guidelines for considering the virtual, warning that 'we must not represent it as a latent double or ghostly prefiguration of the real',[40] and that it 'would be just as wrong to conceive of the virtual as a kind of indetermination, as a formless reservoir of possibilities' that are only identified in their actuality (1997: 49, 50). Finally, it is not the case that we inhabit the actual world while the virtual remains inaccessible, 'the beyond'. Drawing distinctions by using notions like 'our world' (of the actual), as Massumi sometimes does (see for example 1992: 66) for example, despite his otherwise rigorous and helpful 'deviation', should be avoided. This is key in that engaging in the virtual is not only the task of philosophy, but has important ramifications for the study of world politics. 'Our world' is virtual too – it must be, as will be made clear in the following. Again, both the virtual and the actual share one ontic condition and are equally real.

In *Bergsonism* Deleuze draws out the basic distinctions of what will become in *Difference and Repetition* the virtual and the actual, which will be taken as the operative notions in the present work. But that Deleuze uses various terms to describe similar relations becomes obvious, perhaps with no small amount of frustration to the first-time or casual reader, for in *Capitalism and Schizophrenia*, for example, the virtual will mutate to the very similar and widely misunderstood (see Bonta and Protevi 2004: 62) notion of the Body without Organs and its counter-notion – its opposite pairing, in other words – the organism (*ATP*: 158).[41] Following Bergson, Deleuze contrasts duration (again, the virtual) with space or matter (the actual). Recalling the difference–thought–representation distinction above, it is in duration where the strongest sense of difference subsists. These are differences in kind as compared to spatial differences of degree, but both coexist in a single Nature. Again, these are not proper opposites but rather forms of each other: 'Duration is only the most contracted degree of matter, matter the most expanded (*détendu*) degree of duration' (*B*: 92); see Figure 2.2.

It is in duration where qualitative difference lies (in itself and for itself) – it is continuous and homogeneous; in matter or space difference is of degree (outside itself and for us) – it is discontinuous and metricized. Thus in Deleuze's *Bergsonism* duration is commonly characterized – in the secondary literature ad nauseam – by intensities that cannot divide without changing their nature (see for example Boundas 1996: 6). Deleuze (and others) often offers the examples of speed and temperature. These qualities are intensive because they are not an aggregation of smaller speeds and temperatures; and thus they cannot divide without changing their nature.[42] For example, although one can arrive at the distance of 100 metres by adding unit metres: 1+1+1+1+ …, one cannot arrive at water heated to twenty degrees by the same process. Or put the other way, a litre of water heated to 75 °C divided in half yields two quantities of 500 millilitres, but the quality of heat remains unchanged. One can reduce such intensities, but not divide them, in the sense that 'no part of it exists prior to the division and no part retains the same nature after division' (*DR*: 297). Bergson discusses this in considerable detail in *Mind and Matter*. Any given emotion cannot be seen as possessing extended magnitude, and any impression or sentiment that it does so is the failure of 'psychological analysis' (1929: 13). Love is an example of an intensity: it is non-quantifiable and cannot be divided (without changing its nature). Bergson goes on to extend this principle to sensation and finally to time and space, treating the latter as a form of the former. Thus difference in nature – virtual difference, true difference – differs from itself qualitatively. There is

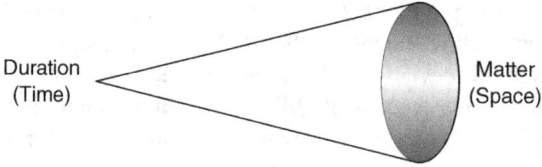

Figure 2.2 The virtual–actual in *Bergsonism*.

nothing negative about this (*DR*: 295); at the level of the virtual, true difference, we cannot compare two entities by what one is not as in, 'This man differs from Socrates insofar as he is not Socrates'. In space, on the other hand, extension differs quantitatively. It repeats itself in that it is incapable of changing its nature; only varying in degree. Thus we have all kinds of measurement of space and time and the corresponding (representational) differences which such characteristics are capable of determining.

In this schema any given thing (person, physical object, group, thought) is at once virtual and actual. It is as if any given actual thing is 'plunged' into the virtual (*DR*: 260). 'Every object is a double without it being the case that the two halves resemble one another, one being a virtual image and the other an actual image' (*DR*: 261). The nature of the virtual image is qualitative and intensive; the actual image is one of quantitative difference and measure. Here, in a *Bergsonism*-derived reading we can see that the virtual is not a ghostly image. It fulfils a very special function, for unlike quantitative difference – that is, without, in effect, space – virtual elements are able to differentiate in infinite variety. It is precisely these divergent series (differen*t*iation, below) that provide the dynamism for Deleuze's metaphysics. It is also important to bear in mind that everything has these two halves, according to Deleuze. It is not the case that there are uniquely virtual objects or uniquely actual objects (*D*: 112).

There is a further important point to remember at the outset. It is that although the model sketched in *Bergsonism* gives a general idea or a good introduction of Deleuze's metaphysics, Deleuze departs substantially from it in *Difference and Repetition*. To my mind the main reason he does this is to provide a description of the movement or the process from the virtual to the actual. It is important to keep this in mind as one could use the *Bergsonism–Difference and Repetition* split to divide commentators and to keep their respective fields of influence in the secondary literature straight. On the one hand, for example, we have Constantin Boundas relying very productively on the Bergsonian reading. On the other there is Manuel Delanda's hugely influential *Intensive Science and Virtual Philosophy* (2002) which was amplified by John Protevi's *Political Physics* (2001) and has garnered considerable attention in recent years. What Delanda's analysis lacks, however, is a certain mobility between the virtual and the actual, making his analysis sometimes rather uni-directional; that is, it seems to run only from the virtual to the actual. This also means adopting, tacitly at least, a unidirectional arrow of time – a characteristic of complexity theorists drawing on the tradition made popular by Prigogine and Stengers (1984), a point which will be followed up in the next chapter. It also means that those who draw heavily upon Delanda's reading – Mark Bonta and John Protevi, for example, in their highly original *Deleuze and Geophilosophy* (2004), perhaps the first to address Deleuze's work in a more or less social scientific context – share this view of time. In the case of Boundas we have a much more flexible relationship between the virtual and the actual. Here it is the ways in which entities move back and forth (2006: 5) that are crucial. Time – not surprisingly an important aspect of Deleuze's work – here is treated much more rigorously and in fact corresponds to recent developments in the field of physics which challenge not only classical but also relativistic notions of time.[43]

On the other hand the advantage of Delanda's (and subsequent commentators') reading of Deleuze is its emphasis – complete with detailed description – on movement and dynamism. Such is lacking in Boundas, for example, who is rather vague on exactly how the virtual is actualized due to his emphasis on virtual differences or differences in kind being qualitative. The following will seek to locate such a mechanism – thereby improving on the *Bergsonism*–Boundas reading – without falling into the 'complexity trap' of Delanda's reading. This trap entails tending to blur the distinction between virtual and actual systems through the relentless relying on physical models. For Deleuze these models are examples of virtual systems, but do not make them up in their entirety. This is evident, for example, when he writes '[M]athematics and biology appear here only in the guise of technical models which allow the exposition of the virtual and the process of actualisation, along with the exploration of the two halves of difference' (*DR*: 273–4). When relating virtual systems and 'certain physical concepts' Deleuze uses the phrase 'adequately expressed' (*DR*: 43), not *is*. In other words physical concepts *express* the virtual, but do not in themselves constitute it. The main danger here is a conception of linear time (the arrow of time) which very clearly runs against Deleuze's insistence that the divergent series which make up systems of simulacra (the virtual) move at infinite speed (*WP*: 118), effectively meaning that they are 'simultaneous' (see *DR*: 151).[44]

Looking at the variation within Deleuze and the resulting Deleuzisms amongst secondary sources – and I have only scratched the surface here – one might be tempted to wonder why such divergent readings. When it comes to unpacking extremely dense aspects of Deleuze's work we can consider a few possibilities. First, that like his ambiguity regarding the line of flight as mentioned above, Deleuze in fact never got it straight and it is impossible to draw one consistent version from his opus. A second likely scenario is that in English at least there is massive translation problems from one text to the next and within single texts themselves.[45] Complexity literature in the social sciences was in its nascency at the time of these translations and in any case it seems that both Massumi (who translated *A Thousand Plateaus* in 1987), and especially Patton (*Difference and Repetition* in 1994), probably did not dwell on its implications at the time. A third likelihood is that there is a consistent position that is accessible via the translations but various commentators choose to ignore or suppress different aspects according to their own ends and whims. A final possibility is that a consistent position is accessible – perhaps with a little digging – and yet has not been 'gathered' from the literature. This last is the most optimistic view it seems to me and will be the perspective of this investigation. In the face of possible failure in this task, the very least one can do at this stage in Deleuze research is posit a bare minimum or consistency in Deleuze's position. That is, not to buy in wholly to either the two different readings that have just been characterized as following Boundas or Delanda. What we will see below through such a 'bare minimum reading' is that series in an intensive spatium (systems) interact through differentials (intensive quantities). Intensities – what characterized the differences between heterogeneous series – unable to relate to each other numerically or metrically relate to each other immanently and interact through their pure difference which, far from an innate quality or essence, differentiates them and causes the pattern of their actualization (or differenciation – the processes by which difference is cancelled). But what precisely are these intensities and what do they do?

In *Difference and Repetition* Deleuze asks us to consider two propositions: 'only that which is alike differs; and only differences are alike.' (142). The first proposition is what we could refer to as Aristotelian-based difference: difference within the concept. The second proposition, the alternative, is the goal of Deleuze's metaphysics. The criteria are: 'difference must be articulation and connection in itself, it must relate different to different without any mediation whatsoever by the identical, the similar, the analogous or the opposed' (143). Or, again, recalling the above discussion of difference–thought–representation: What Deleuze is seeking here is a 'primary system of differences', and this gives us a hint as to the nature of the virtual. It also tells us something of the nature of the actual: in the actualized real, representations 'become no more than effects of the primary difference and its differentiation' (143). This, in short, is a contrast between the 'in itself' of pure difference (difference in itself) and the 'for itself' of representation (repetition for itself). The question remains, however, what describes the movement between pure difference (the virtual) and its effects (the actual)? This is not a question that Deleuze addresses very directly or succinctly. In fact, one can read Chapters 4 and 5 and perhaps also the conclusion of *Difference and Repetition* as the prolonged or perhaps repeatedly deferred response to this central question. The following revisits these chapters in order to clarify the logic of Deleuze's argument. Such a labour is justified given the density and difficulty of the material and the hastiness with which a great deal of commentary deals with this aspect of Deleuze's thought.

The virtual is characterized by Deleuze as pure *spatium*. The nature of this *spatium* is much misunderstood and is the source of a great deal of confusion amongst commentators. I would also argue that this misunderstanding has caused substantial logical blockages, for seeing the *spatium* of the virtual as strictly qualitative makes it impossible to understand or to draw on much of the crucial discussions in *Difference and Repetition*. We said above in the discussion of *Bergsonism* that duration was characterized by intensive qualities as opposed to extensive quantities. But in *Difference and Repetition* it is crucial that intensities are *quantitatively* different precisely because this kind of difference is inherently different from extensive difference, which in fact exhibits the only qualitative difference of the entire schema. Again, unlike a *Bergsonism*-derived reading, Deleuze is not simply placing all qualitative differences within intensity (the virtual) and all quantitative difference within degree or extension (the actual). This view is further supported by the fact that in later works, for example, in the discussion of Freud's Wolfman in *A Thousand Plateaus*, it is precisely these intensive quantities to which Deleuze and Guattari are drawing our attention. What they end up emphasizing here is depth which is *quantitative*: 'Difference becomes qualitative only in the process by which it is cancelled in extension' (*ATP*: 30–1). In other words it is through the process of actualization that difference becomes qualitative. Otherwise it is quantitative: intensive quantity. But what exactly is this intensive quantity?

Intensities have three characteristics. The first is unequalness in quantity (*DR*: 291) or 'difference in itself' (293). This is the quality of quantity; the fundamental movement in quantity. For example, ordinal numbers: 'ordinal number becomes cardinal only by extension, the extent that the distances enveloped in the *spatium* are explicated, or developed and equalised in an extensity established by natural number.' Furthermore

> [i]ntensity is the uncancellable in difference of quantity, but this difference in quantity is cancelled by extension, extension being precisely the process by which intensive difference is turned inside out and distributed in such a way as to be dispelled, compensated, equalised and suppressed in the extensity which it creates.
>
> (292)

Second, intensities affirm difference (293). One must note here that Deleuze is very clear here that this is not negation (294, 295) and thus not expressible in terms of *not* being something. Finally, an intensity is an 'implicated, enveloped or "embryonised" quantity'. Difference implicates or envelops distance. Deleuze explains it thus:

> In this sense, difference in depth is composed of distances, 'distance' being not an extensive quantity but an indivisible asymmetrical relation, ordinal and intensive in character which is established between series of heterogeneous terms and expresses at each moment the nature of that which does not divide without changing its nature…[I]ntensive quantities are therefore defined by the enveloping difference, the enveloped distances, and the unequal in itself which testifies to the existence of a natural 'remainder' which provides the material for a change in nature.
>
> (298)

Intensities 'direct the course of the actualization of Ideas and determine the cases of solution for problems' (306). One way of putting it is that intensities, in their variation, create the new; new individuations and singularities, new series to be actualized. But how do they do this precisely? Deleuze tells us that there are divergent lines along which differential relations are actualized (306), a process he calls individuation. Individuation does not suppose differenciation, it gives rise to it. But how does intensity imply such individuation or the creation of lines along which it is differenciated? Here we learn that it does so 'by virtue of an essential process' (307) of individuation which is like the act of solving a problem. 'Individuation is the act by which intensity determines differential relations to become actualised, along the lines of differenciation and within the qualities and extensities it creates' (308). This seems then to be synonymous with the flash of phenomena (280) or differentiators. These are the individuals which populate the system and are formed of intensive quantities. Basically what we have is a differential relation or an individuation which is a differentiator. Actualization arises when this inequality is cancelled and difference is cancelled, or put another way, the 'problem' of the Idea is solved.

Deleuze defines a system as two or more series made up of terms, the difference between the latter as that which defines the series. Now, assuming as he does that these series communicate (*DR*: 143), and that series are defined by terms which are in turn defined by the difference in distance between them (first degree difference) in the intensive spatium, then 'this communication relates differences to other differences, constituting differences between differences within the system' (143). These second degree differences play the role of what Deleuze calls a differenciator, that is, they relate first to second degree difference. These second degree differences, or intensities, are, as is evident from Deleuze's schema, constituted by 'a difference which itself relates to other differences' by way of an infinite regression (144). For any two points on a series, $E - E^1$, E refers to $e - e^1$, e refers to $\varepsilon - \varepsilon^1$ and so on – in both directions (that is, $E - E^1$ is in itself a sub-series). A differenciator is composite 'because not only are these two series which bind it heterogeneous but each is itself composed of heterogeneous terms, subtended by heterogeneous series which form so many subphenomena' (280–1).[46] Crucial here is that as soon as these series begin to communicate the system begins to fill with what Deleuze calls spatio–temporal dynamisms: the coupling of series causes resonance and an increase in amplitude to the extent that these further series take on new intensive quantities. At this point the space of the system becomes 'populated' by what Deleuze calls 'larval subjects' and 'passive selves' (144). These are the proto-subjects which exist, in the biological model, on 'the borders of the livable ... under conditions beyond which it would entail the death of any well-constituted subject endowed with independence and activity' (145). Deleuze offers the example of the embryo: in the initial stages an adult would be torn apart by the 'torsions' and 'drifts' involved in the unfolding of the life form. In any case these are the 'subjects' of the dynamisms which these couplings effect. Finally it is the dynamisms which cause the qualities and extensities to develop (see Figure 2.3 below).

A key question is, what causes these two series to communicate in the first place? Enter the much referenced 'dark-precursor' of Deleuzo-complexity adherents. In the case of *Difference and Repetition* the discussion in fact precedes both Deleuze and orthodox complexity theory, coming from Nietzsche's discussion of the doer and the doing using the example of the lightning flash (Nietzsche 1989: 45), which Deleuze also uses to illustrate his point. It is the nature of the dark precursor (also called object = *x*, nonsense, abstract machine, or Event) to join two heterogeneous series. But, like Nietzsche's lightning flash, it is only visible in reverse from the perspective of the phenomenon which induces it into

76 *Deleuze and politics as becoming*

the system, and thus 'it has no place other than that from which it is "missing", no identity other than that which it lacks' (*DR*: 146). Any logical or physical characteristics retroactively attributed to such a dark precursor are only a condition of its representation. It cannot be represented in itself, and for this reason Deleuze likens it to an effect – very much in the same sense as an optical effect.

These differential relations communicated through a dark precursor or Event create corresponding singularities in the system which will be actualized into the extensive parts through a process of individuation. Here the differential relations themselves become – through speed and slowness, acceleration and deceleration – the qualities or species. This is the process which precedes generic, specific, and even individual differences which Deleuze sets as his criteria for a univocal ontology as described above. Deleuze sums up the virtual–actual thus (see Figure 2.3):

> It is as though everything has two, odd, dissymmetrical and dissimilar 'halves' ... each dividing itself in two: an ideal half submerged in the virtual and constituted on the one hand by differential relations and on the other by corresponding singularities; an actual half constituted on the one hand by the qualities actualising those relations and on the other by the parts actualising those singularities. Individuation ensures the embedding of the two dissimilar halves.
>
> (*DR*: 350)

From this schema we get the transcendental illusion of sensibility which says that difference tends to be cancelled in the quality which covers it. And this is key, for although this cancellation really occurs, it is nevertheless an illusion because it falsely suggests that the nature of difference is to be found in the qualities and parts. Difference is not *found* in that by which it is covered. It 'is intensive, indistinguishable from depth in the form of a non-extensive and non-qualified *spatium*, the matrix of the unequal and the different' (*DR*: 335). Of course there is the obvious question: 'How, then, do these two aspects of differenciation connect with the two preceding aspects of differentiation? How do these two dissimilar halves of an object fit together?' (262). Again, Deleuze's answer (262–3) is that the actual is the local solution or local integration of the

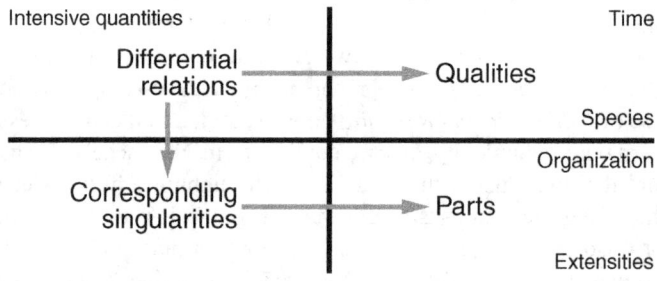

Figure 2.3 Individuation.

differential relations in the Idea (the virtual). In other words the halves are joined together through the solving of problems, the cancellation of difference.

So we have, in sum, the *spatium*, the series which make up the systems in the *spatium*, and the differences between these differences (differential relations; intensities). The movement to the actual is the result of the solving (differenciating) of these differential relations. 'When the virtual content of an Idea is actualised, the varieties of relations are incarnated in distinct species while the singular points which correspond to the values of one variety are incarnated in the distinct parts characteristic of this or that species' (257–8) as Figure 2.3 shows. With actualization, 'a new type of specific and partitive distinction takes the place of the fluent ideal distinctions.' This is carried out by 'spatio-temporal dynamisms' (266) and means simply that things in their actualization are 'distinguished by the orientations, the axes of development, the differential speeds and rhythms which are the primary factors in the actualisation of a structure and create a space and time peculiar to that which is actualised' (266). Deleuze's example involves a division into 24 cellular elements which all have similar characteristics. By observing them as a simple state of affairs it is not possible to tell what the dynamic process by which this division was obtained – 2×12, $(2 \times 2)+(2 \times 10)$, or $(2 \times 4)+(2 \times 8)$, and so on (268). But then the difficult and persisting question becomes how to relate these dynamic processes (spatio–temporal dynamisms) to actualization?

Deleuze's answer: *drama*. Dynamic processes dramatize the Idea. This is the crux of Deleuze's concept of complex repetition: that things have movement through their differences. Actual states of affairs have no movement – it is only the virtual which repeats. They do so in two ways, predictably: spatially and temporally. First, spatio–temporal dynamisms create (or trace) a space 'corresponding to the differential relations and to the singularities to be actualised' (*DR*: 268–9). Additionally, and this is crucial to Deleuze's metaphysical system, the constitution of these spaces interact because of the relationship between complex Ideas; it is not just a matter of tracing an internal space. For example, living beings are not defined genetically (by the dynamisms which determine them internally), but by other external movements of other Ideas, that is, environment(s). These spaces are the incarnation of differential relations between elements. So in essence spatio–temporal dynamisms incarnate further differential relations. Second, spatio–temporal relations constitute a time. These times are rhythms, rates of growth, accelerations and decelerations. In terms of how things come to be actualized as this or that particular quality and extensity, it is all a matter of arriving too soon or too late, or at just the right time.

Thus there is the duality of species (quality) and parts (extensity) (*DR*: 270) which exists in the outcome only (actualization). The relationship is complementary. '[T]he species gathers the time of the dynamisms into a quality (lion-ness, frog-ness) while the parts outline its space' (270). This is the differenciation of differentiation (just as there is difference of difference). But it seems we have not proceeded much further in trying to understand precisely how this dynamic process works; by what mechanism is it propelled? What exactly are these spatio–temporal dynamisms? Where do they come from? Deleuze says (270) his model differs from Kant's *schemata* in that the latter are of the possible (it converts logical possibility into transcendental possibility) whereas dramatization denotes a power *internal* to the concept: 'Dynamism thus comprises its own power of determining space and time' (271), though this explanation still remains rather vague. Here is Deleuze not getting closer to what Nietzsche criticized in 'old Kant': 'by the faculty of a faculty' (1966: 18)?

Deleuze's ultimate answer is repetition.[47]

> Repetition is everywhere, as much in what is actualised as in its actualisation. It is in the Idea to begin with, and it runs through the varieties of relations and the distribution of singular points. It also determines the reproductions of space and time ... In every case, repetition is the power of difference and differenciation: because it condenses the singularities, or because it accelerates or decelerates time, or because it alters spaces. Repetition is never explained by the form of identity in the concept, nor by the similar in representation.
>
> (273)

Thus the order (or rather a model for the order) of reasons is differentiation–individuation–dramatization–differenciation, driven by repetition. One of the difficulties in understanding all this, especially for social scientists, is imagining heterogeneous systems that coexist in duration and spatium and yet are distinct from one another, that is, there is distance (depth, quantitative intensity) between them. But nevertheless it is precisely this which describes a truly immanent ontology and satisfies the requirements of univocity. The ontological and ontic status of all the series and points is equal but not the Same. Deleuze refers to this as *perplication*, series and points 'undifferenciated and coexisting with other Ideas' (314).

This dovetails to Deleuze's notion of a signal–sign system wherein two or more heterogeneous series communicate with each other. What flashes across the system (every phenomenon, qualities) and brings them into communication is a sign. Every phenomenon (or sign, or second-degree difference or differentiator) is a composite because the series which bind it are composite *and* it itself is composed of heterogeneous terms, subtended by other homogeneous terms which form further sub-phenomena. 'We call this state of infinitely doubled difference which resonate to infinity *disparity*' (*DR*: 281). This is the sufficient reason of all phenomena. 'The reason of the sensible, the condition of that which appears, is not space and time but the Unequal in itself, *disparateness* as it is determined and comprised in difference of intensity, in intensity as difference' (281). But in order to understand how this works we have to look again at intensities.

Deleuze re-forms his question thus: '[W]hat happens when Ideas are expressed by intensities or individuals in this new dimension of implication [of intensities]'? (314). Here we get to a crucial and overlooked passage in

Difference and Repetition – and one perhaps which, after the above retracing of Chapters Four and Five, we might wish Deleuze had been more forthright with. The key seems to be this implication of intensities. We know that intensity (difference) expresses differential relations and determines their corresponding points. It distinguishes them to the point where they 'are in a sense separated: instead of coexisting, they enter states of simultaneity or succession' (314). But as we saw from the notion of disparity, differential relations are defined by an infinite regress. Each intensity both determines difference and is itself determined by sub-difference. Deleuze calls this enveloped and enveloping, that is, every intensity is itself a sub-differential relation and at the same time contains within it sub-differential relations. Because each intensity is related to every other, each intensity 'continues to express the changing totality of Ideas, the variable ensemble of differential relations' (315). It is here of course that we begin to see the reasons for Deleuze's fascination with Leibniz in terms of the nature of a virtual multiplicity whereby everything is immanently connected,[48] and how Events subsist in the same time (the Aion). However, getting back to the intensities, each one can only clearly express those relations which it envelopes, that is, when it plays an enveloping role. When it plays an enveloped role – when it is enveloped by other intensities – it still expresses all relations, but this time confusedly. These roles, due to the nature of the relationships at work (disparity) are reciprocal and inseparable. The key point is that when an intensity expresses certain differential relations clearly (the ones it envelopes), it still expresses all of the other differential relations and points confusedly. And it expresses these in the intensities that it envelopes. So it expresses two intensities: the primary ones on which it is clearly focused, and the secondary ones (the ones by or in which it is enveloped) which it expresses only confusedly. Thus these latter (enveloped) are within the former (enveloping). The enveloping intensities or depth constitute the field of individuating differences (individuation). The enveloped intensities or distance constitute the individual differences. Thus distance is within depth, and depth is primary.

We have, then, two intensities, primary or enveloping, and secondary or enveloped (Table 2.1). From this we can attempt to answer our original question pertaining to dynamism and understand the relation between the virtual and the actual. The distinction between the two, if it can be called that,

Table 2.1 Enveloping and enveloped intensities

Primary	Secondary
Enveloping intensities	Enveloped intensities
Express certain relations/variations clearly and precisely	Express all relations/degrees confusedly
Depth	Distance
Constitute field of individuation and individuating differences	Constitute individual differences

depends on whether an intensity is enveloping or enveloped. It is a question of perspective. The key point here is that the enveloped, or that which has distance, expresses all relations (of the virtual) confusedly, not clearly. 'We call individuating factors the ensemble of these enveloping and enveloped intensities, of these individuating and individual differences which ceaselessly interpenetrate one another through the field of individuation' (317). Thus, and in a way to come full circle, we can detect the nature of difference in Deleuze: it is simply a differential characterized by a quantitative intensity. Representational difference results from a process (actualization) caused by this differential and in doing so is cancelled.

What does this mean more practically for the process of the actualization of the virtual? Perhaps the most important relation between the virtual and the actual is that the actual does not resemble the virtual. It is rather the virtual that gives rise to or rather produces the actual. 'While actual forms or products can resemble each other, the movements of production do not resemble each other, nor do the products resemble the virtuality that they embody' (*B*: 105). This was the case with the apple and the orange above. They resemble each other – indeed, they are both fruits, as Aristotle would likely point out. However, in the process of actualization or differenciation that gives rise to them one cannot say that there is resemblance, in the sense of apples resembling oranges. Actualization as a double-differentiation, on the one hand qualitative (differentiation) and on the other extensive (differenciation) – qualification and partition in physical actualization; organization and determination of species in biological actualization. 'That is why we proposed the concept of different/ciation to indicate at once both the state of differential relations in the idea or virtual multiplicity, and the state of the qualitative and extensive series in which these are actualised by being differenciated.' Thus the intensive quantities make possible the differentials, the asymmetry of which result in different/ciation and the cancellation of difference (actualization, extension). 'Intensity is the determinant in the process of actualisation' (*DR*: 306). It is the motor which drives it forward.

A good example of the virtual is the concept. In *What is Philosophy?* Deleuze and Guattari write – in a passage strongly reminiscent of *The Logic of Sense* – that the concept

> is an incorporeal, even though it is incarnated or effectuated in bodies. But in fact it is not mixed up with the state of affairs in which it is effectuated. It does not have spatiotemporal coordinates, only intensive ordinates. It has no energy, only intensities; it is anergetic (energy is not intensity but rather the way in which the latter is deployed and nullified in an extensive state of affairs.)
>
> (21)

Deleuze often likens actualization or differenciation to the local integration or local solution to a problem.[49] Thus, for example, organisms are solutions to problems, just as their parts are differenciated organs: the eye solves the light 'problem' (*DR*: 263). One of the most important things this process of actualization/differenciation provides for Deleuze is a theory of generation or emergence. There is no need here for a realized possible, only an actualized virtual as series which are differentiated on the basis of their intensive differences. Representational thought cannot see or tends to ignore the virtual (because of the transcendental illusion). It only deals with the actual and tends to treat the virtual as merely the possible; when in fact in an important sense the virtual is the cause, is primary – the actual an effect.

It seems necessary, especially given the discussion to come in Chapter 3, to clarify at this point what Deleuze refers to when he talks about systems. Indeed, what Deleuze sees as a system serves as a nice illustration of the metaphysical schema described and analysed in this chapter so far. When Deleuze speaks of open systems or rhizomes (see *N*: 31) he is talking about the virtual, or more specifically, the heterogeneous series which resonate in the intensive *spatium*. He sums it up thus:

> Systems of simulacra [the virtual] affirm divergence and decentring: the only unity, the only convergence of all series, is an informal chaos in which they are all included. No series enjoys a privilege over others, none possesses the identity of a model, nor the resemblance of a copy. None is either opposed or analogous to another. Each is constituted by differences, and communicates with the others through differences of differences. Crowned anarchies are substituted for the hierarchies of representation; nomadic distributions for the sedentary distributions of representation.
>
> (*DR*: 348)

A closed system (the hierarchies and distributions just quoted), on the other hand, is an actualized one where the parts have no more ability to resonate and create new individuations. A good example of this is to be found in classical physics experimentation where the virtual is purposefully shut out by way of controls, thus allowing for predictable patterns within certain parameters or conditions (see Prigogine and Stengers 1984: 9).[50] This distinction will become crucial when we deal with organizational systems and networks in Chapter 3, but for now it is important to remember that no system is perfectly open or closed, despite the fact that many systems seem closed. The *homo sapiens* system seemed closed until concepts of evolution took hold in the nineteenth century. The state system seemed closed (or is still treated as closed by some) until people began to admit that international relations is perhaps more complicated than aristocratic diplomats fully representing homogeneous entities through anarchical relations.[51]

A further important implication of Deleuze's immanent metaphysics concerns time, which in the Western tradition has always been a problematic though underproblematized subject, both metaphysically and in terms of human experience. Classical Greek philosophy, of course, has left a legacy of highlighting the problems of time, most notably with Zeno's paradox and likewise, perhaps predictably, Deleuze has no simple, discrete theory of time. The first thing we should realize about time in Deleuze is that it cannot be thought of in terms of sequential, chronological time, for the virtual exists as duration, as a whole, 'in a single Time which is nature itself' (*B*: 92). Time for Bergson–Deleuze is essentially a relaxed and contracted field, with the past being the most relaxed and the present being the most contracted; the future being the anticipation of further contraction. Thus time is infinitely layered: 'It is a case of there being distinct levels, each one of which contains the whole of our past, but in a more or less contracted state' (*B*: 61). For Deleuze, the succession of instants through which we generally understand time is but one aspect of this single time, and not the principle one nor, it is probably fair to say, the most important one. Although the most familiar, it is certainly the least significant and challenging in terms of the discussion here. The topological (as opposed to metric) has very special implications for time, and it is here that we find the importance of becoming in Deleuze, as we shall see later. Deleuze's concept of time also offers another way of looking at differenciation. As Boundas points out, it is possible to think the relationship between the virtual and the actual as essentially temporal. In all the variations that Deleuze presents to us, including duration/space, Aion/Chronos, the difference lies between the 'heterogeneous time of difference' and the 'spatialized time of metrication with its quantitative segments and instants' (1996: 92). In order to integrate this into a system of human experience – drawing this time of Hume, Bergson, and Nietzsche – Deleuze proposes three approaches, or syntheses to time.

The first synthesis of time corresponds most to time as duration, or what Deleuze often refers to – especially in *The Logic of Sense* – as the Aion. Drawing inspiration from Hume, Deleuze associates habit with the first synthesis. This habit is a form of contemplation common to all organic life. Time here is in the form of a 'living' present (*DR*: 117) where both the past and the future are divided infinitely in both directions (*LS*: 170) and exist as aspects of that present. It is a form of biological or organic time independent of any subject's understanding. It is 'not merely prior to the recognition or representation of these, but prior to the being sensed' (*DR*: 93). Deleuze therefore calls this synthesis 'passive' wherein the future is in the form of organic expectation or need, the past as cellular heredity.

The second synthesis of time is constituted on the basis of a pure past that allows the present to pass. This active synthesis is characterized by an understanding on the level of the subject that comes about through memory, which Deleuze associates with Bergson. The empirical character of the presents (that is, the phenomena) which 'make up the world' is determined by representation via contiguity, succession, causality, resemblance, and opposition. However, their noumenal character is virtual: the relationship between the levels of what Deleuze calls 'the pure past' (*DR*: 105). The presents are mere actualizations or representations of one of these levels. In other words these levels actualize into the phenomena of a succession of presents to make the time of Chronos. 'In short, what we live empirically as a succession of different presents from the point of view of active synthesis is also the ever-increasing coexistence of levels of the past within passive synthesis' (*DR*: 105). Of course from the point of view of their actuality (in metric, linear time) which functions according to representation, the series *are* successive – one coming 'before' and the other one 'after'. However from the point of view of the virtual, the essential point is the 'simultaneity and contemporaneity of all the divergent series' (*DR*: 151). The virtual is a

> gigantic memory, a universal cone in which everything coexists with itself, except for the differences of level. On each of these levels there are some 'outstanding points,' which are like remarkable points peculiar to it. All these levels or degrees and all these points are themselves virtual. They belong to a single Time; they coexist in a Unity; they are enclosed in a Simplicity; they form the potential parts of a Whole that is itself virtual.
>
> (*B*: 98)

Deleuze refers to two types of causes (*LS*: 7). States of affairs are causes amongst themselves or elements in a system: one billiard ball colliding with the next, causing it to move. Quasi-causes – what we earlier described as differentials – on the other hand, take place in the virtual and so give rise to actualizations, although since they do not resemble that which they actualize, they do not 'cause' them in the full sense of the mixtures of states of affairs. They are incorporeal transformations or effects. These quasi-causes are Events, which are very different from 'events' in the sense of things happening 'in the world', as in 'last week's events were significant'. First, events in the world relate to each other through successive time (one event happening before or after another) whereas Events are the opposite: 'All the meanwhiles [*entre-temps*[52]] are superimposed on one another, whereas times succeed each other' (*WP*: 160). Second, the Event is always a singularity, 'or rather a set of singularities or of singular points' (*LS*: 63). It is, perhaps ironically, outside of time.

> It is no longer time that exists between two instants; it is the event that is a meanwhile [*un entre-temps*[53]]: the meanwhile is not part of the eternal, but neither is it part of time – it belongs to becoming. The meanwhile, the event, is always a dead time; it is there where nothing takes place, an infinite awaiting that is already infinitely past, awaiting and reserve.
>
> (*WP*: 160)

One of the consequences of this is the relations Events have amongst themselves. Because Events are outside of time they interchange and interact without mediation. The *entre-temps* 'makes them communicate through zones of interdisciplinarity, of undecidability: they are variations, modulations, intermezzi, singularities of a new infinite order' (*WP*: 160). The result is that we cannot speak of things 'happening' in the virtual, but rather it is here that everything becomes. Significantly no amount of representational thought will ever be able to apprehend the Event, but rather it is 'the concept that apprehends the event, its becoming, its inseparable variations; whereas a function grasps a state of affairs, a time and variables, with their relations depending on time.' (*WP*:160). Thus we have the continuation of the above definition of the concept:

> The concept speaks the event, not the essence or the thing – pure Event, a haecceity, an entity. The concept is defined by the inseparability of a finite number of heterogeneous components traversed by a point of absolute survey at infinite speed.
>
> (*WP*: 21)

This leads to the notion of pure or complex repetition, which, as Deleuze makes clear in the introduction to *Difference and Repetition* (26–8, 30) is difference without a concept, or non-mediated difference. He says it is covered in the sense that it is hidden by the material repetition of the actual. Drawing on this distinction Deleuze cautions against the fallacy of taking repetition 'to be an extrinsic difference between objects represented by the same concept' (*DR*: 29). This raises the question of a 'plurality' of things: how can we have, say, 42 Boeing 747 aeroplanes, or 11 football players, or how do we relate the series of 'tocks' of the clock to each other? This pertains to the notion of repetition itself that will not be found in an appeal to the 'facts' with, as Deleuze points out, the simple question, 'Are there repetitions – yes or no?'. He suggests the answer lies rather in forensic science – at how no two fingerprints are exactly alike; no two revolvers. Deleuze is looking for a repetition which 'bears witness to singularity as a power of Ideas', one that is not 'reducible to difference without concepts' and not to be confused with 'the apparent character of objects represented by the same concept' (*DR*:30).

This is the third synthesis of time. The repetition of the different or, as Nietzsche put it, the eternal return. This is the repetition of pure difference which does not presuppose any identity (*DR*: 302). It is 'a repetition of the whole on diverse coexisting levels' as opposed to 'a repetition of successive elements or instants' (*DR*: xviii). The eternal return is difference as differen*t*iation, or what was referred to above as the dramatization. It is what injects the dynamism into Deleuze's metaphysics and has nothing to do with the actual, the transcendental illusion, or in other words, representational philosophy: 'The Negative does not return. The Identical does not return. The Same and the Similar, the Analogous and the Opposed, do not return. Only affirmation returns – in other words, the Different, the Dissimilar' (*DR*: 372). It 'constitutes a future which affirms at once both the unconditioned character of the product in relation to the conditions of its production, and the independence of the work in relation to its author or actor' (*DR*: 117). In more practical, political terms this manifests itself in Nietzsche's Übermensch, that is, the one capable of willing the eternal return, thereby aligning herself and opening herself up to the immanent relations of the virtual. Such a poise does offer an ethic, though not a morality. Willing the eternal return, or as Deleuze puts it in *The Logic of Sense*, not being unworthy of

Table 2.2 Syntheses of time in Deleuze

First synthesis	Second synthesis	Third synthesis
Aion	Chronos	Übermensch
Contemplation	Understanding	Eternal return
Passive	Active	Static
Habit	Memory	Caesura
Hume	Bergson	Nietzsche
Living present	Pure past	Future as such
Larval subjects	Actualized subjects	Fractured self
Foundation	Ground	Groundlessness

what happens to us (*LS*: 169), does not entail passivity or fatalism, but rather an openness to the third synthesis of time, to the untimely in the sense of *unzeitgemäß*. This will become significant when we explore subjectivity in Chapter 4, but for now Deleuze's notion of time can be summarized in Table 2.2.

Counteractualization

So far in this chapter we have been looking at Deleuze's metaphysics almost exclusively in terms of how the virtual is actualized, but there is also the important process of counteractualization. The notion of counteractualization is much misunderstood and glossed over in the secondary literature, thanks in no small part to Deleuze's shiftiness in deploying this term. In fact, he seldom does, instead referring to counter-effectuation, deterritorialization (in several varieties), and the more well-known Deleuzo–Guattarian notion of the line of flight. It would be difficult to delineate all of the variations on counteractualization, but a few suffice to give an impression of the wide interpretations. James Williams sets himself apart from most commentators in calling actualization 'differenciation' and counteractualization (the actual to the virtual) 'differentiation' (2003: 21). Boundas consistently identifies the move from the virtual to the actual, though links the counter-process to the notion of vice-diction (2006: 5), as does Egyed (2006: 82).[54] The *Deleuze Dictionary* has an entry for neither counteractualization nor vice-diction, and Tamsin Lorraine's entry for line of flight is somewhat opaque, and in the context of this discussion, ambiguous: 'A "line of flight" is a path of mutation precipitated through the actualisation of connections among bodies that were previously only implicit (or "virtual") that releases new powers in the capacities of those bodies to act and respond' (Parr 2005: 145). Bonta and Protevi also have neither definition in their glossary that forms the bulk of *Deleuze and Geophilosophy*, but offer something more accessible with line of flight, distinguishing here between absolute and non-absolute lines of flight: '[A]n absolute line of flight is an absolute deterritorialization to the plane of consistency, the creation of new attractors [dark precursors] and bifurcators, new patterns and thresholds' (2004: 106). Despite a characteristically loose reading of Deleuze, Žižek injects an interesting discussion of the latter's 'two logics': that of immaterial becoming (reaching the virtual) as the effect of body–material causes, and that of immaterial becoming as production, that is, the virtual actualizing itself (2003: 21ff.). What makes his simple observation so refreshing is that Žižek evidently bases his reading on *The Logic of Sense*, a book which many basically ignore, especially in terms of the relationship between the actual and the virtual, the latter which the book somewhat ominously calls a 'sterile double'.

I provide this overview of the commentaries to illustrate the extent to which this notion has baffled readers – let alone first-time ones. From all this confusion perhaps it is not difficult to see why some of the clearest expressions of the movement from the actual to the virtual are offered in Deleuze's last major publication, *What is philosophy?*, as if in response to a broad misunderstanding. Here he and Guattari describe movement to the virtual not as a return to the absolute, primordial, and chaotic virtual but 'rather virtuality that has become consistent [hence the "plane of consistency"],[55] that has become an entity formed on a plane of immanence that sections the chaos' (*WP*: 156). Moreover, here they explain that although the relationship between the virtual and the actual is always a relative one, this is not on the same line. In other words it is not the perpetual shifting backwards and forwards between the two, but rather the formation of new lines. This formation constitutes a creation through the progressive actualization on new lines 'followed' subsequently by a counteractualization that returns the entity to a new plane of consistency (new frontiers with chaos, different intensive quantities) and so on. This will be important to remember when we get to the notion of becoming. A key characteristic that counteractualization lends to Deleuze's metaphysics is that no matter how stratified or ossified a system is, it is still prone to counteractualizations which reimmerse it into the immanence of intensive quantities. 'The most closed system still has a thread that rises towards the virtual' (*WP*: 122).

What is interesting and indeed crucial, and what sets Deleuze's notion of creative lines apart from many of his contemporaries, is the way that lines of flight are not outside or external to any given system. They are, rather, an integral part of it – and must be as a consequence of his immanent metaphysics. 'Far from lying outside the social field or emerging from it, lines of flight constitute its rhizome or cartography' (*DP*: 187). It is precisely these lines that define a system as opposed to, for example, its contradictions, or characteristics that focus on essence. Thus deviations in a system's functioning are an internal result of its processes of actualization and counteractualization which are ultimately based on difference itself. Everything is related relatively to everything else, but not in terms of definition or representation, but relative to its movement either towards actualization or counteractualization.

To clarify the relationship between the jumble of terms in Deleuze, the very familiar deterritorialization simply refers to the process or movement of what we have just called counteractualization, whereas the line of flight describes this path.[56] There are essentially three types, though again it can be confusing in the primary and secondary literature as a line of flight 'traditionally' refers to absolute deterritorialization. In any case, the schema is quite simple. All things (systems, people, ideas) are actualizations that also counteractualize. If we use the model of stratification provided in *A Thousand Plateaus* (39–74), which Deleuze often does, wherein the virtual layers are at the 'top' or beyond the top of sedimentary layers and the actual resides in the ever 'deeper' layers of stratification and sediment, some deterritorializations are relative (also known as molar or segmentary). These result in essentially no movement outside the system or beyond the stratum. A good model of this, as has already been mentioned, is found in classical physics which strives to shut out the virtual through its quest for closed experiments. On the other hand some counteractualizations are migrant or molecular. These result in certain systemic changes and relative displacements. Deleuze and Guattari offer the example of regime change here: the movement from one hierarchical political system to another. A counteractualization is absolute when it extends to the virtual, creating new immanent connections. Thus it creates a 'new earth' (*ATP*: 510) and explains how newness comes about in Deleuze, in this case with Guattari. But as will become evident in Chapter 4, this is not a utopian invocation, but rather the recognition of complex repetition; repetition of the virtual. It is worth pointing out that such a model, extensively used by Deleuze, does not completely correspond to the complexity theorist-inspired Deleuzian readings in the way that the latter sometimes confound the actual–virtual. Considering the model of stratification and sedimentation just given, it seems that in the complexity–Deleuze literature that bifurcation, gradients, and thresholds occur at some intermediary level between virtual and the actual, whereas based on the discussion of the present chapter such dramas take place in the virtual or perhaps better still, as part of the actualization of the virtual. There is, however, a second possibility that Deleuze provides in *Dialogues* where 'the molecular line would appear only to be oscillating between the two extremes, sometimes carried along by the combination of fluxes of deterritorialization, sometimes brought back to the accumulation of reterritorializations' (102). It is this version that corresponds best to and explains most fully the metaphysical position found in *Difference and Repetition*. In any case, that there is such leeway in the texts supports the basic reading wherein systems, phenomena, individuals, and things should be understood as arrayed along a term or a series of terms which have two poles or a relative movement: one towards the virtual and further communications through intensive quantities and the other towards further actualizations.

This relative movement offers an innovative way of understanding entities and structures through the figure of the assemblage or *agencement*, about which there has been considerable work in recent years.[57] Simply put, the assemblage is perhaps best understood as that which replaces essences and things in Deleuze and Guattari. Deleuze himself borrowed substantially from Foucault, and his reading of *The Archaeology of Knowledge* asserts that Foucault discovered two forms of historical formations: content and expression[58] – two terms borrowed from Louis Hjelmslev and central to Deleuze's thought. These are things (the visible) and words (the sayable) and are in reciprocal presupposition, and which, according to Deleuze, receive their clearest treatment by Foucault in *Discipline and Punish* (*DP*: 188–9). The way in which the forms of content and forms of expression join the virtual and actual is called an assemblage, and its diagram is called the abstract machine. The assemblage allows for the analysis of Deleuze's materialist universe: it is a substantive without essence. To illustrate these agencements one can investigate institutions (in terms of their form and content) as Foucault does, but the stirrup as it developed in early medieval Europe provides a simple example. As Deleuze and Guattari write, 'It is always the assemblage that constitutes the weapon system' (*ATP*: 399). The stirrup, an abstract machine, is an occasion of the man–horse assemblage, which is itself a variable with differing effects. Its form of content is the stable distribution of the rider's weight on the mount allowing for the range of motion required for mounted combat (which is also the form of expression of the metal-worker and the saddle maker); its form of expression is a new hierarchy of military power (which can be viewed in turn as the content of a new political system – feudalism). To be sure the stirrup existed elsewhere before the reign of Charlemagne – indeed, Europe was very late in adopting it (White 1966: 15–16) – but on the margins of other agencements that did not bring about the specificity of the European medieval cavalry and the further actualizations that came with it. It is important to note here that Deleuze is not positing a facile dualism (nor was Foucault, for that matter) – both content and expression are forms that occur independently of any dual-natured object (or subject). Furthermore, to be clear, this is not an analogy dealing with a thing and its representation. Deleuze is therefore careful to map out the elements of an assemblage, rather than begin from a system of fixed essences. Assemblages differ from Foucault's notion of *dispositif* in that they effectively add the virtual–actual dimension to the forms of content–forms of expression axis of Foucault. Thus whereas Foucault has some difficulty explaining the precise relationship between forms of content and forms of expression, Deleuze can relate them through the movements of actualization and counteractualization (*ATP*: 88).[59] In other words forms of content engender forms of expression which in turn become new forms of content in increasingly fixed or stratified states of affairs (institutions, identity), and at the same time are open to evolution, change, and influences from other series or what Foucault calls 'neighbouring practices' (2002b: 230). The task of the researcher is to map series in immanent relation (or, the connections amongst a dispersal of elements as in Foucault) by means of Deleuze's transcendental empiricism (which corresponds to Foucault's genealogical approach), which will be discussed in more detail in the next chapter.

This lends itself particularly well to conceiving of all things not as individuals or groups, but rather in their singularity. It is important to note that for Deleuze the process of the actualization of the virtual is the same at any scale or level of analysis, whether for a group or for what we normally call an individual. Both are actual multiplicities resulting from the different/ciation of virtual multiplicities. Thus a single human being is as much a 'population' as an organized (or disorganized) group of human beings. According to Deleuze, everything is a population, and these individual populations or specificities are logically superior and methodologically preferable to categories of the greatest difference. As was posited at the beginning of this chapter, according to Aristotle the individual in its specificity remains unknowable; only species are real. But for Deleuze '[i]t is not the individual which is an illusion in relation to the genus of the species, but the species which is an illusion – inevitable and well founded, it is true – in relation to the play of the individual and individuation' (*DR*: 311). The reason for this, as we saw above is that individuation precedes the species in principle:

> Every species is thus an arrest of movement; it could be said that the living being turns on itself and *closes itself*. It cannot be otherwise, since the Whole is only virtual, dividing itself by being acted out. It cannot assemble its actual parts that remain external to each other: The whole is never 'given'. And, in the actual, an irreducible pluralism reigns – as many worlds as living beings, all 'closed on themselves.'
>
> (*B*:104)

The implications this has for the individuals–group problem of analysing alter-globalizations (and for the more traditional structure–agency problem) should seem obvious by now, and will be addressed further when we turn to the problem of the level of analysis in the next chapter.

The philosophy of becoming

In light of the discussion of counteractualization above, the remainder of this chapter and a considerable portion of the next will deal with change, newness, and how things evolve. In the current cultural climate obsessed as it is with the new, and an academic environment often largely fixated on change, it may seem rather superficial or even disappointing to say that a philosophy or a politics of becoming is all about 'newness'. It is as if we would like the new to be something much more timeless, more poignant, more radical than we generally understand it to be. But to the extent this is true, it is so only because of the dogmatic image of thought whereby we generally tend to think of even newness in fixed terms, in terms of identity, the Same, and hence representation. We can only say that 'the new' is truly emergent when we drop identity as a point of departure and point of destination, that is, point-identity A leading to point-identity B, where we have no satisfactory way of explaining genesis itself. Deleuze's becoming, due to the nature of his immanent political philosophy, is truly emergent or more accurately creative – as Deleuze puts it, a veritable becoming-mad, or in the case of Alice (in Wonderland), becoming larger than she was, but smaller than she will be; that is, both directions at once. Deleuze and Guattari express it thus in *What is Philosophy?*: 'Becoming is an extreme contiguity within a coupling of two sensations without resemblance or, on the contrary, in the distance of a light that captures both of them in a single reflection' (173), for example, the becoming-whale of captain Ahab in Moby-Dick. The genius of

Melville's classic lies not in its account or representation of what captains, sailors, and whales actually are or do, but its nomadic, *un*centred – that is to say, without centre – converging of captain series and whale series.[60] 'It is a zone of indetermination, of indiscernibility, as if things, beasts, and people ... endlessly reach that point that immediately precedes their natural differentiation' (173). In terms of this chapter it is an approach that prioritizes the reinsertion of counter-actualizations into the virtual realm which allows for them to enter into pre-individuating communications with other series. As Delanda writes, 'The Deleuzian ontology ... is ... one characterizing a universe of *becoming without being*. Or, more exactly, a universe where individual beings do not exist but only as the outcome of becomings, that is, of the irreversible process of individuation' (2002: 84). Although I would be tempted to omit 'irreversible' here due to the fixed nature of time and the non-dynamic nature of the process of counteractualization it implies, the point is taken. To understand what this becoming without being is like we can recall Nietzsche's example of the lightning strike. People see the strike, and believe that the lightning has caused it. They attributed the effect, the strike, to a cause, or an entity, called lightning. Surely, of course, there is something that causes lightning strikes, a complex relationship of energy and forces and so on. The point is, there is no such thing as this lightning, this thing, which is the cause of the lightning strike. What we are moving away from here is an entity with being called lightning with certain characteristics or identity. What lighting *is*, is simply the being-caused of lightning strikes. In non-representational terms it can have no identity. The task is start to think about lightning as pure effect; as pure becoming.[61] What we would need here for an investigation of world politics and the case of alter-globalizations is an approach that does away with being and identity. This is why complexity theory – at least certain aspects of it – present the best tools for analysing such becomings, which will be the subject of the following chapter.

But before getting to that we must refine somewhat or further flesh out Deleuze's philosophical and consequently political schema. The above discussions have analysed in some detail the relationship between the virtual and the actual, how intensive quantities lead to differentiations which spark spatio-temporal dynamisms which are in turn differen*c*iated or actualized. But so far it is unclear how these play out in the sensible world, or more specifically here, for questions of social science investigation. In *The Clamour of Being* Badiou offers us a reading of Deleuze wherein the latter's fundamental ontological position leads him to deploy what ends up being a rather simple metaphysical schema in a number of 'cases', each of which is a starting point (though, to be sure, a point in the middle[62]) or that which causes thought. It is these cases which offer numerous examples in Deleuze's own work and, more significantly – certainly for contemporary Deleuze-inspired investigations of social and political phenomena – fill the plateaus (that is, 'chapters') of *A Thousand Plateaus*.[63] For all that, Badiou sees Deleuze's work as rather 'monotonous', 'composing a very particular regime of emphasis or almost infinite repetition of a limited repertoire of concepts, as well as a virtuosic variation of names.' Surely the monotony of

Deleuze's work is a matter of opinion, but Badiou makes a compelling argument here, seeing all the 'cases' of *A Thousand Plateaus* as the various applications of Deleuze's fundamental metaphysical position. By this reading we can distil a list of pairs of notions, with one term tending towards the virtual, the other the actual, each relative to its counterpart. Table 2.3 lists some (a very small number, in fact) of the pairs to be found in Deleuze's work, both his own and those composed with Guattari. At the top of the list are some of the fundamental metaphysical aspects discussed above. Further down are more 'names' for the virtual–actual, and finally are included a few physical examples, though these obviously do not describe material processes.

The relationship between these pairs can be illustrated with felt and weaving. A piece of felt, in itself but especially and most significantly during its production, has no centre, nor any defined edge. In itself it has no formal restrictions or patterns, but is actualized into whatever use it is put to. Weaving, on the other hand, is regulated by the warp and the woof, is restricted, at least longitudinally by the size of the loom. Making felt tends to be a communal, intuitive task, whereas weaving is a technical, specialized task. Likewise with chess and go. The former is determined by a finite number of functional rules governing play on a field of fixed coordinates. The latter is a game only of relations, operating on simple principles which determine a sequence of de- and re-territorializations. To be fair, especially when considering abstract philosophical notions, it is worth pointing out that two distinct and exclusive poles is not exactly what Deleuze (and Guattari, here) are driving at. It perhaps could be better expressed as two lines or two directions.[64] Nevertheless, to repeat, Deleuze and Guattari often speak of the virtual and actual in relative presupposition and for this reason they are presented here as two poles, even if they are not two ends of the same line. Note also that multiplicity is not on this table. This is because multiplicities – a

Table 2.3 Pairs of notions in Deleuze

virtual	actual
duration	matter
memory	space
qualitative	quantitative
difference in kind	difference in degree
crowned anarchy	representation
intensive ordinates	spatio–temporal coordinates
molecular	molar
non-denumerable	denumerable
rhizome	root
smooth	striated
Aion	Chronos
consistence	reference
topological	metric
nomad	state
felt	weaving
go	chess

term much vaunted in *Capitalism and Schizophrenia* and perhaps associated overly with the virtual or nomadic[65] – are both virtual and actual, or rather there are both virtual and actual multiplicities.[66]

> Functions and concepts, actual states of affairs and virtual events, are two types of multiplicities that are not distributed on an errant line but relate to two vectors that intersect, one according to which states of affairs actualize events and the other according to which events absorb (or rather, adsorb) states of affairs.
>
> (*WP*: 152–3)

That these pairs of notions are in relative opposition is a confusing aspect to Deleuze's work – and the source of inconsistent and inaccurate readings and deployments. For in effect it sometimes seems, in literary, political, or aesthetic discussions especially, that Deleuze (and Guattari) prioritize or valorize one pair of the couplet, or put another way, valorize only one aspect of a 'term' which in fact has two poles. But Deleuze and Guattari are very specific regarding the relative opposition between, for example, the consistency of assemblages (virtual) and the stratification of milieus (actual):

> But once again, this opposition is only relative, entirely relative. Just as milieus swing between a stratum state and a movement of destratification, assemblages swing between a territorial closure that tends to restratify them and a deterritorializing movement that on the contrary connects them to the Cosmos.
>
> (*ATP*: 337)

In fact these two poles are mutually implicating aspects, as is evident in their discussions of royal versus nomad science:

> What we have ... are two formally different conceptions of science, and, ontologically, a single field of interaction in which Royal Science continually appropriates the contents of vague or nomad science while nomad science continually cuts the contents of Royal Science loose. At the limit, all that counts is the constantly shifting borderline.
>
> (*ATP*: 367)

The same holds true for the Apparatus of Capture and the War Machine.[67]

What tends to happen in Deleuze-inspired readings of social phenomena – due no doubt in no small part to a certain amount of, again, what Valentin calls fascination and mystification (2006: 186) – is the prioritizing of one pole at the expense of the other, for example (the usual suspects) rhizome, line of flight, and nomad (for tree–root, reterritorialization and state form, respectively). A 'two poles' reading emphasizes a comprehensive analysis of how an entire assemblage (or system) works, thereby providing a useful theoretical framework for analysing contemporary political and social conditions. This opens up the perspectives offered by the various theoretical approaches in Chapter 1 considerably, as will be discussed in the next chapter. But for now we can say that in understanding the AGM, for example, we need not be uniquely interested whether any given organization or event is liberal, green, democratic or otherwise, but rather the extent to which it tends to respond to its immanent and necessary – for 'purely actual objects to not exist' (*D*: 112) – virtual connections. In other words, rather than define a socio-political phenomenon by its putatively right- or left-wing slant, moral stance, or contradictions,[68] such a reading of Deleuze insists on defining an entity (group, individual, event) by its line of flight. Such an emphasis looks not at the putative 'newness' of the organization – as if the AGM were necessarily a new being different from others (for example civil society) – but the extent to which and ways in which it varies, adapts and mutates. Leaving aside a potentially pure revolutionary aspect for the moment, what this does for the study of the processes of globalization or world politics is to open the door to theoretical possibilities for accounting for systemic evolution and change. And perhaps most significantly it accomplishes while also being able to account for the fixed, striated structures and bounded organizations (and individuals) that appear to populate the everyday world of politics. In Deleuzian terms we are looking, through transcendental empiricism (to be discussed in greater detail below), for counteractualizations that will combine with others in intensive relations, the product of which will actualize into new species (of political participation, of global governance) and parts (organizations, networks, etc.). Such a view, in its post-structuralist credentials, sees no structure, organization, or process as necessary in itself or enduring, nor for that matter inherently suitable as a point of reference (for example, the state system). On the other hand, unlike other shades of post-structuralism, it does not preclude the possibility of empirical investigation. What will make this empiricism 'superior' is the fact that it is not based on the model-copy or representation, nor, perhaps more significantly, on a linguistic or discursive analysis.

In considering the breadth of his writing, Deleuze's philosophy does not make for easy reading. In all likelihood Deleuze's terminology is too ambiguous between books. Moreover, there is little development in Deleuze's thought in terms of an argument being refined or an empirical application being perfected. On the contrary, although Deleuze's philosophy is far from static, it does maintain a certain monolithic-ness through its insistence on univocity. It is for this reason that Badiou's comment about the principle and its cases should resonate with all but the most casual reader: there is the basic (though no less dense for it) ontology and the 'simple' metaphysics – all the rest is merely the description or playing out of an infinite variety of cases. Furthermore, unlike his friend and colleague Foucault, his rather dry or at least impersonal writing style precludes him from ever confiding in the reader that he just might have got something wrong the last time around.[69] From his admission about his 'muddled'-ness of the line of flight it is easier to assert that there is a certain liberty in his use of terms.[70] Other examples abound.

The reading of Deleuze provided in this book emphasizes the fact that everything (individuals, organizations, ideas, things) has two ontically equivalent halves: one in the actual and the other plunged into the virtual. But there is no such thing as a uniquely virtual object. It is true that Ideas are expressions of the virtual, but this does not mean that they can be separated from their solutions, from their actualizations. Likewise no state of affairs, no system is stratified to the extent that it loses its virtual image (*C1*: 16, 17). It is also true that through the transcendental illusion the virtual is hidden – this is the nature of the actual. But nevertheless the virtual persists. It is the goal of transcendental empiricism to uncover these hidden centres of envelopment and follow the lines of actualization back to their virtual becomings, just as it is the task of philosophy to point to the virtual. Maintaining this perspective when analysing and in turn deploying Deleuze in the investigation of world politics is a robust way to guard against fascination and mystification that not only can blind the researcher to the deeper and more productive aspects of Deleuze's political philosophy, but moreover render Deleuze-based investigations in the social science flighty, empty, and ineffective. A rigorous reading of Deleuze involves rejecting representation but especially any transcendent principle. The result is a superior empiricism which demands that each case or expression of the virtual–actual couplet be uncovered via its immanent criteria. Such an uncovering does not seek an essence or a universal process, but rather the specifics of a system's own becomings. This explains Deleuze's rather controversial interest in jurisprudence, a topic to be addressed further in Chapter 4.

To conclude this chapter it is worth emphasizing that as overwrought or even downright far-out as Deleuze's metaphysical position might sometimes seem, and as difficult as it is to get one's head around Deleuze's 'cases', with his philosophy of immanence he has achieved its goals:[71] through a univocal ontology a metaphysics that relies neither on the possible or representation. This means no essences, no model–copy, no teleologies, no dialectic, no 'progress'. Furthermore no transcendent point, no privileged positions of observation and thus no hierarchies of thought. There are systems, but they are neither entirely open nor, more importantly, entirely closed. It is a materialism in which the material forms itself, as opposed to hylomorphism (the view that substance is organized according to some external principle or form and cannot be organized from within).[72] Thus we can still talk about things, we can still investigate structures, only without assuming an external force or architect that creates or causes them. This is what Deleuze sometimes calls starting in the middle. The question is what does all this mean for the study of socio-political phenomena or in our case expressions of the AGM? The answer to this question is the subject of the following chapter. For now we can recall that it means no universal object (no thing which persists outside its actualizations) and no strict level of analysis. No longer will we be talking about groups and individuals,[73] structures and agency, but of multiplicities and populations. As for political agency and the subject itself, this will be the subject of Chapter 4.

3 Deleuze and world politics

New directions

The previous chapter explored the political philosophy of Gilles Deleuze as it might pertain to social scientific investigations in general and to the study of world politics in particular. This was by no means a comprehensive analysis, but provided mainly a fleshing out of his ontological principle of univocity and the consequent two-pole – though non-dualistic – metaphysics of the virtual and the actual. The present chapter will take this philosophy and see what it says about world politics both in terms of continuity and change, and more specifically about political topographies surrounding the AGM. It will not be the continuation of the direct analysis of Deleuze's philosophy as presented in Chapter 2, but rather a 'plugging in' of this theory into an already existing literature in order to sketch a general theoretical perspective on world politics – a nomad science of world politics – as well as to deliver a more comprehensive understanding of the AGM. The basic question here is what a Deleuzian version of world politics looks like. How are we to understand and operationalize things like the AGM, the state, so-called global flows, and global civil society, among others, with no recourse to representational thought as a founding principle? In other words, how can we imagine a theory of world politics that is truly immanent? What does this nomad science look like and how do we go about it? After having addressed these questions, the next chapter will then ask precisely what kind of agents can act in such a socio-political field and, in terms of the AGM, just what participants might be resisting, or what new forms of political practice they may be engendering.

The general argument of the present chapter is that the AGM is best described through non-representational thought and is, moreover, symptomatic of contemporary political practice. Deleuze's philosophy as presented in Chapter 2 provides an innovative and productive approach to an investigation of the AGM: innovative in the sense that it acts as a sort of ontological bridge, joining current scholarship in IR, complexity, and systems theory studies with social movement theory and a rigorous take on political subjectivity. Most notably it overcomes difficulties with space, time, and level of analysis. It is a productive approach in that it presents a coherent framework for theoretical reflection and a methodology for empirical analysis.

An appropriate question might be: In an analysis of the AGM as a global political force, why do we need Deleuze at all? Why this dense ontology and metaphysics? The reason is that, simply put, theoretical innovation has not kept up with empirical findings, as we can recall from the investigation in Chapter 1. In many fields of inquiry, from IR to social movement theory, one detects the general sentiment that the socio-political world is a fluid process for which commentators and researchers lack a theoretical approach. There is the general sense that in the contemporary world uncertainties have replaced regularities (Rosenau 2003: 12), and that flows have replaced structures (Lash 2002: vii). Even the nation state – widely viewed as one of the most stable institutions of global politics 'is everywhere characterised by floating populations, transnational politics within national borders and mobile configurations of technology and expertise.' (Appadurai 1999: 230). Some argue the basic impossibility of even seizing on anything 'fixed, total, comprehensible or global' (Penksy 2005: 2), what John Urry – more on his research later – calls 'liquid modernity' (2005a: 35). The ephemerality of contemporary global socio-political activity is perhaps in general better addressed by social movement theory, which typically seeks to understand the shifting terrain of political activism. And yet here too there has been little headway achieved in terms of 'emerging grammars' capable of describing contemporary social actors and their conflicts, with the sociological theory deployed in this context 'remaining embedded in conceptions of instrumental mobilization of collective identity aiming at the political system [i.e. states]' (McDonald 2002: 124). As Tim Cresswell puts it, 'Maybe ... our ways of knowing are just not mobile enough and we are stuck in a sedentarist metaphysics – a way of knowing that valorizes the apparent certainties of boundedness and rootedness over the slippery invisibility of flux and flow' (2006: 57). Ruggie's observation that we lack the vocabulary and the dimensions of analysis for contemporary political thinking (1993: 142–3, 167) has perhaps never seemed more poignant than today.

Likewise Tormey points out that political theorists, faced with the apparent realities of contemporary global politics and society, lack 'the vocabularies to begin moving towards this weightless world of flight, speed, intensities and velocities' (2005b: 428). But if we are to accept such a statement, what remains to be done is to question what such a 'moving towards' might entail and to sketch out some sort of map to get us where we want to go. Is this moving towards a cognitive or conceptual change? Is it a theoretical insight? A methodology? A moral stance? What will be shown in this chapter is that this moving towards is an uncovering or unmasking of a basic political form – an immanent one, corresponding to the notion of the virtual in the previous chapter – which is papered over by or embedded in various stratifications of international order, localization, or what in the last chapter was called actualization. In other words, it is the hiding of the virtual in the actual – the transcendental illusion. What is important to note at the outset is that it is the immanent relations, not the actualizations, which are primary. What characterizes the contemporary 'weightless' world is, then, the persistence of the virtual, or from the perspective of actualizations, of deterritorializations. But as we will see below, that we are confronted by this now is neither predetermined nor necessary. Indeed, there have been other times and places in human history which have also been characterized by a propensity to deterritorialization, and in turn these too were confronted by new ways of thinking. As Hedley Bull pleads in *The Anarchical Society*,

> Is there not a need to liberate thought and action from these confines by proclaiming new concepts and normative principles that would give shape and direction to the trends making against the existing system, as Grotius and others gave intellectual coherence and purpose to the trends making against an earlier political order?
>
> (1977: 265)[1]

A positivist approach is surely ill-suited to developing today's new concepts and principles – indeed, positivism is emphatically against the creation of concepts, as by definition it adheres to a representationalist metaphysics. As Ruggie has noted, positivist theories 'cannot, ontologically, apprehend fundamental transformation' (1993: 171). In Deleuzian terms it is a science of bounded entities and closed systems (a science of the actual). But beyond this there is a crucial point to be made here at the outset which differentiates the present offering from other critiques of socio-political thought. By positivist here we cannot mean empirical – or at least for the purposes of this study we must hold positivism and empiricism firmly apart. As will become clear by the conclusion of this chapter, in order to arrive at a (more) workable theory of the global – the lack of which commentators in IR and world politics have been lamenting for some time – we need to hold on to an empirical thrust, but come clean on the question of representation. Empiricism need not denote an unfailing ability of humans to represent their environment via a pure science of observational method. It need only retain its realist impulse in that there are – outside of human experience and discourse of that experience – bodies and states of affairs. Certainly, approaching these states of affairs in a scientific manner is no mean task: there are any number of forces which come together to engender – to actualize – any given state of affairs. The questions therefore pertain to which one[2] and how. And here we must be careful of ready-made positivist representation (positivism being just one form of representational thought). It may be more useful to talk of bringing enquiry to bear on a 'system of dispersion', as Foucault argues in *The Archaeology of Knowledge* (2002b: 41).

If one considers the putative desire of the social sciences to become more like the physical sciences in terms of rigour and methodology, there is a certain irony at work. For although innovations over the last decades in the social sciences are indeed mirroring developments in the physical sciences, just as our physical reality is not based on such firm foundations as we once thought, social sciences are also unchaining themselves from representationalist philosophy and finding resonances in aleatory points, strange attractors, complexity, and chaos. Deleuze's philosophy offers a compelling ontological and metaphysical underpinning for such investigations. In other words the theoretical insights, as described in Chapter 2, are capable of addressing some of the problems associated with a representationalist approach such as positivism, while still maintaining an empirical and indeed a materialist impulse. What is certain is that a great deal of research over the last decade or two in the social sciences about emergence, complexity, chaos, and systems has many parallels and indeed seeks to overcome many of the same shortcomings as Deleuze's non-representational thought. Or from another perspective: the ontology and metaphysics of Deleuze can support or inform many of the insights of the 'complexity turn' in the social sciences. To get to the bottom of this, the present chapter will address the question of emergence by looking at complexity, chaos, systems and chance. But in order to better understand the role such perspectives might play in theorizing about the AGM and world politics in general, this chapter begins by looking at two of the most fundamental aspects of the study of human politics: space and time.

Space

Over the last decades space has been taken less for granted across a broad range of socio-political investigations. On the one hand in the AGM or global social justice literature space plays a seemingly central role. Any given forum, journal, conference, meeting (face-to-face or otherwise), or website 'creates a space' that exhibits any number of conditions such as newness, genuine resistance, change, safety, sharing, and real expression. For example, Lacey writes about 'the creation of dialogues and practices of social justice in contested spaces' (2005a: 406). A valid question that is seldom posed, however, pertains to the exact nature of this political space. Is it primarily discursive? productive? geographical/locational? How different in its linguistic use is space from a 'forum'? On the other hand many in political science and IR in particular have been implicitly interested in space for a long time in terms of territoriality, and explicitly interested in it for at least two decades in other terms, that is, *questioning* the whole notion of territoriality itself. This recent interest has stemmed from space not being taken as a given, and of course becomes the principle focus of critical geography and critical geopolitics (see for example Ashley 1987; Harvey 1990; Augé 1995; Ó Tuathail 1996; Hirst 2005). One general observation is that through the influence of Derrida and to a certain extent Foucault space has come to be understood as discursive across a number of fields, including geography, the sociology of development, IR, and social movement theory. This section, however, will 'withhold assent' on this notion of space and attempt to determine whether there is anything valuable to be said about space following Deleuze's materialist impulse. In doing so it is useful to be aware of the double thrust of dealing with space that can be found very often in social movement literature. In one sense many are interested in analysing 'new spaces' of resistance or action, while at the same time power is ultimately assumed to reside in the state, as discussed in Chapter 1. The dichotomy or conflict consists then in a discursive, open kind of space on the one hand and a more stable, institutionalized, territorial space in the state on the other. A pertinent question, would be, however: are these two notions of space – both as discursive location and territory – the same or related somehow? If the latter, then how? This section seeks to develop a Deleuzian notion of political space that is neither primarily territorial nor discursive. In other words this chapter is not concerned with actors or geographical lines in themselves, but rather, taking from James Anderson, focuses specifically 'on the shifting space–time of the stage itself (1996: 143).

The central argument here is that the notions of space in the social sciences in general – the challenges from the discursive realm aside for the moment – are derived from a specifically modern European form, namely the kind of geometric space discovered by Euclid and brought to full force in the sciences by Newton. This means homogeneous, divisible space, a kind of space which, as might already be guessed, corresponds to the actual in Deleuze.[3] As is often remarked, the development of such a notion of space is tied up with other changes in the way humans have described their surroundings and themselves. The adoption of the single perspective in painting by Masolino in the fifteenth century and then later exploited by Raphael a century later marks a shift to a homogeneous, metricized notion of space which flows forth from the viewer and ends in the vanishing point. Similar advances in cartography relate the viewer to the represented space in fixed, geometric terms. This allows the observer not only to locate herself on a map, but also relates individual elements on the map to each other in a uniform way, something that medieval maps or Roman *itineraria picta* or *peripli* did not explicitly attempt to do with any degree of accuracy. 'Accurate maps', writes Stephen Kobrin, were required for

> the idea of a modern international system based on mutually exclusive geography and territorial sovereignty even to become possible. The very idea of conquering and controlling external space requires a modern mind-set: the ability to see it as something finite, bounded and 'capable of domination through human action.'
>
> (1999: 169)[4]

The corollary argument taken up in this chapter is that although this notion of space closely corresponds to the modern European experience and although such space did have practical political and social consequences, it was by no means a stable concept or uniformly applied and understood. The purpose of such a line of argument is to cast doubt on and ultimately undermine methodological nationalism that clouds socio-political thought right up to the present.

One classic example of careful research – also inspired by global political movements – that nevertheless remains tied to a kind of methodological nationalism is Ronnie Lipschutz's influential article, *Restructuring World Politics: The Emergence of Global Civil Society* (1992). In it he paints the picture of 'many heterogeneous transnational political networks' which represent 'an ongoing project of civil society to reconstruct, re-imagine, or re-map world politics' by 'challenging, from below, the nation-state system' (391). In identifying the concept of global civil society, we are to 'look for political spaces other than those bounded by the parameters of the nation state system.' (392–3). What is suggestive in Lipschutz's approach is the emphasis on space that is non-territorial: 'These political spaces are delineated by networks of economic, social and cultural relations, and they are being occupied by the conscious association of actors, in physically separated locations, who link themselves together in networks for particular political and social purposes' (393). Next he maps out some of this space among various policy issue networks including the environment, development, human rights, and indigenous peoples' issues. He then picks up on Ken Booth's omelette analogy of the international system (various ingredients including international regimes, diplomatic culture, and neoliberal institutions) and adds to it this emerging global civil society. But what distinguishes this last ingredient from the others is that it is not state-centric (398).[5]

He then goes on to trace its emergence, noting that 'prior to the Treaty of Westphalia and the emergence of the state system, there existed a relatively vibrant trans-European civil society, linked to territories but not restricted to territory' wherein a 'universal authority' allowed princes to interfere in each other's rule (as well as to persecute political and religious heretics). In this sense 'Westphalia represented a coup from below' (400). After marking the transfer from royal sovereignty to popular sovereignty in the eighteenth century, he shows how in our time the incompetence of the state is being picked up by the competencies of global civil society in a variety of sectors, which, however, as he states in his conclusion, might not represent the smooth transfer to 'a more peaceful and unified world' (419). What is promising in his approach – and what made his article compelling to so many – is his comprehensive and ultimately rather open-ended overview of global civil society and the historical contingency which he injects into the state as an institution. Thus the state need not be the only game in town as far as conceiving world politics goes; contrary to what some realist and neo-realist IR scholars – as well as social movement theorists – are prone to claim implicitly.

As erudite as Lipschutz's analysis is, it leaves a number of open questions, however. First, it is not obvious what precisely these spaces of (global) civil society are. He tells us they are networks and presumably they are non-geographical, but this is not made explicitly clear. He does find it significant that these networks operate over or within space (on the face of the earth), so geography does seem to play a role. Just what that is, however, is left to the reader. Second, his merely adopting a non state-centric approach does not go far enough to get rid of the state. For in the very attempt to leave it behind, he in effect re-entrenches the notion of the state and inflates its role as an international actor. Global civil society, as he points out, must interact with the state system after all, a state of affairs that leads to the well-rehearsed arguments that an emerging civil society only strengthens the role of the state, especially through appeals to rights (see for example Baker 2002). Finally, he prioritizes the state again by tracing its historical emergence. Although he obviously does not treat it as a primitive element in his conception of the global, nevertheless he uses it as a sort of independent variable when explaining its emergence: at one point in history this thing called the state did not exist, then it did, and today it is in peril. To truly explain the historical emergence of the state he either needs some other independent variable (society, in its vagueness, is used by a great many), or some other means of relating the state to the global. All of these questions point to a need to more profoundly examine the ontological foundations of the state and (the spaces of) non-state aspects of world politics such as civil society.

It is important to note that such a line of reasoning is certainly not unique to Lipschutz; his article is merely an example of an approach which is indeed pervasive. We can see another example in the more recent AGM literature. Given the latter's many connections with critical theory and post-colonial thought, one might expect it to be particularly sensitive to these fundamental problems of political space. However, it tends to be for the most part remarkably isomorphic to social movement literature and IR. Hayden and el-Ojeili describe globalization as the intensification of

> cross-border interaction and a growing interdependence between national and transnational actors through a 'deterritorialization' whereby social spaces, distances and borders lose some of their previously overriding influence as political, cultural, social and economic relations become more global over time.
>
> (2005: 4)

In other words, deterritorialization (unfortunately a term left unexplained in the text) leads to cross-border interaction and interdependence between all actors, national and transnational. The result is that space, distance, and borders lose influence. Apart from the fact that the final clause is merely a repetition of the first, it is unclear why cross-border action does increase, as opposed to lower, the influence of borders. Whatever the case, their argument assumes the primacy of nations and borders in the first place. The goal, however, should be to talk about such intensifications without using the state/borders – nor concepts of global civil society – as an independent variable. Due to such slippages back to the state, we must extend the designation of methodological nationalism to any account which ontologically prioritizes the status of the state. Let us examine this in more detail.

Since the 1990s it has become fashionable in many fields to herald the death or at least tremendous decline of the nation state. From a rather cynical point of view, the academic interest circles around 'endless controversies about whether states are here forever or are about to disappear into some global cosmopolis' (Walker 1993: 14). In order to put these controversies in perspective, however, it is worth remembering that the debate concerning the disappearance of the nation state has been a subject, if not a central focus as it is today, of IR literature for some time.[6] As Kratochwil reminds us (in 1986), citing Nye, such discussions are perennial, and were ongoing in the 1960s (1986: 27). What this suggests at the very least is that the recent musings on the state's health are not the direct result of some process of globalization driven by recent technological innovations such as the World Wide Web, post-Panamax shipping, and a host of new financial instruments, but rather reveals the inherent ontic instability of the nation state – even during the twentieth century, even at the height of the cold war.

And yet not only are current debates about the nature of global (dis)order bound up with the state, but future visions (the global cosmopolis) and even trans-temporal (historical) or transcultural studies are as well. Buzan and Little write about the Westphalian straightjacket wherein even pre-modern history (in IR) was understood 'largely by way of reference to specific cases that shared the assumption of the anarchic structure of the Westphalian system: the Greek and the Italian city states or the Chinese "warring states"' (2001: 25). Far too little attention has been paid to the grey areas, unruled lands, or overlapping structures, in short, the aspects of human interaction on earth which fall outside – and thus tend to undermine or challenge – the notion of a formally similar and homogeneous state, which is now putatively under attack. This straightjacket oversimplifies and is unable to account for the nuances of, for example, the Mongol Empire of the (European) Middle Ages or the *pax romana*, seeing all forms of social organization and disorganization in its own image. In essence this is a form of Eurocentricism that extends beyond the walls of the academy to the media and popular culture whereby it is difficult to theorize what came before, around/outside these ordered state systems – the fluid, polycentric, overlapping, and ambiguous nature of most of human political history – and what is to come in the future. What Buzan and Little call for is a more comprehensive understanding of the system of world politics – in order that we might begin to contemplate its future:

> Without a fuller understanding of all the forms that international systems can take, and all the variables that shape them, one cannot theorise properly about either structure or process, and can hardly theorise at all about system transformation. Because the interstate system has obviously existed throughout the modern era, little or no thought has been given to the conditions under which other international systems come into existence, evolve and are transformed. Consequently there are real difficulties in trying to conceptualise where our current, increasingly globalized, system might be going.
> (2001: 33)

In the literature methodological nationalism or the Westphalian straightjacket is the quintessential modernist position, but for Deleuze it is more broadly an example of the image of thought, what in *A Thousand Plateaus* is called the Royal Science which goes back much further, as explored in the last chapter. An examination of global political practice which followed a Deleuzian ontology and metaphysics would seek to render the elements of such a system without recourse to representational thought, or in the idiom of *A Thousand Plateaus*, seek a nomad science of world politics. But of course this is not to say that the state – as a system of human practices – does not or has never existed; only that it has no necessary and enduring essence. As Paul Veyne notes, to hold onto the notion of a state as an ideal type is a paradox: 'we understand that each society has its own list of what we call the tasks of the State: some societies want gladiators, others want social security ... In short, we believe that no state resembles any other and also that the state is the State.' In other words we believe in the State only as a word. Even when we move from a theoretical list of characteristics to an empirical one – what the state has done in all its manifestations

> we 'record' what tasks the State has found itself asked to perform to date ... we continue nonetheless to fix our sights on it, instead of trying to discover, beneath the surface, the practice of which it is simply a projection.
> (1997: 162–3)

The discovery and analysis of this practice, or more specifically, forms of content and forms of expression, is what Deleuze calls transcendental empiricism which will be discussed later in the chapter. For now it is worth emphasizing that Deleuze does not measure variations of the state (copies) to their ideal type (form or Idea). There is movement and differentiation, but the variables are completely different and moreover highly flexible and mobile. It consists of relating the virtual realm where aspects of human organization mix in an immanent field, and the variety of ways in which these mixtures are actualized in chronological time and metricized space. This shifts the focus from a science of the state to an understanding of how various state-forms come into being through the analysis of the transition from one regime or actualization of social relations to another. According to Deleuze and Guattari, this is the mapping of actual states of affairs, through to the virtual realm (counteractualization, deterritorialization), and then the subsequent – or more accurately, consequent – actualization in a new state of affairs. In terms of the status of the state – current, past, or future – what will be relevant is the relative movement between a completely open system of organization and the most regimented forms of government. This context refocuses questions concerning space, sovereignty, and the state somewhat away from a quest for a theoretical insight which would explain something called the state (or its putative rival, globalization) towards a methodology which explores state-ness or 'stating'.

In IR literature this is reflected in discussions on the issue of the false binary of the state. Anderson, for example, questions the apocalyptic nature of claims surrounding the so-called death of the nation state.

> Talk about the 'end' of territorially based sovereignty, postmodernist ideas about the 'death' of states and their replacement by regions, or glib notions of a 'borderless world', or a 'space of flows' replacing a 'space of places', are all clearly wide of the mark.
> (1996: 135)

He suggests a view of world politics that it is somewhere in between – that it is never an assessment in terms of one or the other. And this is precisely where the relative opposition of Deleuze's two poles comes in. It is never a matter of total ephemerality nor the rigid essences of human organization, but rather the movements between these two poles. John Agnew as well challenges the either/or quality of questions pertaining to the state and its relevance. He suggests that it is perhaps better to look at the state 'in terms of its significance and meaning as an actor in different historical circumstances' (1994: 54).

This raises the question of the status of such an actor. It is unclear why sociopolitical theorists tend to believe that sovereignty is so stable, monolithic, totalizing and unassailable, when history suggests that it has always been more or less nebulous, shifting, and contingent. The problem has traditionally been, however, that exceptions to the 'rule' of the state were viewed as an anomaly or as something external to a system of ideal types. From Bull (1977) to Rosenau (1990) and of course beyond, IR theorists have been well aware of 'sovereignty-free' or 'non-state' actors, but whatever their approach, they still have tended to view these as outside the state system. This leads one to wonder about the solidity of the state in the first place which was, from the Babylonian Empire to the Treaty of Westphalia to even cold war geopolitics, both conceptually and actually, a much more fluid beast. As will be argued below, in the case of the Roman Empire it was the patron–client relationship, more than the inside/outside of the state or imperial system, that played the most important role in delineating the 'frontiers' of the empire – an aspect overlooked by many historians, sociologists, and political scientists.[7] What this teaches us about a present or future world politics is to challenge assumptions of statehood as a fixed idea – especially when we are today inundated with exceptions in the form of entities such as supranational regimes, professional organizations, regulatory agencies, bond-rating agencies, NGOs, and the AGM. But recent debates on globalization (the positive image to the 'death of the state' debate) have actually served to further reify the state. As Mathias Albert points out in discussing Justin Rosenberg's (2005) influential if somewhat caustic article,

> globalization theorists, by emphasizing that globalization constitutes a massive trend toward transcending the Westphalian, sovereignty-cum-territoriality principle of the state, in fact reproduce a methodological nationalism by falsely assuming the existence of a 'preglobalization' era without significant transnational ties.
>
> (2007: 172)

What we can say is that the modern era was, at least conceptually, dominated by its own particular state form, although as will be shown below in the discussion of territoriality, the reality of the bounded nation state hardly measures up to its power as an ordering principle. Through the philosophies of Hobbes and especially Hegel, modern representational thought exhibited itself in the belief that the state form was the terminus of human organization. In the former, the main argument, the one that makes the Leviathan possible in the first place, is the notion that the state is something over and above a civil society (1967: 90). In the latter, civil society, as in Hobbes, is based on selfish ends (1967: 67) against which the state is the actuality of ethical life, the culminating expression of the universal mind (216) through a process of linear world historic time (see Patomäki 2003). Such a conception of civil society being distinct from the state is in fact one of the hallmarks of liberalism and has become so deeply embedded in IR as not to be questioned, and what it in fact does is reify the state form. It is a binary field or space wherein we cannot have one element without the other. Such a belief, however, goes much further back in Western thought, of course. Aristotle held the idea of individuals belonging to the state – granted, not exactly the juridico-territorial entity of modern times – as something inherently proper to humans. Moreover he maintained that, 'the state is by nature clearly prior to the family and to the individual, since the whole is of necessity prior to the part.' (1984b: 1988 [253a19], 2029 [1278b15]). This idea was incorporated by the scholastics, most influentially in Thomas Aquinas, as justifying the Christian religious state (see Bigongiari 1953: i). Thereafter an embryonic form of what we know as the modern state formed during the Hundred Years' War as rulers began to justify their aggression (as well as labour and tax regimes) along nationalist – and increasingly territorial – lines (see for example Spruyt 2002).

In practical terms, however, the state and especially the modern nation state – to the extent that human practice exhibited characteristics which we associate with 'stateness', or in Deleuze's terms, 'to state' – must be seen as an exception in human history. Following Roland Robertson, the state or even the national society is historically unique and moreover abnormal, and ultimately serves as just one way among many for the 'analysis of the global human circumstance' (1990: 25). Thus the state must not be conceived as an eternal form, or a model in the Platonic sense, but rather viewed in its specificity, uniqueness, and historical context, or, as Agnew writes, as historically and geographically contingent and not as an ideal type (1994: 64, 70). This is not to argue that there is no commonality amongst expressions of the state in any given era or region, nor likewise that it is pointless and moreover unproductive to analyse something called 'European modernity'. Rather it is to highlight, again, the implicit fluidity and heterogeneity of such conceptual generalizations, to avoid working from static forms and fixed categories, and consequently to emphasize the non-necessary and transient nature of any visible stability, thereby focussing on the state's emergence and metamorphosis.

It may be difficult to bookend an era which was characterized by the modern nation state. The typical starting point in IR is the Peace of Westphalia in 1648 which established territorial exclusivity amongst the hitherto warring states of Western Europe, thereby replacing the more fluid, ambiguous, and complex system of kingdoms, principalities, and alliances which characterized the preceding era. The endpoint of the modern era is normally associated with the cold war – its beginning, middle (the US in Vietnam), or end. From a more sociological perspective, one might begin with the discovery of society late in the eighteenth century (see Polanyi 1968: 111ff.) and end with its famous disavowal by Margaret Thatcher in 1987. Another candidate could be the sea-change in thinking brought about by the French Revolution and the relative stability of the post-Napoleonic era through to the breakdown of the post-war system signalled by the social unrest of 1968 or the dismantlement of the Bretton Woods system in 1971. In any case most would agree that what one might call the modern era is bound up with the European Enlightenment embodied in such thinkers as Descartes, Hobbes, and Montesquieu. It ends – thus heralding the so-called postmodern era – it is generally agreed, in the last quarter of the twentieth century, signalled by such phenomena as the ascendency of the US dollar as a world currency, post-industrialization and the rise of service industries, the fall of the Berlin Wall, the end of the cold war, digitization, the new role of finance capital, among others.

But of course such firm demarcations are problematic. Benno Teschke, for example, has challenged the view of a clean start to the modern political era, arguing that in order to understand the Westphalian system, we have to 'unpack the social relations of sovereignty that underwrote the Westphalian order to reveal its non-modern nature' (2003: 3). He sees 1648 not as the beginning of something new but as the culmination of a dynastic system of order. Likewise heralding the dawn of the postmodern era turns out to be fraught with problems. Following the discussion of Deleuze in Chapter 2, the relations – social, political, economic – between human beings take place fundamentally on a plane of immanence, or in other words are 'underdetermined' in an open system. The Enlightenment, in these terms, is an actualization of these relations or series into a variety of more closed or stratified systems which 'overdetermined' or, to use a Deleuzo-Guattarianism, 'overcoded' human activity and interaction. Significantly these stratifications have been characterized by countless counteractualizations or lines of flight of social organization, art, and thought. Some of these deterritorializations were relative and constituted what Isaiah Berlin called the Counter-Enlightenment. Others, such as Nietzsche's untimely 'war machine', were more absolute. The point is here to emphasize that the modern era was far from monolithic and was characterized by flux.[8] Walker, for example, splinters the modern period, mapping the early modern Enlightenment onto mid-twentieth century theories (especially in IR) about space and time (ones with all the assumptions about subject and object, rational action), and the late nineteenth and early twentieth century (Marx, Nietzsche, Bergson) onto postmodernism and post-structuralism. He presents a more or less cyclical account: progressives checked with romantics, or 'Enlightenment and Despair', as he calls it (1993: 9–12). Similarly Foucault asserts a preservation of a unity in the face of the decentrings of Marx, Nietzsche, and Freud (2002b: 14). From this perspective Deleuze's history of philosophy can be seen as an account of the 'history' of the revolutions of thought and explains why he sees such important connections between the Stoics, Scotus, Spinoza, Nietzsche, and Bergson in the face of Plato, Aquinas, Descartes, and Kant.

One important thing to remember is that based on Deleuze's political metaphysics there can be no *reason* for the waxing and waning of certain stratifications such as the state form, or, in other words, the actualization of a given state of affairs. Recalling the discussion in the previous chapter, the process of individuation (which follows differentiation but precedes differenciation) is determined simply by speed and slowness: series 'happening' to converge and diverge, or put more crudely, things just bumping into each other. The relation between states of affairs are not effects amongst themselves; strictly speaking, effects are what Deleuze reserves for 'quasi-causes' in *The Logic of Sense*. The latter are in fact Events which cause states of affairs, but there is no reason or structure to them nor do the ensuing processes resemble that which they actualize. This is post-structuralism in the strictest sense, and from this perspective Rosenberg's critique of globalization (2005) becomes a non-starter: there is no explanans of globalization. There can be no process we can name to explain it. Likewise Harvey (1990) can write so fluently about postmodernism (and make use of Deleuzian terms such as rhizome and deterritorialization), but shows his difference from Deleuze through his reliance on economic materialism. It is very clear to him why we have things like time–space compression. Deleuze, as we have said, is also a materialist, but the material in this case is self-forming.

The putative death of the nation state today in terms of a borderless world or the flows of global capital is part of a long process – or rather an ebb and flow – that must be seen as a fundamental part of the de- and subsequent reterritorialization of human interaction. But what marks today's deterritorialization (as opposed to, say, the 'globalization' of the late nineteenth century) are things such as post-industrialization, finance, spectacle (the disintegration of the sign, fractured subjectivities, etc.) – in short, a qualitative change in the fabric of society. Other seemingly stable systems such as the Hellenistic or the Aztec World had their own deterritorializations also, with their own attendant specificities. The conclusion is that modernity is a contraction, abstraction, or papering-over of the fundamental immanence of relations, and 'the modern period' with its notions of space and the state must therefore be seen as an anomaly (in a sea of anomalies – each one being a singularity) and understood in its specificity. In terms of space, an investigation of this specificity can begin with territoriality. Here the central attribute of modernity in international politics has been a peculiar and historically unique configuration of territorial space (Ruggie 1993: 144), but the following will also show that this configuration was far from homogeneously understood or applied.

Territory is the demarcation of geographical (Euclidean) space with the use of borders or what function variously as frontiers between one space and another. It is this demarcation that upholds the historically unique nature of the modern state system with its emphasis on mutual exclusiveness, functional similarity, and sovereignty (Ruggie 1993). But like the broader notion of the state, finding an example of territory as an ideal type is difficult. Indeed, what would seem to be a simple question of geography (looking at a map to find a state) becomes extremely complex. In practice the boundaries, borders, and frontiers which tend to define territory are far more fluid, blurry, and complex than most deployments – whether in history, sociology, or political science – would imply. As

Kratochwil argues, the notion of 'territoriality, like property, is not a simple concept, but comprises a variety of social arrangements that have to be examined in greater detail' (1986: 27).

We could start by looking at Roman geography, which is particularly pertinent, as many of the territorial borders of the modern era around the Mediterranean are based on the territorial groupings of various stages of the Roman Republic and then Empire. The peoples conquered by the Romans were subject to certain administrative and hence geographical structures. By imposing the provinces of *Germania Superior* and *Germania Inferior*, for example, Julius Caesar distinguished its inhabitants from Gaul and thereby effectively 'created' Germany. Although the Rhine River served as one of the most clearly demarcated frontiers throughout most of the imperial period, it is, however, a mistake to liken such a boundary to its modern equivalent – and the Rhine is perhaps one of the strongest and most consistent frontiers in Roman history. One of the causes of this mistake is a reliance on Roman sources. Thomas Burns argues that although these sources give the impression of more or less precise borders based on exclusion, archaeological evidence suggests that the Empire never had the manpower or resources that such exclusivity would require. 'Permanent exclusion was never the goal. Rather, Roman efforts were directed towards controlling the process of inclusion, first among conquered provincials and then among those living beyond the frontiers who had proved worthy.' (2003: 18). It was legal distinctions (including citizenship) which formed the basis of exclusion and were very often held out as rewards to the barbarian peoples. But these of course are not geographical distinctions of territory, rather they describe a relation between a subjected person and the imperial centre. Once an individual attained citizenship it was a valid sort of inclusion throughout the empire and indeed beyond. In other words, the 'borders' of the republic but especially of the expansionist empire were much more fluid, porous, and smooth than might be imagined from the perspective of territorial–juridical thinking.[9]

The lures of citizenship were a later phase of a relationship that was first determined by the rules and traditions of Roman patronage. But strikingly what this implies is an empire without end. 'Because patronage was the earliest and most enduring relationship among Romans and between Rome and the barbarians, all Roman clients would have been included to some degree as being "within" the empire' (Burns 2003: 146). The key here is 'to some degree', meaning that in practice the distinctions would have been nebulous, unfixed, and most certainly variable and again, non-territorial. 'This conceptual rather than geographic boundary, beyond which there were no clients, would have been impossible to locate on a map precisely because patronage itself was regarded as essentially personal rather than territorial.' An illustration of this from the primary sources is that Roman authors rarely speak of conquering territory but rather conquering people. For Julius Caesar '[d]espite his desire to declare the Rhine as a cultural boundary, his narrative reveals a transition zone in which life-styles and peoples merged around shared topographic features – for example, along the lower Rhine' (Burns 2003: 137). That such a 'weak' conception of territory (I am not arguing here that the Romans had no concept of geographical space whatsoever) was based on the fact that the Romans were more interested in ruling people than land is illustrated in conceptions of what an empire was precisely: 'we see over and over that Julius Caesar did not think in terms of a limit to empire. For him there could be no geographic limit to the networks of patronage defining and channelling Roman power' (Burns 2003: 130). It is not difficult to see how this would apply to the Mongol Empire of the thirteenth century (see for example Saunders 2001: 73, 76), or the successive dynasties in China. That Chinese rulers often played on the limitless nature of the Chinese empire is reflected in the very term for China, 中国 or 'middle kingdom'. Such a sense of a boundlessness can be detected in the smooth space of empire in modern conceptions of power throughout seas and oceans, as well as ideas like the sun never setting on the British Empire, and so on. In all of these cases the physical borders, where they existed, were membranes and as such were porous, transparent and usually existed primarily for the purpose of taxation (see for example Saunders 2001: 52). Even the physical evidence belies the nature of these boundaries. As Kratochwil reminds us, neither the Great Wall nor Roman *limes* constituted a boundary in the modern sense, though they appear to be an example of linear boundaries showing some exclusivity. As for the latter, 'The political and administrative domain often extended beyond the wall or stayed inside it at a considerable distance' (1986: 36). Boundaries tended to be about property in the legal sense, not about jurisdiction.

In the same article Kratochwil traces what Deleuze would call the reterritorialization (from their beginnings as nomads to suzerains of the Manchu empire) of the Mongol people who at their height under Kublai claimed a vast space from China to Syria as their own – what is generally referred to as the world's largest contiguous empire. Their success was based on what Deleuze and Guattari call the war machine, about which there has been considerable interest in recent years (see for example Reid 2003). They view it as an expression (admittedly idealized) of the form of conquest of the nomadic people of the Eurasian steppes who operate not in the striations of territoriality, but in the smooth space of an open empire, who do not acquire space, but rather fill it. It is the creative aspect of such a machine that the State must harness (*ATP*: 483) through the apparatus of capture, and indeed this is what happens with various imperial dynasties (Yuán, Mughal). Kratochwil points out that a firm sense of territoriality was lacking in this part of central Asia through to modern times. Though the Treaty of Peking between Russia and Imperial China was indeed a case of reterritorialization (here the fixing of frontiers), in practice space remained fluid in most cases. For example the Xinjiang region remained considerably independent until the 1940s. We can remember that Imperial China, like the Roman Empire, was based on clientship. So even though modern state boundaries were introduced to the region, they did not function as Westphalian orthodoxy would have it: 'Local leaders and Russian and Chinese liens made the attributing of the area to either state problematic in spite of its internationally settled boundaries' (Kratochwil 1986: 31).

Kratochwil goes on to explore what is in fact the fluid nature of territory in practice. He writes that boundaries come in two classes: manipulation of location as in, for example, the balance of power in Europe, or management of the types of exchanges. The latter he maintains played a key role in modern European imperialism. 'Institutions such as buffers, protectorates, spheres of interest (or influence), suzerainties, and neutral zones were commonly used to impose European rule on more or less recalcitrant "locals" and to manage potential conflicts with other expanding European powers' (1986: 37). Much like in the case of the enduring legacy of the Romans in Europe, it was only later that these boundaries became permanent for former colonial areas. Other examples of the fluid nature of territory include frontier zones such as the Balkans in the nineteenth century; protectorates; condominia like Samoa under Germany, Britain, and the US; spheres of preponderance; neutral zones (often exploited by brigands); and buffer states (as in the case of eastern Afghanistan in 1879). This shows that throughout the modern period, although the territorially-defined state may not have been a gross exception, the vast majority of the world's inhabitants lived under more blurry and fluid regimes than a strict interpretation of territoriality would reveal, or indeed much more ambiguous than contemporary cartography would suggest. Territorial sovereignty belonged to but a few powers; what have just been described above are the forms of 'fluid' territory that were the means by which 'states have tried to modify the exclusionary nature of territorial sovereignty and thereby to maintain their relations' (Kratochwil 1986: 41–3). Even in 1986, at a point of heightened tensions of the Cold War when interstate relations seemed rather more straightforward, Kratochwil points out that there were contradictory tendencies: although territorial sovereignty putatively became the universally recognized differentiating principle of international life, interdependences in modern economic life tended to erode these boundaries.[10] Moreover, there was also the question of ideological and informational transaction which demanded new conflict management methods as well as 'spheres of responsibility' (1986: 46). Finally Kratochwil highlights the difference between the old European state system and the 'modern international system': 'The accommodation that occurred in the late sixties and early seventies was not backed by explicit agreements, and the rules of the game that have emerged in regard to spheres of influence resemble "unspoken rules"'. Here spheres of interest or influence were usually the result of 'bilateral, explicit agreements'. Thus we have (during the Cold War, at least) the so-called tacit rule: Agreements need not be based on 'explicit verbal agreements' interpretable through ordinary language, but should be understood by looking at motives and other non-verbal acts: 'its institutionalization is weak; no explicit discourse about the tacit rule is possible, and therefore neither scope nor applicability to certain contexts can be discussed' (1986: 48–50).

Thus we see the imperfections of what is supposed to be a state system characterized by territoriality. As Anderson argues, the domestic–foreign distinction is rather fictionalized: society has always been transnational, rather than simply national. 'In principle there is nothing new in cross-border relations undercutting state sovereignty; and the reality of geopolitics is that powerful states have frequently ignored the "sovereign rights" of weaker countries' (1996: 147). Moreover the assumption of territoriality is a stark expression of Eurocentricism: Anderson adds that multi-perspectivism in the form of multiple identities and hybridization is not novel at all to people in colonies or ex-colonies, which is one of the themes of post-colonial research (see for example Bhabha 1994). Likewise there is no reason that such multi-perspectivism was alien to the people of Germania two millennia ago, or to those on the fringes of the Tang Dynasty (618–907 CE) in China.

Another oft-cited example which undermines 'the myth of territoriality' is the embassy chapel question. The notion of an embassy actually belonging to the territory of the home country came from the problem of national religious services in other countries, which caused considerable disorder in the sixteenth century for pre-modern European states. Mitigation was achieved by deeming chapels to be the territory of the sending embassy.

> Rather than contemplate the heresy of a Protestant service at a Catholic court and vice versa, it proved easier to pretend that the service was not taking place in the host country at all but on the soil of the homeland of the ambassador. And so it gradually became with other dimensions of the activities and precincts of embassy. A fictitious space, designated 'extraterritoriality,' was invented.
>
> (Ruggie 1993: 165)

Of course this caused havoc, for example, when Catholics living in England tried to attend mass at the French embassy chapel (see Trimble 1946: 107) and similarly with Protestants in France. Other 'exceptions' to state-centric orthodoxy include transnational organizations such as the Catholic Church, common markets, international fairs that enjoyed special privileges,[11] and political communities that fell into two or more territorial jurisdictions (Anderson 1996: 145) such as the Xinjiang region mentioned above.

The tendency to use territoriality to underwrite the state system is heavily criticized in Agnew's well-known article, *The Territorial Trap* (1994). In Anderson's words, the territorial trap is 'an ahistorical reification of states as fixed units of sovereign space; a dichotomizing of domestic and foreign or inside and outside which obscures cross-border processes; and a view of the state as the preexisting container of "society"'. From this he lists inadequate and now inappropriate perspectives: idealizing the state as timeless and unchanging (wherein in fact it has been constantly mutating and will most certainly continue to do so); which consequently fosters the life or death of the state debate; the tendency to equate society with 'national society'; and the separation of political theory (internal) from IR (external) which tends to place traditionally inner-state actors (interest groups, classes) out of IR. Moreover '[c]ollapsing most issues to the one level of the state usually meant that other levels above and below the state remained relatively undifferentiated and unexplored' (1996: 139).

That the entire notion of territoriality is contingent, as we saw with Kratochwil above, suggests an enormous variation of stronger and weaker borders, not only as sketched on the earth's surface – in itself a highly contestable process (see Ó Tuathail 1996) – but also of differences in general that divide people. Looking back to Chapter 2, we are not talking about difference in the concept such that Space A is different from Space B, but rather a process of differenciation (as the consequence of a differentiation) or actualization of all kinds of structures and stratifications, including geographical ones. The notion of mutually exclusive states – what has turned out to be an anomaly both in terms of population living under such regimes and geographical area – must be viewed not as natural or necessary but as a sort of 'cooling'[12] of immanent relations. Moreover, as the above discussion has shown, the spaces that are generally considered to be striated are in fact much 'smoother' than they appear.

The consequence of such a line of argument is that states as such – as an essence – do not exist, but rather persist as various becomings of ebb and flow. We can see the expression of this argument in many contemporary studies. Bob Jessop (2003: 13–15), for example, detects a false opposition between the claim that the state is losing importance in the face of globalization, especially when territorially defined states are contrasted with a global economy that operates within a borderless whole. He detects several conceptual errors in such an argument. The state, he concludes, is not a thing as such but rather a 'power connector' or a node. 'Thus we should focus on the changing organisation of politics and economics and their respective institutional embodiments and see frontiers and borders as actively reproduced and contingent rather than as pregiven and fixed' (2003: 13–14). Essentially Jessop turns the standard globalization question around. Rather than asking how states are affected by globalization (a question that presumes the conceptual stability of states – in effect the classical representationalist position), it asks how these institutional embodiments called states (re)produce borders as part of the globalization process(es). In what is in fact a very Deleuzian register,[13] he does not talk about globalization as an explanans:

> far from globalization being a unitary causal mechanism, it should be understood as the complex, emergent product of many different forces operating on many scales. Hence nothing can be explained in terms of the causal powers of globalization. ... Instead globalizations themselves need explaining in all their manifold spatio–temporal complexity. This does not exclude specific hypotheses about the impact of clearly specifiable processes on particular sets of social relations.
>
> (2003: 3)

Thus in empirical terms we can investigate how finance affects the state's capacity to set interest rates and achieve employment objectives. We cannot, however 'meaningfully investigate the wild and overly general claim that "globalization undermines the power of the state."' In other words it is not a zero-sum game between globalization (economy) and the state (politics). Saying that the former puts pressure on the latter is misleading. Sovereignty is 'only one aspect of the form of the modern state' and can be reorganized: 'The processes that generate globalization can only put pressure on particular forms of the state with particular state capacities and liabilities, such as the Keynesian National Welfare State in Atlantic Fordism or the Listian Workfare National State in East Asian Exportism.' Moreover the effects are felt in different ways by different elements of these societies. And, 'since globalization is not a single causal mechanism with a universal, unitary logic but is multicentric, multiscalar, multitemporal, and multiform, it does not generate a single, uniform set of pressures', and some aspects of globalization actually enhance state capacities (2003: 13–15). Thus states are not so much declining as being transformed, becoming hybridized. In the Deleuzian sense we can understand the state as a becoming – a becoming-state[14] or, again, state-ing – rather than a reified, stable, socio-political entity. This involves no return to a form or essence of political organization. The state must be understood merely as a (contingent) ordering tendency. That is, it is a process that is highly singular in that no two states are alike and ultimately imperfect in that there are always innumerable lines of flight. As we shall see below, contemporary global society is not reverting to a new medievalism – though it may share resemblances – but is rather becoming something else entirely. Likewise, institutions such as the EU are also not bound by dualisms but are rather characterized by lines of flight. In this sense the EU exists neither in an intergovernmentalism of the member states nor in a 'United States of Europe', but perhaps is already here in an ' "intermediate" form which is distinct in its own right rather than merely transitional' (Anderson 1996: 134).

The world then is made up of many different elements or actors in a constant state of becoming which we can truly define as a multiplicity: it is a non-denumerable set expressed in infinite variety. It is at this point where Deleuze's critique of difference in the concept as discussed in the last chapter comes to the fore. Such difference only functions amongst entities which share in the Same, that is, have characteristics or differences that make them part of a set. Multiplicities have no such fixed differences and so no such location within (or without) the concept. Saying that the world is a multiplicity is quite a different claim than that the world consists of a plurality of actors, for the latter implies a very great number of things with essences which are, therefore, countable though they be infinite (or are claimed to be infinite, at least). Such a stringent critique of difference (within the concept) offers further methodological innovation. If there are not essences, no basic units, if all kinds of elements and actors such as states, supranational bodies, legal regimes, and epistemic communities are in a constant state of becoming, then the question of a level of analysis becomes irrelevant and moreover inherently false. In IR terms, challengers to the state have largely been seen to be state-equivalents: super states (state writ large) or regional governments/devolution of power (state writ small) – in other words, merely a change in geographic scale. For critics this is known as the 'Gulliver Fallacy' which 'is rooted in a way of thinking about geographic space which sees it as "absolute and homogeneous" (as in Euclid's geometry and Newton's physics), rather than "relative and variable" (as in Einstein's universe)' (Anderson 1996: 140).

And yet the notion of level of analysis as a precondition of scientific investigation is a cornerstone of mainstream socio-political theory, though it remains under-problematized. Walker, in a passage strongly echoing Deleuze's argument on good and common sense, argues that

> [i]t is striking that much if not most of modern social and political analysis can be understood as an exercise in classification of some kind, and yet the literature on the practices of classification is, to say the least, rather Spartan. ... As an expression of the inbred common sense of modern political discourse, this schema hides most of its ontological significance under a chaste appeal for analytical clarity and explanatory parsimony.
>
> (2005: 136)

The ontological significance from the perspective of this book is the perpetual reliance on representational thought which assures difference in the concept and thereby stable entities. Deleuze does not have this problem since every element – from the supranational regime to the individual voter – is seen as a population, that is, as a non-denumerable set of series connecting and diverging between the virtual and the actual. The roots of such an understanding can be found in Leibniz and Whitehead, where 'microcosm and macrocosm are coordinated, linked to one another in a seamless web of process' (Rescher 1996: 21) and receives fuller attention in complexity theory as will be shown below. The laws that govern the world (adhesion, attractions, of contact)

> are like statistics because they pertain to collections, masses, organisms, and no longer to individual beings. Thus they do not convey primary forces or individual beings, but they distribute derivative forces in masses, elastic forces, forces of attraction, and plastic forces that in each case are determining the material linkages.
>
> (*LB*:118)

It follows that we can no longer speak of subjects but of populations because the (virtual) events which actualize as actors are a multiplicity and thus non-denumerable and irreducible, resulting in an actual multiplicity. Thus the actions of the political agent (of whatever 'scale') are better described as a flock of birds or a herd of caribou (or the movement of a mob) than a point of sovereign subjectivity 'steering', as it were, a corporeal body. Accounting for, understanding, or mapping such activity through transcendental empiricism is thus more statistical than algebraic. The individual elements themselves, especially in terms of political subjectivity, will be further discussed in Chapter 4, but for now we can sense the significance of an approach to world politics that includes smooth space (or virtual, immanent relations), rather than politics only happening in the striated or geographical and metricized. With such an approach it will not be possible to talk about rational actors conducting cost–benefit analysis of discrete bits of information, to say the least.

This problem of the level of analysis is perhaps the reason for Appadurai's comment that a framework relating the global, the national, and the local has yet to emerge (Appadurai 1996b: 188). Or perhaps it is better to say that the statement itself belies the fact that since these elements are not reified entities but related to each other through processes of becoming, then the quest for a 'framework' is a non-starter. The world is not one big system with successively smaller subsystems within it. As Anderson argues,

> The contemporary world is not a ladder up or down [on] which processes move from one rung to the next in an orderly fashion, the central state mediating all links between the external or higher levels and the internal or lower ones. That was never the case, but it is even less true today.
>
> (1996: 151)

This exposes a problem with Delanda's notion of embedded assemblages (2006: 17ff.)[15]: giving the impression of subsystems within systems ignores relations that take place outside what are normally thought of as distinct levels. In terms of scalar interaction, the world is not the state writ large; the state is not the community writ large, and the community is not the family writ large. Rather we have scalar complexity. In terms of level of analysis – because of enveloped/enveloping as discussed in the last chapter, and in the relationship between the world and the individual as discussed in the next chapter – the world is a complex web resembling more a game of snakes and ladders than matryoshka dolls: it is an 'adventure playground' (Anderson 1996: 151). Some contemporary sociological research reflects this in attempts to understand the connection between the global and the local (see for example Lachernmann and Dannecker 2008), as does neo-institutionalism, which explores the decoupling of the state from a global–local continuum (see Meyer *et al.* 1997).

Time

Before we move to map out a political metaphysics that would be appropriate for a political terrain not primarily inscribed in hierarchy, territoriality, or exclusiveness, we must take a look at time itself as a notion. Just as we hesitated to take on board the established truths of space and territory and thus the state, so too in terms of time care must be taken. The first step in such care is to question the whole notion of a natural, metricized time moving from past to future with the force of inevitability, as addressed in the previous chapter. Ilya Prigogine and Isabella Stengers in their seminal *Order Out of Chaos* caution against such assumptions. They raise the question of why people – in the West in particular – applied the 'analogy of the watch' to nature in general. The answer, they submit, is bound to the Christian belief[16] that there is a secret which can be unveiled, and studying science was studying God, from Aristotle right up to Newton's *Principia*. In contrast, in traditional Chinese cosmology, they point out, there is nothing external – such as (a/the) God – to nature, society, and the heavens. These are in a process of harmony and resonate with each other, rather than follow a hierarchical form (God–nature–society) (1984: 45–8).

Somewhat ironically for Deleuze, it is movement characterizing the Event which resides in the time of the Aion; the realm of Chronos is in contrast static and fixed. Traditionally, instants in Western political thinking are climaxes in a succession of states that share the nature of a higher form or essence ('discovery', 'brilliance', 'eureka!'). Beyond the teleological nature of such temporal narration, which has been much criticized in recent decades through the critique of the notion of progress, such a treatment of time privileges the individual moment, an approach of which Deleuze, perhaps not unsurprisingly, is very wary. Privileged instants, he argues, are, rather, 'remarkable or singular points which belong to movement, and not as the moments of actualisation of a transcendent form.' They require an 'immanent analysis of movement, and not a transcendental synthesis' (*C1*: 6). What he is after here is not a representation of some (eternal) form that serves as a *prise* or snapshot of some transcendent – or perhaps worse, the expression of such – but rather what he calls a synthesis that forms points that belong to a movement that in effect express the Aion. Evidence of a nomadic aesthetics of time is that other art forms besides cinema (which for Deleuze is the art form of the virtual par excellence), such as dance, have relatively recently abandoned poses 'to release values which were not posed, not measured, which related movement to the any-instant-whatever.' This art 'became actions of responding to accidents of the environment; that is, to the distribution of the points of a space, or the movements of event' (*C1*: 5). The goal for Deleuze is to do to thinking what is already evident in art, namely, to abandon representation (fixed in time) in favour of the virtual (*DR*: 346). In a similar way all the arts have become fluid, or more accurately – and here Deleuze adds a whole other dimension to this observation – non-representational. They are no longer *about* anything. They do not represent or signify, but rather think or philosophize. They literally produce.

Thinking of time in more practical terms one can point to the shift, generally recognized in academia at least, from progress to chance: from the modern linear life sequence to a risk society. The significance of this shift is that parts of the world that lean towards global urban cultural patterns (in other words, approaching that 'global cosmopolis') can be seen to be much more sensitive to the movement or the Event (becoming) rather than the more cumbersome changes of states of affairs in the actual.[17] Contemporary life in such a society is more akin to living in the perpetual present, as evidenced by the observation that forward thinking (that is, modern in the strict sense) culture is being replaced by pastiche, contextless cultural motifs, and 'retro' (see for example Smith 1990: 176–80). In this perpetual present one speaks of 'life chances' or 'being at the right place at the right time'. To be sure the notion of scientific progress is an enduring one – which in itself, however, is beginning to be questioned as people lose faith in a technological fix in terms of health and the environment in particular – but the high modernist perspective of the 1960s is almost completely absent in the global cosmopolis. Very little in the way of music, art, and design are forward thinking and progressive, but tend rather to be endlessly recycled, a process which some claim in effect erodes the distinction between 'high art' and mass culture (see for example Jameson 1983: 112).

Moreover there is the loss of historical sense (as expressed in 'who needs to study history?') that is bemoaned by some, especially in the English-speaking world, with, for example, the study of history being seen as increasingly unnecessary from an educational policy point of view (see for example Dillon 2006). The loss of historical sense can also be seen in the narrowing of temporal scale in the form of real-time everything, ever-shortening news cycles, and mobile access to friends, work, and information. Global, affluent culture is increasingly living in a thick present, a 'time out of joint' as Deleuze would say. This is a schizophrenic time,[18] which has often been theorized by those writing about postmodernism(s) as the breakdown of the relationship between the signifier (a material object, sound of a word or text), the signified (the meaning), and the referent (the real object to which the signifier refers). Such schizophrenics live in a perpetual present with no 'sense of the persistence of the "I" and the "me" over "time"' (Jameson 1983: 120).[19] When the signifier loses its connection to its signified, it becomes transformed into pure image. From a societal point of view, we thus have an endless, fluid 'chain of signifiers', rendering all media a mechanism for historical amnesia.

These are just a few aspects of time that are highlighted by the turn away from modernist actualizations – there are of course many others. But what we should take away from this discussion is the role of the Aion. Similar to smooth space being uncovered by contemporary political practice, the Aion too becomes increasingly exposed. For example, just as the smoothness of cyberspace differs from the striations of modern regulated space, so too does the smoothness of flexitime differ from modern regulated time characterized by Fordist punchcards. Granted, grasping the notion of the Aion is more difficult than that of smooth space, but what it in fact entails, recalling the discussion from Chapter 2, is that the present is infinitely subdivided by the past and the future in both directions, so that in effect everything just happened and is also just about to happen. Sometimes Deleuze describes this as everything 'happening' at the same time; the homogeneous directional time of the second synthesis (Chronos) that we experience through memory as a succession of instants is but the actualization of the virtual Aion (see *DR*: 105). The point is that there is no underlying pure or refined 'clock time' that seemed so strikingly present in the modern period, but absent previously and afterwards. The pure time is the time of the Aion and contemporary experience of postmodernism and cultural schizophrenia exposes this immanent world.

Neo-medievalism and the postmodern

Having looked briefly at the development of the nation state during the modern era and exceptions to its rule which have persisted up until the present, as well as the role of time and space in general, we now must reassess an approach to thinking of the AGM outside the theoretical restrictions of the state. We can now look towards understanding it in terms of a global process that is in a constant relative movement between de- and re-territorialization, or, put differently, between lines of flight and apparatuses of capture. What would it mean to engage with and analyse the political terrain that in effect, or at least primarily, is without frontier, border, limit, or possibilities? Many, especially in IR literature, and in international political sociology in particular, have looked to what in the Western context is the most readily and well-documented example of a period which was not characterized – however accurately or not – by the modern, sovereign nation state, namely medieval Europe. As Agnew notes, 'In medieval Europe there were few fixed boundaries between different political authorities. Regional networks of kinship and interpersonal affiliation left little scope for fixed territorial limits' (1994: 60).

In *Back to the Future; Neomedievalism and the Postmodern Digital World Economy*, Stephen Kobrin makes an extensive argument highlighting the similarities or parallels between the European medieval era and the current global system. He notes the changes in space, geography, and borders that have been explored above. He adds the ambiguity of authority which was dispersed, overlapping, and often trans- or supranational. Such authority was not bounded by space (and territory) as it tends to be during the modern period. Rather people, land, and property often fell into more than one jurisdiction and there was interpenetration by other systems, namely the Church. This was exemplified in multiple loyalties as well as the influential role of transnational elites in a system where the distinction between private and public property was not yet fully developed. Finally, Kobrin points to the presence of unifying belief systems and supranational centralization (1999: 168). In contrast to the spatialization and territorialization (reterritorialization in Deleuze) of authority that putatively characterized the modern period, in such a deterritorialized or smooth space of the Middle Ages, belief systems had the potential, at least, to unify – in a sense, to have immanent effects. Of course the main difference between medieval Europe as characterized by Kobrin and the global situation today is that Europe at the time had elements from the outside or radically external phenomena such as 'the Orient' or the horse-people of the steppes. Overlooking, for a moment, the fact that society was dominated by the transcendent form of God, this decidedly dampens any sense of medieval immanence. Contemporary human existence, on the other hand, is characterized by everything being part of a globalized whole, which has been variously theorized as the emergence of a world society,[20] as delivering a note of promise,[21] or something far more sinister.[22]

Temporally as well there are striking similarities, which become more clear in light of the brief discussion of time above. Although time may be understood as a precious commodity and constantly under scrutiny in many aspects of contemporary life, it has been in many important respects decoupled from the many gradients and markers that were characteristic of the modern era. This can be seen in the flattening of the life cycle. For example, early childhood development along with constant retraining and job shifting[23] dissects previous educational stages which made up life patterns. An emphasis on youth over experience in many fields, along with university degree programmes for seniors both makes age less significant and in many cases reverses what were viewed previously as essentially natural processes. Consumer cycles also have been largely obliterated, with reasons for shopping and gift-giving blending seamlessly throughout the year. Working habits such as flexitime, holding multiple jobs, ubiquitous 24-hour shift systems as well as time zone differences for those engaged in service industries or emotional labour – overseas call centres, for example (see Bryson 2007) – strip the day of its regular, modern cycle. In this sense so-called postmodern time has more resemblances to European medieval time, which, before the public use of clock-work, followed the sun and moon and little else. In short, both eras have a similar character of undifferentiated time where any given instant, hour, or day tends to be, in itself, unremarkable and indistinguishable from any other. This is precisely what is implied in the virtual time of the Aion. Finally history itself loses its cultural traction as witnessed by the 'dark ages' on the one hand, and its relegation to mere nostalgia as it becomes yet one more referent among many (Jameson 1991: 19). But it should be noted that these are not subjective shifts, as if individuals are merely experiencing an even, homogeneous time differently than they have in the past, but serves rather to illustrate the undifferentiated nature of the Aion which, consequently, can be variously actualized in Chronos. The same holds regarding the discussion of space above: it is not a matter of space being perceived or measured differently – or rather, not only that – but of the principally smooth nature of space and the immanent relations between entities in the virtual realm. Deleuze's point is not a shifting human consciousness or mode of intervention, but rather that everything in effect takes place at the same time (*C1*: 58). Human historiography with its notion of passing time is (but) one of the actualizations of this Whole.

Given these spatial and temporal similarities it is possible, as Bull argued, that we are witnessing 'the decline of the states system and its transformation into a secular reincarnation of the mediaeval order' (1977: 258). But the question as to the extent of these similarities, though interesting, need not be the most relevant aspect of medieval time and space for the purposes of understanding contemporary world politics. Many argue (Ruggie 1993: 169; Anderson 1996: 142; Kobrin 1999: 167) that in order to understand the shift from the modern period to the postmodern one (or alternatively from the cold war more-or-less industrial-based world to the post-cold war flexible capital 'new economy' world) we should look at what might be analogous changes which characterized the shift from the medieval to the modern period. As Kobrin writes

> Mutually exclusive territoriality is not a transhistorical, fundamental principle of political organisation. Political power and authority were not

geographically defined in medieval Europe and may not be in a digitized world economy organized through overlapping electronic networks. Discrete and meaningful borders and the clear separation of the domestic from the foreign, indeed the very idea of the international, may be a modern anomaly. Conceptions of space may again be symbolic and relational rather than geometric and physical.

(1999: 182)

The important thing here is the difference between smooth and striated. In the characteristically striated space of the modern period (including the Cold War), difference could easily be seen as highly representational: comparable, metricized – and thus it lent itself to positivistic analysis. But in the postmodern period a much more fitting and indeed useful perspective is difference in intensity. The question in the present discussion thus becomes: what is actualized by these differences in intensity, or how to precisely account for this shift in eras – either from the medieval to the modern or from the modern to the postmodern (remembering of course that to talk about fixed eras is a gross oversimplification). In fact, we cannot, following Deleuze, tacitly rely on some spatial or temporal structural essence that would serve as a baseline against which one could measure variations. What we are addressing here is a plethora – in fact a true multiplicity – of aspects which determine the social and political world, of which space and time are but two, albeit important ones. The more specific question we must ask, therefore, is how are we to explain shifts, changes, and evolutions at all? Persistent structures or stratifications traditionally in the West have largely gone unquestioned, which in the context of the Deleuzian discussion where becoming is primary is in fact ironic; it is being that needs to be explained.

In any case, to reformulate: How precisely does this change, this becoming operate? Here we will explore the idea of newness or emergence borrowing from complexity, chaos, and systems theory, showing, as was mentioned in the introduction to this chapter, how Deleuze's philosophy overlaps in many respects with these fields. The next section will outline this overlap, and then look at some ways in which they differ. Although no doubt Deleuze's philosophy would benefit – and surely will benefit in the future – from recent discoveries in complexity theory, such a question is beyond the scope of this chapter. With this caveat in mind, the following encounter will show the relevance of complexity/ systems theory for the study of world politics, and highlight how Deleuze's theory can inform, shape, or limit these research trajectories.

Emergence

Simply put, emergence is a way of talking about change without essence or form. One might say it is a way of talking about change without structure – a typical reading of post-structuralism – but this would be an overstatement, since structure is hardly possible without essence. In other words, the key point is not that there are no fundamental, enduring structures (there are not), but that structure in itself is simply not possible without essential or fundamental 'things' to support them. In the Royal Science – the science of Descartes, Newton, and Durkheim, for example – form comes to matter from without. Matter, in other words, is differentiated by these forms or what this book calls essences. As was mentioned in the previous chapter, this is known as hylomorphism. Emergence, we could say, is the opposite of hylomorphism. It is matter developing its own 'form' and it is in this sense that true emergence is materialist; materialism without essence. In light of the discussion here of the virtual–actual, emergence is becoming, ultimately involving the relative movement between the actual and the virtual. And as we will see, it is the special virtual–actual couplet that provides the basis for such an encounter with complexity–chaos literature. Without such a gap, divide, or distance between the virtual and the actual, it is difficult to understand how things come to be or emerge, beyond saying they come from the realm of possibilities. The absence of a possible as a means of explaining emergence as discussed in Chapter 2 makes Deleuze's materialist philosophy particularly well suited to the kinds of questions addressed in the present chapter. Without the realm of the possible, emergent properties must come from within matter itself, and it is the movement of the virtual–actual lines and the inherent qualitative/quantitative relationship as well as differen*t*iation/differen*c*iation that provides the friction or the differential for this process. Looked at from the other way, a transcendent philosophy which relies on something outside matter is hardly the place to start building a metaphysics of emergence.

Many liken the kind of metaphysical lineage to which Deleuze subscribes, and its subsequent meeting with complexity, to vitalism. This has been a cause for hesitation, as many are wary of vitalism's association with humanism, for it is not difficult to see how the vital impulse or *élan vital* could be attributed to a human subject. As Scott Lash points out, vitalism usually presupposes a philosophical monism (Bergson, Deleuze), whereas mechanistic doctrines (Descartes, Kant), tend to be dualistic (mind–body). 'The mechanistic heuristic invades the study of human life itself in the varieties of positivism and behaviourism, while in vitalism, the power of self-organization is extended from humans to all sorts of matter.' (2006: 324). Thus he links the Bergson–Durkheim antagonism of the last century to the current distance between Deleuze/Negri and, for example, Pierre Bordieu, that is, the vitalism–neo-positivism divide (2006: 324). However, there is a subtle twist to Deleuze's 'vitalism' in the form of the machine which would clarify Lash's account. Deleuze uses the machine, in particular with Guattari in *Anti-Oedipus*, to show the subjectless nature of hylomorphism. That is, it is not some active, wilful subject which enacts its vitalism, but rather vitalism (or, to put a more Nietzschean spin on it, the will to power), which enacts the subject. Thus we have machines producing, rather than essences doing, breaking down distinctions between the human and the natural.[24] Protevi puts it thus:

> Deleuze exorcises the ghost in the machine, but in doing so leaves us with a different notion of machine, that of a concrete assemblage of heterogeneous

> elements set to work by the potentials of self-ordering inherent in the virtual singularities of the actual system.
>
> (2001: 10)

Such a rigorous understanding of mechanism is capable of keeping humanism well outside the very special metaphysics described here.

The invasion of humanism is exactly the danger. The problem is that even though, for the most part, contemporary scholarship is very aware of the unstable, shifting, and dynamic character of the objects of investigation – that is, it often repudiates, de facto, the very notion of essence – it nevertheless is saddled with an ontology that, as was argued in Chapter 2, goes back to Aristotle's understanding of perfect difference (within the species or concept). So even though few would claim to adhere to a Platonic idealist essentialism, we mentioned earlier a 'taxonomic essentialism' wherein scholars 'reify the general categories produced by their classifications' (Delanda 2006: 26). In other words taxonomic essentialism means taking 'finished' products and logically analysing them into giving up enduring properties and shaping these into an essence. Thus, although social scientists in general do tend to critique basic Euclidean notions of space and Newtonian conceptions of time, they nevertheless act as though they are fully and uniquely real. Recalling the Paul Veyne quote above regarding the state, even though there are endless examples that challenge the notion of bounded, metricized space and an unending list of exceptions to territorial sovereignty, researchers tend to essentialize products such as the State. To counter this we must look at the historical or, more accurately, morphological processes which produce these products. Thus the object of study is always a process – and a precarious one subject to destabilization. Genera and species have no ontological status; there is only individuals (of various scales) or again, haecceities. As we will see in Chapter 4, such individuals can be anything: people, societies, or even thoughts.

One of the main causes of this taxonomic essentialism resides in the very foundations of Western scientific method which relies on closed, repeatable experiments that ensure that findings can be verified and compared.[25] Notwithstanding the enormous effects of such a methodology, many of which can be seen as positive 'advances', it tends to overlook the self-ordering properties of matter. As Prigogine and Stengers argue, classical, reversible, deterministic models generally only occur in a closed experiment, artificially 'putting matter into a box and then waiting till it reaches equilibrium' (1984: 9), thus divulging what appear to be essential characteristics. This prolongs the illusion that the artificial is deterministic and reversible. However, the wealth of evidence collected over the past decades shows that the natural world in fact is much less stable and more random than such a methodology would suggest. If we reject such a black box view of the universe, then our vision of matter must move towards the study of emergence and complexity, leading to 'a new view of matter in which matter is no longer the passive substance described in the mechanistic world view but is associated with spontaneous activity." (Prigogine and

Stengers 1984: 9). It is here where we see the connection between Prigogine and Stengers and Deleuze, as expressed by the former in *La nouvelle alliance* (1983: 387–9). Deleuze and Guattari later solidified that connection in their distinction between philosophy and science,[26] the former dealing with the immanence of the virtual (concepts moving towards the plane of consistency), the latter with the states of affairs of the actual.[27]

The rejection of the black box of science entails waking up to the necessity of emergence, in other words, to how complex things form out of simple stuff – though at the same time not being afraid of the endless anomalies, leftovers, and things that will not seem to fit in predetermined categories. This involves a reversal in method. As Frederick Turner notes,

> The issue is not how higher, more active realities emerge out of lower, more passive ones, but how to stop this from happening when we do not wish it so. The art of the elegant and closed experiment now stands revealed as a way of trying to make sure matter in bunches does not show its proto-spiritual bent for creativity.
>
> (1997: xxiv)

In short, this shows how dualistic or modernist approaches cannot cope with the becoming nature of things, but are interested predominantly, or necessarily – because of their methodology – with being. In the social sciences researchers have begun to investigate the open system, what Deleuze calls nomadic distribution or the perfect game, where 'all singularities are influenced by their neighbours with no over-governing rules' (*LS*: 70). One of the most obvious examples or lines of inquiry in this investigation is complexity theory.

The basic rationale and central message of those writing about complexity in the last ten or 15 years is that the social sciences are 'waking up' to its implications. It is said that the current world is characterized by its complexity,[28] though of course in the physical sciences the application of the idea of complexity has been around for some time (Urry 2005b: 1). But given the argument so far in this chapter, and here we really see its elegance and attraction, the world – that is, its underlying metaphysical structure – in itself is complex, but this complexity is sometimes blanketed or painted over by more regular, linear systems (stratifications in the actual or the transcendental illusion in Deleuze). In terms of world politics, complexity is revealed or expressed in the world when aspects of the monolithic stratifying elements of nationalism or culture or an apparatus of capture like the state begin to accelerate. Under such circumstances the relations between groups and individuals are not regulated by hierarchies, determined life pathways or master signifiers, but are related much more immanently, despite the persistence of stratifications and arborescent structures. This is not to say that human interaction was not complex during the modern period, however. In many aspects it most certainly was,[29] though perhaps not on the levels around which traditional objects of analysis for the social sciences and especially IR have hovered, such as warfare, economics, diplomacy, and especially the state. What we have today – what characterizes the postmodern – is a relatively high degree of integration and connectivity on a wide variety of levels and spheres. In world politics this refers to the multitude of actors that engage from various levels of representation, legitimacy, and participation, including NGOs, IGOs, supranational bodies such as the EU, and various transnational organizations and movements such as the AGM. 'The key question' writes Cerny, 'is whether the resulting organisational mix can be understood through traditional analytical lenses or requires a new analytic paradigm.' (1999: 188).

In a basic sense, complexity means that something new – what we would normally think of as an object, phenomenon, or characteristic but must (in the context of this book) be seen to be a process or becoming – emerges that was not there before, that is, that the product is not describable in terms of its parts, at least not as static parts. It is characterized by its unpredictability.

> Complex adaption is characterized not only by a high degree of interaction among component parts, but also by the way that the particular nature of this interaction – the way that the system is organized – generates outcomes not linearly related to initial conditions. Whereas linear organisation is generally predictable in its consequences, emergence is characterized by a non-linear mode of organisation that can generate non-obvious or surprising consequences.
>
> (Mihata 1997: 32)

Likewise Deleuze often writes of entities crossing thresholds or gradients in their deterritorialization or becoming. But when this happens in the plane of immanence or in the virtual – technically through the process of differentiation – new divergent series are created, which are further actualized in qualities and parts that bear no resemblance to the 'initial' state. The 'limit', in effect, becomes not some characterization of what a thing is, but an aspect of its power. From an empirical point of view it is a matter of

> knowing whether a being eventually 'leaps over' or transcends its limits in going to the limit of what it can do, whatever its degree. ... Here, limit [peras] no longer refers to what maintains the thing under a law, nor to what delimits or separates it from other things. On the contrary, it refers to that on the basis of which it is deployed and deploys all its power.
>
> (*DR*: 46)

We can compare this to *relative* deterritorialization, a movement which is reterritorialized before it crosses this limit or threshold into the virtual. Thus both deterritorializations – relative and absolute – are reterritorialized, but only the latter have this characteristic of emergence which entails new properties or individuals.

Complexity, just as vitalism, does away with the need for essences. Here the connections to Deleuze's position of univocity become clearer: In ontological terms both belong to a realist project wherein one makes substantive claims about reality. There is no transcendent figure, no further nature of being that would relate elements to each other. Of course, in what may be perceived as a downside, it turns out that when we arrive at that reality, it ends up being a lot different – that is, complex and indeterminate – than we might have thought or hoped. In this sense it cannot be stressed enough that complexity in the sciences is not an alternative pathway to determining essence or form – a fallacy of some applications of complexity as we will see below. It is rather that complexity science functions without essence or form. But this need not be a reason for complacence or negativity, as if the shifting ephemeral world would make researchers throw up their hands in despair at the closure of the Enlightenment project. David Byrne sees the complexity programme as taking the best of both worlds of realism (belief in the real world, of observation) and of postmodernism (contingency, the importance of locality).

> Complexity/chaos offers the possibility of an engaged science not founded in pride, in the assertion of an absolute knowledge as the basis for social programmes, but rather in a humility about the complexity of the world coupled with a hopeful belief in the potential of human beings for doing something about it.
>
> (1998: 45)

Perhaps one of the most important issues in complexity is the notion of massive effects. Many point out that under complex conditions variations at one level create effects at other levels (see for example Toffler 1984: xv; Lee 1997: 22). Although this must not be thought of in terms of simple subsystems of systems, as in Delanda's embedded assemblages as described above, what it does account for is slight local changes creating turbulence which effects the system as a whole – the so-called butterfly effect. In the social sciences this is often referred to as scalar complexity: things at the local level are connected to the supra-national, transnational to state-level and local. Such an approach accounts for relatively recent innovations such as glocalization (Robertson 1995) and translocalization (Appadurai 1996a). Deleuze would say that even a seemingly insignificant line of flight can trigger massive changes in far-off fields.

The whole notion of complexity hinges on the relationship between order and chaos, the latter being the means by which newness is injected into the system. In Deleuze's terms chaos corresponds to the virtual and is, as was argued in Chapter 2, the most significant value-added of Deleuze's offering. It already has, ready-made, a theoretical understanding of true difference – that is, difference in itself, not difference within the concept – which serves as an engine of complex evolution or emergence. For Deleuze:

> Chaos is defined not so much by its disorder as by the infinite speed with which every form taking shape in it vanishes. It is a void that is not a nothingness but a *virtual*, containing all possible particles and drawing out all

possible forms, which spring up only to disappear immediately, without consistency or reference, without consequence. Chaos is an infinite speed of birth and disappearance.

(*WP*: 160)[30]

It is in this sense that complexity explains the distinction between order and chaos, which, as Urry writes, persists in all physical and social systems (2005a: 249). There is no 'natural equilibrium' or balance in nature. 'The "normal" state of nature is thus not one of balance and repose; the normal state is to be recovering from the last disaster' (Urry 2005b: 6). And in Deleuze we find essentially the same point: there is no 'normal', foundational model in nature or in anything else for that matter. As we saw in the previous chapter, the idea of fixity, or normalcy, or adhering to a norm (model–copy) was born, in the West, in Plato and solidified through Aristotle. But elements persist in a much more processual way, or in Deleuze's terms, a state of becoming. In terms of complexity this is neither complete order or complete chaos: 'Order and chaos are in a kind of balance where the components are neither fully locked into place but yet do not fully dissolve into complete instability or anarchy' (Urry 2005b: 8), what Mitchell Waldrop calls the 'domain between deterministic order and randomness' (Byrne 1998: 16). Likewise Deleuze, as was emphasized in Chapter 2, argues that the virtual and the actual are always in relative opposition.

This highlights the split in the application of science, or rather the kinds of science on offer, between one that tends only to study order (Royal Science) and the other which is sensitive to the complex (Nomad Science). Toffler points out that according to Prigogine and Stengers, during the Age of the Machine – analogous in Deleuze and Guattari to the Royal Science – emphasis was placed on enduring characteristics, order, stability, uniformity, and equilibrium. This is typified by a concern with closed systems or the actual realm. In terms of the amount of shift or change possible in such investigations, the linear kinds of inputs associated with such methods yielded relatively small and hence more-or-less predictable results. The shift came, says Toffler, with the transition from industrial to technological/information society, or what is known as post-industrial or postmodern society. The latter is characterized not by order or uniformity, but by chaos and disjunction.

> What makes the Prigoginian paradigm especially interesting is that it shifts attention to those aspects of reality that characterize today's accelerated social change: disorder, instability, diversity, disequilibrium, nonlinear relationships in which small inputs can trigger massive consequences, and temporality – a heightened sensitivity to the flows of time.
>
> (1984: xvi–xvii)

The reason for the success of linear approaches that favoured closed systems (the actual) lay in the tasks being relatively modest. Of course as sciences, both physical and social, began asking tougher questions, the viability of such an approach wore thin. As Mandelbrot points out, the linear relationships of Euclidean geometry are perfectly acceptable for building houses or assessing the quality of drywalling, but we need more for understanding mountains, clouds, and rivers (1993: 2). Put in the context of the present work, the linearity of closed systems may suffice for exploring the behaviour of (supposedly) mutually exclusive, functionally similar states with identifiable interests, for example.[31] However, the chaotic nature of something like the AGM – and, it must be said, the shifting nature of state authority today – requires a different approach.

From this overview of complexity we can see a great deal of promise in its application to questions such as the ones posed in this book. Many scholars argue that the kinds of behaviour expressed in the AGM are better understood through chaos and complexity rather than order (see for example Robinson and Tormey 2005: 217). Perhaps the biggest benefit of embracing a complexity-oriented approach to socio-political investigations is the way that it bulwarks against reductionism. Because it rejects the notion of essences in favour of what we have here called becoming, there is no simple biological, physical, or structural framework that could result in theoretical inertia. In such cases, taking an example from Mihata, saying all human behaviour is a matter of biology says very little, in fact, about human behaviour, from a scientific point of view. 'If human behaviour exhibits qualitatively unique properties that cannot be reduced to biology, much less to physics (e.g. consciousness), then emergence is intrinsic to any internally consistent epistemological and ontological framework for the study of human behaviour' (Mihata 1997: 35). As Deleuze notes, it is the abstract or the universals that need explaining (*N*: 145).

But there is also cause for hesitation. First and perhaps most strikingly, a great deal of the literature on emergence and complexity – especially in the social sciences – is rather repetitive and sometimes grossly superficial. In many cases it consists largely of the glossing of points that were made in the mid-nineties when complexity literature became more mainstream. Perhaps one of the main reasons for this underdevelopment is the simple fact that complexity is, in a word, complicated. There is no particularly easy way to talk about it and precisely what it might do remains stubbornly opaque. It requires an enormous divestment of the excess baggage of Western philosophy and modern scientific method, as has been argued above. As Mihata writes:

> It is difficult to conceptualize, much less operationalize, emergent phenomena. Thus, as intuitive and even obvious as the idea of emergence may be, it has not advanced much beyond rhetoric, metaphor, or disclaimer. If anything, the effect has been to trivialize emergence as either too obvious or trite to be theoretically useful, or too complicated to be practically useful.
> (1997: 35)

The result in some of the literature, especially in empirical investigations, is that complexity tends to be treated as merely complicated. That is, its contribution amounts to replacing the search for simple models and answers with a wide focus on a *great deal* of factors, tantamount to saying that 'there's a lot to consider'.

This very often results in a second problem, namely complexity theory's reliance on one of its key methodologies, modelling. The goal of modelling, as described by Barabási, is to understand how something works, rather than merely representing it. If we were interested in the science of a Ferrari, he argues, rather than just drawing a perfect picture of one, 'we need to know how to build one just like the original' (2002: 91). Similarly, as Turner argues,

> In a sense the most powerful proof that one understands something is surely that one can build one that works. And if it is objected that we cannot really know what is going on at each step of the process, this itself may be an insight about the real nature of the universe – the universe does not know either, so to speak, until it has done it, and it can forget what it did quite soon in a sufficiently complex process.
>
> (1997: xxvi)

The problem with modelling, especially in the social sciences, however, is that despite providing evocative illustrations of how complexity research actually works, it tends to be rather reductionist, as hinted at above. It ultimately requires the oversimplification of both the variables and their environment that come very close to definitions. In other words the models end up enacting possible interactions amongst bounded entities. Deleuze was not only interested in thresholds and massive effects, but the actual drifting of elements: sliding sideways, becoming-whale.[32] Transcendental empiricism is truly rhizomatic in that it is not just sensitive to elements in a cumulative time-process, but capable of mapping what flees subterraneanly to pop up somewhere else, completely unpredictably. In other words Deleuze is profoundly interested in changes in nature. Modelling is ill-equipped to address such change: the complex, non-linear effects of contemporary social science computer models are poor analogies to the pure changes of nature in intensities. With such distinctions in mind, research in emergence should be ever vigilant to keeping the inherent creativity of matter *in* matter, and not let it leak outside to preconceptions and assumptions.[33] Ultimately there is the lingering question of what complexity theory or the study of emergence actually does for social science investigations, and in general there appears to be a considerable time-lag between talking up the promise of complexity theory and actually delivering results.

Third, complexity literature, despite its responsiveness to the seemingly chaotic nature of physical and social systems, often does not seem to go far enough or ask the right ontological and metaphysical questions. A greater understanding of process philosophy in general would be required to reap the benefits of a complexity research paradigm. Books such as that by Nicholas Rescher (1996) provide a concise overview of the metaphysical questions involved, addressing notions of space and time, substances and things, and so deserve greater currency. Finally complexity literature has difficulty accounting for subjectivity or, more precisely, the subject. The idea of complex connection can be a productive one provided that we do not think of these nodes as fixed individuals, as in 'we're all just connected', when the 'we' means basically normal, rational, political agents. This will be picked up later in Chapter 4 with the question of the subject in Deleuze's metaphysics.

As mentioned in the previous chapter, in terms of the recent convergence of Deleuze and the social sciences complexity literature, there is a danger of reading Deleuze as a self-described complexity theorist. Not only does complexity theory mostly overlook the issue of the subject, it also tends to have a far more narrow conception of time than Deleuze. The time of the Aion does not appear to be addressed by chaos/complexity literature, and Bonta and Protevi's gloss over the difference between the Aion and Chronos (similar, in fact to Delanda's) masks the real productive nature of this distinction (see 2004: 160). Time, as Prigogine and Stengers tell us, is decidedly irreversible, contrary to the approach of Newtonian physics, where physical properties are constant and therefore infinitely repeatable and reversible, the endstate having no bearing on future outputs. But in a completely different way for Deleuze, a foundational or underlying metricized time, just like differenciated space, is an effect of immaterial (or incorporeal, as he says) Events. In other words metricized time, reversible or not, is an illusion; a very important and persistent illusion, but hardly the starting point of a truly immanent metaphysics. Nevertheless, there is a significant connection between Deleuze and complexity. Although it is perhaps an oversimplification to apply concepts of chaos and complexity directly to Deleuze as Bonta and Protevi tend to do,[34] there is ample evidence to show that ideas of complexity can be brought out through Deleuze's philosophy. In short, the science of complexity, when strictly regulated by its own principles, is one which adheres, at least theoretically or potentially, to the fundamental aspects of Deleuze's ontology and metaphysics.

To go back to the empirical example in this book, rather than as entities with essences, the AGM and its aspects must be understood as an assemblage or system, in communication with other assemblages and defined by its line of flight. In the context of Deleuze and complexity theory we can detect two idealized poles along a spectrum of types of systems. On the one hand we have stratified systems which have the least immanent communication and do not freely associate and connect with their environment. On the other hand we have open systems that, through immanent relations, have virtually no border with their environment; they freely associate and connect. What interested Deleuze in particular was the idea of a science of open systems:

> Systems have in fact lost absolutely none of their power. All the groundwork for a theory of so-called open systems is in place in current science and logic, systems based on interactions, rejecting only linear forms of causality, and transforming the notion of time. ... What I and Guattari call a rhizome is precisely one example of an open system.
>
> (*N*: 31–2)

One of the difficulties in bridging Deleuze and complexity is that in the social science literature there is variation in what these systems (open, closed, or better still: opening, closing, becoming) are called. Eyal Weizman, in discussing appropriations of Deleuze by the Israeli Defense Forces, sees networks as primarily open and systems as closed. Weizman argues that despite the rhetorical appeals to 'self-organisation' and the 'flattening of hierarchies',

> military networks are still largely nested within traditional institutional hierarchies, units are still given orders, and follow plans and guidelines. Swarming is only one end of a hierarchical command structure, and what they call networks should be called 'systems'.
>
> (2007: 212–13)

Paul Hirst, on the same theme, has a reading of Deleuze focussed on reterritorialization: 'Networks are generally nested in hierarchies, nomads stick to riding camels and raiding, and war machines run on coal and petrol.' (2005: 4).[35] Barabási (2002) on the other hand ignores the notion of a system altogether and – perhaps given his mathematical background – essentially makes a strikingly similar argument that complexity theory makes, namely that modern science (that is, Royal Science in the Deleuzian sense) has treated the relationships between elements as closed, but is waking up to the ubiquitousness of open networks. There remains, however, one crucial difference. Although in Barabási's network theory there are emergent effects of a network, the latter relies fundamentally on essential nodes, for it is the relations themselves that are key in network theory: the airports, social butterflies, and large-volume Internet sites with which network theory deals remain unproblematized and therefore rather static. Castells (1996) similarly leaves the metaphysical status of the entities of networks unquestioned. Thus this kind of network theory tends to favour more positivistic-inspired sociology in that it does not problematize the individual or especially the subject. Straight away we see its incompatibility with complexity theory and especially Deleuze. Deleuze would see 'things' as systems in a process of becoming, not bounded nodes which interact.

John Urry makes an important development, especially in light of one of the themes of this discussion, namely, how to discriminate between the various aspects and expressions of phenomena such as the AGM. He distinguishes between global networks such as McDonald's and Greenpeace, which despite their global reach and adaptability remain rather closed to their environment (they are structured; have hierarchies, goals, leaders) on the one hand, and what he calls global fluids such as money, information, the Internet, terrorism, and the AGM (what he calls the *anti*-globalization movement) on the other. The following, quoted at some length, is an excellent description of a line of flight:

> Global fluids travel along various routeways or scapes, but they may escape, rather like white blood corpuscles, through the 'wall' into surrounding matter and effect unpredictable consequences upon that matter. Fluids move

according to novel shapes and temporalities as they break free from the linear, clock-time of existing socio-scapes. Such fluids result from people acting upon the basis of local information and relationships, but where these local actions are, through iteration, captured, moved, represented, marketed and generalized, often impacting upon hugely distant places and peoples [*sic*]. Such fluids demonstrate no clear point of departure, just self-organisation and movement at certain speeds and at different levels of viscosity with no necessary end-state or purpose. Fluid systems create over time their own context for action rather than being 'caused' by such contexts. This self-organisation can occur dramatically and overwhelmingly, like a flood or a torrent moving between or across borders or boundaries.

(2005a: 246)

From this one could conclude that there are two kinds of globalization: the network (or stratified) kind that in fact produces order, and the fluid (line of flight) kind which produces emergent properties. The big question, of course, for Urry in this context is the difference/relationship between global networks and global fluids. It remains unclear if his distinction applies to discrete processes or entities, and, more crucially, if there is any movement or overlap between the two. To understand the importance of such questions we need only consider one of his examples, the Internet: 'It possesses an elegant, non-hierarchical rhizomatic global structure and is based upon lateral, horizontal hypertext links that render the boundaries between objects within the archive endlessly fluid.' (2005a: 247). Despite the fact that he confounds the Internet and the World Wide Web (the Internet is a network, hypertext links are an aspect of the Web), the problem here is that the Web (what counts mostly for the architecture of information) is quite structured[36] and, as in the case of many political regimes around the world, is a tool for control as much as for the free flow of ideas. As for the cases of Weizman and Hirst as just described, it is perhaps more productive to talk about tendency (to what degree are systems 'open'?) rather than discriminating between purely closed and purely open systems (or networks).

A central problem with all of these analyses is that they tend to take an all-or-nothing approach: networks or systems; open or closed. The value-added of the present reading of Deleuze is that it allows for movement along the continuum between the virtual (open) and the actual (closed). Thus when looking at broad institutional patterns or world politics we should be thinking more about velocity: the rate and direction of change, asking to what extent is any given system or network an open or fluid one. Are some empirically more open, more rhizomatic than others? Do contemporary global socio-political conditions mean that there is an increasing number of such open networks, or networks tending towards open or immanent relations? We must determine if this is a trend to which various political activities are moving, and this can lead to some extraordinary and perhaps counter-intuitive results, from student networks in North Africa to the 'implosion' of the Communist party in China. To take this last case as an example, the idea is that through its putative political repression the Chinese

Communist Party actually becomes more fluid and open; it must respond to its polity precisely because there is no opposition party of any description waiting in the wings (see for example Ogden 2002: 354). In what sense are we witnessing an era of deterritorialization? Where are the (perhaps hidden) forces of reterritorialization at work? How such questions should be approached will be addressed below through Deleuze's notion of transcendental empiricism or nomad science, and will become more significant in the context of Chapter 4.

In any event, system or network, one of the innovations of the nomad science such as Deleuze proposes is its denial of a mysterious, inexplicable outside. When we begin to think of the Whole in itself as a system – that is, the virtual realm in its immanence – then much in the same way as systems theory, change and adaptivity cannot come from outside the system itself, but operate as internal elements (see Albert 2004: 18). Thus patterns which do not fit into what are considered 'norms' cannot be seen as being deviant or outside the system, but must be explained from within, and change and emergence must be viewed as an aspect of the system itself. As Todd May writes,

> rhizomatics [what we refer to here as transcendental empiricism] offers a way of accounting for the other as internal, instead of having to see the rupture to the system as coming from the outside or from another system. This is accomplished by loosening up the idea of a system, by ridding it of its closure, and by making the idea of a system a more or less arbitrary delimiting of boundaries within a field constituted more by singularities than by guiding principles.
>
> (1993: 6)

Following Deleuze then, strictly speaking the world cannot be thought of as a closed system with distinct and stable parts (states, regimes, social movements), but rather an open system of transformation – with various velocities and variable proximities. But it is important to remember that these aspects are not hylomorphic, that is, they do not depend on some outside impetus for their actualizations and counteractualizations (lines of flight). That is to say, the system of world politics, in itself, is self forming, which is consistent of course with the principle of sufficient reason which will be discussed presently. It must also be stressed that world politics as a whole here does not in itself imply an empirical framework ('the entire world') with subsystems, but the whole of world politics as the One-All, of which the parts are but attributes. This theme, especially in terms of individual subjects, will be further explored in the next chapter.

In light of all this, the kind of complexity theory which would adhere to a Deleuzian metaphysics shifts the research emphasis from determinism and predictability to chance and chaos. To be sure, some systems are quite closed and lend themselves to prediction. But whereas tides are predictable, weather is not. It was once thought that in order to be able to predict the weather, more information through denser grids of weather monitoring stations was needed. This, however, has turned out not to be the case. 'Simple deterministic systems with only a few elements can generate random behaviour, and that randomness is fundamental; gathering more information does not make it disappear. This fundamental randomness has come to be called chaos.' (Peiten 1993: 37). The question is, which mode correctly describes the universe: determinism or chaos? According to the approach developed in this book, neither is correct, but rather, as argued in the last chapter, the relationship is always relative. Here we see how both Deleuze and complexity science eschews the false dichotomy between a purely deterministic world and one of pure chance. Complexity

> elaborates how there is always order and disorder within physical and social phenomena, and especially in various hybrids. Order and chaos are often in a kind of balance where the components are neither fully locked into place but yet do not dissolve into anarchy. They are 'on the edge of chaos'.
> (Urry 2005b: 238)

What Deleuze insists on is a non-deterministic universe, the discovery of which is perhaps the most 'decisive conceptual event of the twentieth century' (Hacking 1990: 1). This is not a mechanistic universe, for mechanism implies a closed set.

> The plane of immanence is the movement (the facet of movement) which is established between the parts of each system and between one system and another, which crosses them all, stirs them all up together and subjects them all to the condition which prevents them from being absolutely closed.
> (*C1*: 59)

In standard complexity terms, this means that more closed sets (there is no such thing as a completely closed set) operate at near-equilibrium until they are brought to far-from-equilibrium by some outside force, at which point unpredictability enters the system (see for example Toffler 1984: xxiii). In the case of the Earth's moon, at equilibrium its motion is highly predictable, as humans have observed for millennia. An outside force in the form of a collision or effect of another body might change this however, and, due to the complex nature of the forces at work, as with the weather, no amount of information on such an event would reveal a deterministic universe. It turns out that the billiard ball analogy only holds in extremely closed systems, such as a billiard table – and a perfect or ideal one at that.

But this is not to say that things do not happen for a reason; that things do not have causes. On the contrary, the above discussion draws attention to a special distinction wherein the kind of chance with which complexity theory and in this case Deleuze deals with is not a kind of brute chance. Deleuze's adherence to the law of sufficient reason means that any given condition is determined by its cause, and so is not at all 'random', however, predicting this relationship in chronological time is not possible. Deleuze might say this is a matter of destiny, but not necessity.[37] Part of understanding this involves dispelling the possible from not only the thought process but the metaphysics of the world as well. It is not the case that there is a range of possible outcomes 'waiting in the wings' of nature to be realized, a process determined by chance. It is rather that elements combine or do not, in a process that might be called selection (see Massumi 1992: 48), and in fact lies at the heart of the eternal return. Although dealing empirically with such a form of chance suggests a statistical analysis, the important part that Deleuze stresses repeatedly in *Nietzsche and Philosophy* is that each dicethrow is a singularity and in itself a reaffirmation of chance (25–6). As unappealing as this might seem to some, it avoids one of the biggest central – and in many ways unspoken – problems of contemporary social science research, the reconciliation of deterministic features and apparent random events without recourse to individual wills, a problem which will be discussed further in the next chapter.

Nomad science

It is true to say that Deleuze is against essences; hence his dovetailing with the complexity literature analysed above. At times he has promoted the simulacra, though in later works he develops more diverse concepts to pave the way for his various encounters, such as with the 'cases' of *A Thousand Plateaus*. But how could it be possible to encounter something that has no essence, or that is only a simulacrum, or, in short, has no being but is in a constant state of becoming – indeed is 'defined' by its becoming? How is empirical research in the social sciences possible under such conditions? An appropriate approach in light of the discussion so far in this chapter would reject fixed ideas and eternal models that give entities identity with characteristics. It involves not looking for definable things in a specific space and time, but rather following the actualization processes of unbounded entities. Complexity theory is important here not for its number-crunching potential – at least not in its potential to predict behaviour (see Byrne 1998: 16) – but rather so that we need no longer approach empirical research in terms of things with fixed criteria of assessment, static situations, and linear development. What we really need is a kind of complexity theory in application; only that would invigorate theoretical pursuits while at the same time providing a basis for empirical research.

What Deleuze offers is a method he sometimes calls transcendental empiricism. Transcendental empiricism here means not access to some transcendent value (essence) or guarantor (God), but rather an empiricism that focuses on the virtual and not the actual; or rather shows how a thing's actualization is dependent on its virtual component. As Žižek writes, in contrast to the standard notion of the transcendental as the formal conceptual network that structures the rich flow of empirical data, '*the Deleuzian "transcendental" is infinitely RICHER than reality* – it is the infinite potential field of virtualities out of which reality is actualized' (2003: 4). Although there are more similarities than differences, it is distinguished from the genealogical approach of Nietzsche and Foucault in that it does not treat metricized time in the form of history as a constant.

Transcendental empiricism is a perspective that demands that we not look for the characteristics or attributes pertaining to an entity's identity, but that we seek to understand the immanent (non-hierarchical, undercoded, non-teleological) relations (in the form of an Event) which give rise to a state of affairs; in short, the nature of its actualization. In this sense it is analogous if not identical to Bergson's method of intuition (Boundas 1996: 87). Here we seek the 'intense world of differences' (*DR*: 68) wherein difference in itself precedes the difference of representation. Just as with the lightning strike nothing lies behind this true difference,[38] which implies a world governed by what Deleuze calls nomadic distributions or crowned anarchies (69). Everything has its line of flight and mixes in a stage before individuation and spatio-temporal actualization. In terms of a method we must seek to define an entity by its counteractualizations and its capacities to enter into immanent relations with other elements which in turn lead to further actualizations. Deleuze and Guattari write about things (people, institutions, and even axioms like capitalism) deterritorializing themselves and the reterritorializing as something else (*WP*: 68). If we are looking for the originality or specificity of a thing – what it 'is' and how it functions – we must ask what sort of territory it institutes: how it counteractualizes itself and how it is subsequently actualized. This differs dramatically from representational approaches that are only interested in the actual: 'Actuals imply already constituted individuals, and are ordinarily determined, whereas the relationship of the actual and the virtual forms an acting individuation or a highly specific and remarkable singularization which needs to be determined case by case' (*D*: 115). There are three main implications here.

First, transcendental empiricism suggests an innovative epistemological approach. Not one of determining the truth value of statements but in selecting the relevant true statements from an immanent multiplicity. That is, not of determining the true and not true (representation of an essence) but of sorting the important or relevant from the unimportant or irrelevant amongst a field of truths (*DR*: 238). One could take any given statement, such as 'TNCs rule the world.' The task is not to establish the truth or falsity of this statement, but to map the series that gives rise to the statement as a state of affairs (as opposed to a purely linguistic or textual structure) and to determine its productive value. It is easy to see how this dovetails with Foucault. According to Deleuze, statements (and visibilities) are only invisible insofar as their conditions are not understood as themselves being historical. Visibilities 'are even invisible so long as we consider only objects, things or perceptible qualities, and not the conditions which open them up' (*F*: 49).

Second, a theoretical formulation or empirical study of the elements of world politics which adhered to the principle of transcendental empiricism would eschew the whole notion of origin, fixed identity, and any relation among elements which suggested an ordering principle. Again, this is not to say that there are no sentiments of origin, stable identities, or structural realities; only that they are not primary nor necessary. Any given element is not a reified object but rather a population or pack (like a pack of wolves or a gang[39]) in a process of becoming. The identities and fixed relationships reflect only the actual half of a given object. The task, again, is to trace the lines of these actualizations. This is exemplified, for example, in Ruggie when he shows how the characteristics of statehood were the unintended consequences of an immanent multiplicity (that is, lacking any ordering principle):

> The Crusades were not designed to suggest new modes of raising revenues for territorial rulers, but they ended up doing so. The modern state was not logically entailed in the medieval papacy; yet, according to Strayer, by the example of effective administration it set, 'the Gregorian concept of the Church almost demanded the invention of the concept of the State.' Society did not vote for capitalism when it endorsed the civilizing impulses of commerce; but the bourgeoisie, the social carriers of commerce, embodied it. Later, monarchs did not set out to weaken their constitutional powers by selling offices or convening assemblies to raise taxes; they sought only to increase their revenues. In short, the reasons for which things were done often had very little to do with what actually ended up being done or what was made possible by those deeds.
>
> (1993: 166)

Thus in such cases we cannot look to (modern) theories of statehood to understand how space began to be thought of in an exclusionary way. Rather such thought processes are the unintended result of a multitude of other factors. If we wish to pinpoint precise causes, we will not find a purposeful or structural cause, nor a final cause in any Aristotelian sense, but instead the meeting (or not) of series depending on speeds and slowness, encapsulated by the notion of Event. Transcendental empiricism is a methodology which allows for and indeed insists on the investigation of these lines or series.

Third, a corollary we can draw here is that not only is there no basic causal structure, but Deleuze's position does not privilege nor preclude any cause or 'quasi-cause'[40] in an actualization. This implies that there can be no corresponding analytical tool or, in other words, the method of transcendental empiricism cannot prioritize one analytical approach or another. Thus, all such causal structures and analytical approaches must be contained in Deleuze's basic two-poled schema that was analysed in Chapter 2. All representation, Aristotelian difference, Kantian orthodoxy, as well as sciences of closed, stratified systems such as the State apparatus or even the game of chess are included here as the counterparts to virtual, open, or rhizomatic systems. No analysis of 'the cases' in *Capitalism and Schizophrenia* and no example, be it physical, biological, or psychic, in any of his works previous or subsequent is outside of his basic virtual–actual metaphysics. Thus in *Anti-Oedipus* Deleuze and (here especially) Guattari can decry the Oedipal structure of capitalist politics (222–72) but they do not thereby attempt to deny its reality. Thus they offer 'schizoanalysis' as a method to overcome something very real. Likewise Deleuze and Guattari spend considerable time in *A Thousand Plateaus* investigating linguistic structure, semiotics, order words, and discourse (75–148), but they can no more prioritize these as an analytical approach any more than they can claim their non-reality. Moreover, although they do criticize the apparatus of capture (the State), they do not bestow it with merely a linguistic or discursive reality. The State is a counterpart to the nomadic War Machine. They are part of the same system and both equally real and significant for analysis. Thus such a reading of Deleuze accounts for variations in territorial as well as non-territorial rule, as were discussed earlier in the chapter.

One further way of understanding what transcendental empiricism is, is to distinguish between it and state or Royal Science, something that Deleuze and Guattari devote considerable time to in *A Thousand Plateaus* and *What is Philosophy?* In the latter book they distinguish between philosophy, which through its sensitivity to the immanent creates new concepts; art, which pulls the actual towards the virtual, or the finite towards the infinite; and science which deals with states of affairs and their functions. In the context of the present investigation, it must be emphasized that although positivist science certainly seems adept at investigating certain artefacts – such as the modern, territorial nation state or its forms of government – it is not able to grasp becoming and is therefore not suitable for an investigation of fluid entities such as the AGM, global finance, or global networks of violence. It cannot describe or understand immanent relations that are primary and explain evolution and change (*WP*: 197). In this sense Deleuze is not denouncing scientific thought (as in the social science of Durkheim) *tout court*, but only puts it in its place (see *WP*: 199). The problem with the study of world politics is not materialism or observation, but, as was hinted at in Chapter 1, the reliance on measurement and linearity. According to Deleuze, these can only apply to the actual – that is, actualized states of affairs – overlooking that which is hidden: the virtual connections which speak of the Event and, more importantly here, of morphogenic processes that are the cause of any given state of affairs. Deleuze points out that Nietzsche always favours the question *which one?* over *what?* The former means: 'what are the forces which take hold of a given thing, what is the will that possesses it?' (*N*: 71). This is the only kind of 'essence' we have, one that denotes the sense and value of a thing. To ask questions such as *what is it?* is to fall into 'the worst metaphysics' (*N*: 72).

Deleuze sometimes refers to his method or nomad science as starting in the middle. This captures the sense that in the virtual there are not fixed identities or teleological functions from which to locate start and endpoints. Since there are no essences to work from, such a method deals inherently with specificity, not generalizations or universals. As Deleuze writes of his and Guattari's project:

> We weren't looking for origins, even lost or deleted ones, but setting out to catch things where they were at work, in the middle: breaking things open, breaking words open. We weren't looking for something timeless, not even the timelessness of time, but for new things being formed, the emergence of what Foucault calls 'actuality.'
>
> (*N*: 86)

Thus another way of putting it is to say that transcendental empiricism is a matter of unravelling lines rather than locating points (*N*: 160). The applicability in contemporary world politics is evident when one considers that the 'global flows' described by Appadurai and others have no point of origin, no end, no progression, and are non-linear (1990: 296).

The AGM as an emergent political form

What does this all really mean for a (potentially) fluid, ephemeral aspect of world politics such as the AGM? According to the analysis in this and the preceding chapter, some aspects or elements of it are reterritorialized into familiar forms and patterns that lend themselves to standard methods of analysis. These are the traditional social movements, hierarchical NGOs, quasi-political parties, and liberal-framed activist manifestos. All the exceptions, anomalies, and patterns that do not fit existing theoretical models – all of the anti-power, open identity, and non-hierarchical aspects addressed in Chapter 1 – can be traced on this relative continuum between deterritorialization and reterritorialization. In other words, some activities can be understood through linear modelling with conceptual groups and identity,[41] while others require a methodology sensitive to their becoming as complex effects, that is, to how they exhibit characteristics that are not aspects of their initial conditions. It is important to remember that all entities are characterized by their state of becoming, but for the researcher this is not as obvious in some cases as in others. Some phenomena appear more static and inert. International law, for example, although it changes and develops rapidly, does not obviously transform itself away from a modern juridical system. Moreover, becoming can be successfully repressed by scientific controls (closed experiments, representational determinations) and thus empirical phenomena can be made into workable static models using traditional methods. This double analytical nature suggests that the deployment of a Deleuzian–complex systems approach is a good start, being capable of analysing both the fluid and the fixed. However, one of the problems, hinted at in Chapter 2 in the discussion of the two poles of Deleuze's metaphysics, is that very often such attempts tend to drastically over-emphasize the complex element of the AGM, focussing explicitly on the virtual side of a couplet, thereby missing the stratifying aspects or tendencies. To take one example, Chesters and Welsh – in a book that in its fundamental approach shows considerable promise – write:

> We are suggesting, therefore, that plateaux are combinatory expressions of complexity effects realized through assemblages of material and immaterial elements. They are shaped by the material infrastructure of mobility and communication systems that are a prerequisite of a 'network sociality', and through their emphasis upon co-presence, face-work, meetings and encounters they constitute material assemblages realizing the potential of small-world networks. The resultant rhizome – the alternative globalization movement – is further shaped by an eclectic mix of minoritarian

subjectivities, of free radicals or virtuosi including net-workers of various kinds – activists, hackers, mediatistas, and academivists – whose capacity to resist co-option by party discipline and ideological strictures has grown as a direct result of increasing complexity.

(2005: 197)

In addition to their jargon-laden style, unfortunately in the heat of their fieldwork Chesters and Welsh seem to lump various aspects of the AGM together (into one rhizome), where in fact, as was discussed in Chapter 1, a great many, indeed all of these groups and aspects of what they call the alternative globalization movement are constantly being reterritorialized by locality, identity, and even by capital. Major critiques and rubbishings of the political significance of the AGM are usually argued precisely on the basis of this reterritorialization, the poaching of a high-profile ATTAC activist by the German Green Party (Boy 2008) being but one example of this. A reading of complexity that, following Deleuze, accounts for a relative movement over the continuum between complexity and order (the virtual and the actual) means that the researcher need not make impossible choices as to whether any given element is complex or ordered; choices that ultimately lead to theoretical oversights.

This processual continuum can be detected in the vast differences amongst NGOs, with some based directly on local social movements (more open, complex), and the tremendously influential – especially in financial terms – NGOs funded top-down by wealthy governments and private individuals. These latter are by and large not interested in challenging dominant social and cultural values (indeed, often their funding is contingent on the fact that they do not) and thus undermine the view of a profound new role of NGOs in global governance in terms of a utopian transformation of social, cultural, and political activity (Eschle and Stammers 2004: 341). Save the Children and the Bill Gates Foundation are two good examples of this. Moreover there is the whole phenomenon of NGOs becoming increasingly state-ified with the predominance of government-organized non-governmental organizations (GONGOs) in China, for example (see for example Naím 2007). This is not to suggest that GONGOs are to become a global norm, but illustrates the increasing difficulty in differentiating between organizations like the state (normally thought of as molar or closed) and ones such as NGOs (normally considered molecular or open). Thus Chesters and Welsh must either narrow their conception of the AGM (for them the alternative globalization movement) to a pure, almost theoretical form of immanent, rhizomatic relations, or group *selected* forms of activism and protest into the same group, which is what they tend to do. The former possibility offers little in terms of productive value, as all entities are actualized in some way (there is no such thing as a perfectly open system). The latter obliterates the very important differences overviewed in Chapter 1 that not only make the topic of the AGM interesting, but also divide activists themselves. Indeed, fundamentally it is *the* perennial debate of participants and theorists: whether to push for more complexity and autonomy, or to become more hierarchical and party-like, complete with a more or less fixed organizational structure and trappings such as charters and platforms. This is precisely the debate facing the WSF as mentioned in Chapter 1.

Urry's very powerful and evocative analysis would seem to have similar limitations:

> Central to the self-understanding of the anti-globalization movement is an implicit commitment to the sciences of complexity since they best explain complex webs of life that constitute the interconnected and hybridized character of global relationships. And complexity also seems to describe the networked, leaderless, distributed, fluid character of the movement itself. Like a flock of birds taking off, these movements demonstrate patterned emergence but without either anarchy or centralized hierarchy. They are self-organizing or autopoietic smart mobs or swarms. Complexity analyses seems to capture the ways in which 'mobilization' involves flows of emotional or charged energy that occurs within social movements, flows involving non-linear switches in organisation that can occur once a threshold is passed.
>
> (2005a: 247)

Unfortunately Urry here does not employ his own distinction brought up earlier in this chapter, namely the difference between global systems and global flows. Thus he does not address the movement of different aspects of the AGM between their poles whereby any given point of the AGM (whether thought of as a system as a whole or in addressing one of its parts) has a vector either towards the virtual or the actual. Neither 'it' nor a specific part or aspect of it should be classified as being inherently complex in nature. In a similar manner we can recall how Desai and Said's distinction between isolationist and alternative political activity addressed in Chapter 1 shows some promise and certainly captures the chaos/order, de-/re-territorialization aspects of contemporary political practice. The only hesitation in terms of a Deleuzo-complexity intervention as developed here is the reliance on difference within the concept: that is, taking the concept of the AGM and classifying subgroups based on differences (isolationist, alternative). In order that these groups not be made inert they must be addressed on a case by case basis, mapping each in its process of becoming. To take but one example, in what sense does the MST constitute a line of flight rather than a fixed state of affairs? Determining the sense in which each part of the AGM is a line of flight or a more fixed state of affairs would require a transcendental empirical analysis that mapped the emergence and change of these through immanent criteria. In sum, although there is reason to be excited about open and complex aspects of the AGM, merely asserting its complex nature does not give a comprehensive picture of it and care must be taken when making generalizations about any identifiable aspect, activity, or group.

In light of this, despite the fact that many agree that complex systems can be very robust and resilient (Turner 1997: 18; Barabási 2002: 117) and this may, as

Klein suggests, constitute the AGM's greatest strength (2000: 457–8), claims that complexity wards off co-option become problematic. The problem is threefold. First complexity is not a possession, a talisman that wards off co-option. It is an ontological claim about reality that implies a special approach to all elements of the world (ephemeral or stratified). Second, it is an apt description of certain systems, but this must be seen as a tendency. In other words even the most complex systems have a corresponding tendency too 'cool down' and become (more) inert. The third problem has to do with the fact that the AGM is not the only system becoming more complex. It must also be true that processes of globalization are also gaining in complexity and thus also possess the same resilience or in this case increased potential for domination. Perhaps one could argue that the AGM represents a political movement which potentially has enough complexity to match the complexity of globalization, but without parsing out the various facets of the AGM and how they effect and combine with neighbouring processes, such statements remain rather inert.

We can now also say something about the technical aspects of the AGM such as the relative ease of travel, the Internet, as well as new styles of 'making spaces': social fora, informal meetings, flattened hierarchies, consensus, protest, carnival, and the much-toted ironic or symbolic performance aspects. One could say that these create new spaces in the sense that some have the potential, at least, to engender absolute deterritorialization or to explore the immanent nature of convergent series. Or in other words they counteractualize from the stratified and metricized spaces of the actual towards immanent relations. The latter are not bound by rules, conventions, stereotypes, or lines of power – at least theoretically. This is an important aspect, and one of the things explored in the next chapter is what it means to allow such spaces to develop, to resist the stratification or the reterritorialization of these encounters. But in terms of the technology itself, what in fact is going on is not only time–space compression or time distantiation, for these assume the arrow of (homogeneous) time. These technological and social innovations are in fact exposing the smooth space of the virtual and the pure time of the Aion, thereby highlighting immanent relations. Historically, other deterritorializing technologies would include money (see Scholte 2005: 87ff.), the crossbow (see McNeill 1982: 36–7), the printing press, and the telegraph, though these have their reterritorializing tendencies as well. They create new territories or forms of expression.

The Deleuzian approach developed here accounts for the way in which collective actions of the AGM organize themselves, often seemingly spontaneously; how various subgroups and substructures collude, align, and reform; the fragmentation of politics; the challenges of 'group' decisions and communiqués; and the role of technology. Furthermore, and perhaps most importantly, Deleuze's political philosophy allows us to still refer to the AGM as one thing, as a system, loosely captured as an abstract machine.[42] Within it there is continuity, overlap, collaboration amongst its various aspects or expressions; indeed, this is what makes it so novel and interesting – but these aspects are at once pro- and anti-power; highly organized and expressly disorganized; promote identity or belonging or see these as restrictive. Deleuze's political metaphysics can explain this convergence and divergence, integration and disintegration, organization and dispersal. In broader terms, the emergent forms must be viewed as a characteristic of world politics in general. Just as some aspects of the AGM may resemble political parties and traditional organizations, all organizations and states exhibit behaviour which is distinctly rhizomatic in nature.

Perhaps this is nowhere more true than in global governance. Looking at the AGM as evidence of new forms of participatory governance there is the possibility – indeed, this is the goal of many within the AGM – of a global network of freely participating entities, be they groups, communities, individuals, or peoples. This would stand in contrast to hierarchical institutional forms as represented by the state and its sub and super forms. Eschle and Stammers point, for example, to the democratic relationship between transnational feminist movements and the AGM. 'It seems to us that these ongoing efforts point to an emergent model of democracy emphasizing the importance of open and participatory dialogue and of accompanying efforts to counter the multiple forms of coercive and hierarchical power by which such a dialogue may be constrained.' They offer this as the way forward for political organization in general in that 'it offers an important, if as yet underdeveloped, alternative to the dominance of formalized, liberal, representative models of democracy in arguments about global governance' (2004: 350). The viability of such a form of governance aside, what this suggests is that in studying global political practice we should not only be looking for signs of institutionalized global governance, but rather ways that various lines of flight are injecting, reinjecting and maintaining open, creative forms of political relationships, and then the ways in which they are reinstitutionalized.

Looking broadly at the previous discussion, the biggest stumbling block for complexity theory, network theory, and in this case approaches to the AGM such as those offered by Chesters and Welsh and Urry consists in relating the open to the closed. Deleuze offers a very compelling ontological and metaphysical solution to this problem by focussing on the relative relationship between the smooth and the striated and the nature of the lines of flight that bind them together in an assemblage. An assemblage analysis of the AGM would reject the notion of origin and fixed identity (fixed, static culture, in effect), as well as any relation among elements which suggested an ordering principle (civil society, framing). This is not to say that there are no or have never been sentiments of origin, more or less stable identities, or structural realities; again, only that they are not enduring, primary, nor necessary. With an assemblage theory approach, any given element is not treated as a reified object but rather as an individual in the process of becoming. Such an approach avoids the danger of forcing inappropriate theoretical perspectives that may be completely alien to the object of investigation; perspectives deployed, in effect, in a completely ad hoc manner. It is a sociological approach, but it does not reify aspects of society. It is intimately interested in the process of history, but not in terms of teleology or even linear developments. Assemblage theory rejects (initially, at least) any attempt to understand society in other terms, for example, social movement theory, class antagonism, or globalization processes, but rather seeks to understand society in its own terms from immanent criteria. To be sure, other approaches such as social constructivism, grounded theory, and political sociology also seek to avoid ungrounded and theoretically weak assumptions, but assemblage theory explicitly guards against 'taxonomic essentialism' which, as we saw above, results from taking 'finished' categories and logically analysing them – retroactively, as it were – into giving up enduring properties and shaping these into an eternal, fixed identity or essence.

In terms of evidence, such an approach is inherently materialist, that is, it assumes the existence of a singular (if not fixed) reality to which the researcher has some access. There is, however, no single line of approach or hierarchy of evidence. Thus discourse, for example, may be of vital importance, but can never be a unique determinant; likewise with material production or cultural characteristics. States of affairs are understood to be the actualization of a variety of series in communication with no dominating or ordering principle. In practical terms this would imply broad investigations including but not limited to a text analysis of historical records and academic works, a broader analysis of media products, the direct observation of various social practices, as well as physical manifestations. All of these are not seen as human artefacts of meaning, but rather as self-forming *matériel* that are co-instancing aspects of the forms of content–forms of expression relationship along lines of (re-)territorialization and deterritorialization. The object, again, is to describe the relations between elements of a system without using one of them as the explanans. Indeed, such a genealogical approach is an inversion: it is the explanans that needs explaining.

This rather elegant solution that focuses on process rather than entities can only be thought of as radical in the truest sense: the solution to the problem of Being and beings by going to the ontological root itself. Indeed, one of the goals of the present deployment of Deleuze's philosophy is to normalize the AGM – to 'deradicalize' it, in the loose sense of the term. For as we saw in regards to the state form, the AGM's 'radical' nature persists only insofar as thought limits its objects to an illusory, pure form or essence that only has grounding in actual states of affairs. In other words the AGM is radical only to the extent that it eludes representational thought. But the AGM cannot be seen as something outside of a social system or an anomaly. It is rather an expression of the inherent nature of a Whole characterized by true difference. The next question is what is the role of individual participants in world politics? What about the actors involved in the AGM? It is to the status of these actors as political agents that we turn in the next chapter.

4 Subjectivity and political agency

Politics and the individual

The previous chapter analysed world politics and the AGM as an immanent system such as the study of IR or sociology would require. This final chapter investigates the significance of the AGM as understood as a form of political activity, namely in terms of the subject itself. In other words this chapter will analyse the nature and political efficacy of the subjects that populate the system of world politics. The general question to be addressed in this chapter is, what are the implications of the previous two chapters for political action, or more generally, political participation? If Deleuze's ontological and metaphysical position provides a rigorous account of world politics including the AGM, what does this say about the nature of what are normally considered to be actors themselves; what kind of subjects are on offer here? As will become clear as the chapter progresses, one of the consequences of strictly following the principles laid out in the previous two chapters is that the boundary between the system and the subject – in other words, the structure and the agency – breaks down. Another consequence more pertinent for questions of political agency is that if we take Deleuze up on his political metaphysics, it demands that we abandon several important tenets of Western liberal political theory that form the basis of many if not most theoretical approaches. Significantly in the context of this study, this includes the vast majority of those that challenge prevailing forms of global neoliberalism or even Western liberalism in general. These challenges revolve around the precise nature of the political subject and the rules governing its formation, and, perhaps most importantly, its capacity for truly autonomous or genuinely originary activity. Because Deleuze is a materialist, he must downplay autonomous human will almost to irrelevance. Indeed, it would be impossible to be a materialist *and* believe in such human volition, for if indeed material is self-forming, if thought comes from the outside, then we cannot have a science with autonomous humans acting out their wills. Consciousness is no less a problem for it, and Deleuze must come up with an explanation for our apparent sentiment (and, as argued below, this sentiment is far from universal – indeed, it is heavily bound to the Enlightenment project) of singular, self-motivated action. Put another way, just as the last chapter could be viewed as arguing against methodological nationalism, the present chapter challenges methodological individualism and seeks to develop an alternative.

Of course there is bound to be real hesitation here – and it may explain why scholars are so hesitant to incorporate this kind of philosophy (Deleuze, process, complexity) into a social science research agenda – because it implies the abandonment of any remnants of the modern (political) subject that, generally speaking, forms the focus, the kernel, and the alpha–omega of contemporary political thought. To be more specific and in reference to the problem posed in this book, in the vast majority of writings on the AGM or contemporary political participation – with the exception of post-Marxist accounts, as already mentioned in Chapter 1 and to be addressed below – a bounded, autonomous, originary, or sovereign subject is taken for granted despite decades of sustained challenge. As Heller and Wellbery point out, 'The fact is that, especially in America, the post-structuralist critique of individuality has had only a feeble impact on the persistently individualist imagery of our institutions and popular culture' (1986: 12). Hence the charge, usually made by post-structuralists between themselves, of 'sneaking the subject back in'. In any event, at the outset and to avoid any confusion, the present chapter is not a search for a 'new political subjectivity' – indeed it will argue that there is no such thing as a subject per se – but rather is an investigation of the *individual* as a political agent.

The perspective offered here is novel because although as will become clear in this chapter Deleuze does not evoke a 'morality' or a 'model of just governance', he does, unlike most complexity theorists and process philosophers, hold individuals to be relevant, interesting, and ultimately perhaps the most important problem of his philosophy. Indeed his first monograph, published in 1953, is on Hume and entitled *Empiricism and Subjectivity*, and his later writing on Foucault dedicates considerable time to the problem of the subject. On the other hand, he rarely addresses 'the subject' directly, especially in the main texts that form what is considered here to be his basic political canon, namely *Difference and Repetition* and the second volume of *Capitalism and Schizophrenia, A Thousand Plateaus*. Nevertheless, taken from a wide perspective, Deleuze's research can be read as the search for a science of humanity (*ES*: 21), and far from an ascetic philosopher concerned only with metaphysics and systems, Deleuze is keenly interested in questions of thought, ethics, and action.

Perhaps before examining the subject or subjectivity it would be profitable to roughly define a few of the terms that are generally – and too often indiscriminately – used in discussions of world politics and more specifically the AGM. The term subject is used here generally as an analytical unit for political theory. Deleuze's notion of the subject will not resemble this, as this chapter will show, but this core meaning will be maintained as a base-line for discussion. Thus the subject is loosely synonymous with the more well-known, from a social science perspective, actor: bestowed with or capable of (or perhaps not, as we shall see below) agency. The term body refers to that which has extension in time and space. In specific reference to Deleuze's philosophy, the term individual here means a thing; it could be a subject, person, idea, feeling, structure, or extensive body. With the term individual, we can see how Deleuze breaks with the strict etymology that implies indivisibility, as according to the notion of the real described in Chapter 2, only intensities cannot be divided without changing their nature.[1] In any case, in the general sense of political participation such an 'individual' points to an actualized body. The term self, for the purposes of this chapter, refers to the reflexive aspect of contemplation: a subject contemplating itself.

The subject

Chapter 2 stressed the fact that Deleuze's contributions to philosophy overall can be read through the lens of the virtual–actual couplet, or what one can call a 'two-poles' approach. However, applying this approach in a blanket manner to Deleuze's philosophy can be challenging, for Deleuze in different places tries to do different things with the subject matter at hand which is often, particularly in solo texts, the works of one philosopher. Perhaps more importantly, he very often calls concepts by different names and engages them in different ways. Nothing could be more true of his treatment of the subject. There is not so much the development of a theory of the subject in Deleuze's work but rather, as Boundas speculates, various 'series' which pertain to different questions or problems. For example, the Hume series (how does the mind become a subject?), the Nietzsche–Foucault series (how can we have internalization without interiority?), and so on (1994: 102).

The most enduring and, for the purpose of this chapter, perhaps the most significant contribution to Deleuze's treatment of the subject can be found in Nietzsche, in whom, according to Foucault, Deleuze became interested in the 1960s. The question which occupied Deleuze most at the time was, 'is the theory of the subject which we have in phenomenology a satisfactory one?' (Foucault 1994b: 115). So initially, at least, Deleuze's interest in the subject cannot be read as a reaction to latent positivism or behaviouralism in political philosophy or Enlightenment thinking in general, but phenomenology, as Deleuze himself writes (*F*: 44). Foucault goes on to say that 'everything which took place in the sixties arose from a dissatisfaction with the phenomenological theory of the subject, and involved different escapades, subterfuges, breakthroughs, according to whether we use a negative or a positive term, in the direction of linguistics, psychoanalysis, or Nietzsche.' Thus those who were interested in Nietzsche's work in the 1960s – which is why Deleuze's *Nietzsche and Philosophy* ended up being such a seminal work – 'were not looking for a way out of Marxism. They wanted a way out of phenomenology' (Foucault 1994b: 115). This is an important point, especially given the dangers of reading too much Heidegger into Deleuze. What Deleuze (and Foucault) resist in Heidegger – as perhaps the most widely influential proponent of phenomenology – is intentionality, the idea that 'consciousness is directed towards the thing and gains significance in the world' (*F*: 89).

Deleuze's work in general, but especially from the early 1970s onwards, borrows considerably from Foucault's research, and incorporates Foucault's use of content and expression of form, in several cases with the example of the prison from *Discipline and Punish*, as was mentioned in Chapter 2. Deleuze sees Foucault's subject as the third, necessary dimension (the first two being knowledge and power) of the latter's political ontology:

> If Foucault needs a third dimension, it's because he feels he's getting locked into the play of forces, that he's reached the end of the line or can't manage to 'cross' it, there's no line of flight left open to him.
>
> (*N*: 93)

In other words, the unending play of power and knowledge in effect forced Foucault to engage with the notion of the subject. What Deleuze specifically takes from all of this is the notion of subjectivation. Subjectivation refers not to a subject as in a thing or a person, but rather to a process or relationship. And what is distinctive about this process is that unlike determinate forms of knowledge or constraining rules of power, the rules of subjectivation are *optional* (*N*: 98).[2] There are two important consequences of this. First, it is not possible to speak of an enduring notion of the subject due to the variations in the process of subjectivation from one period of history to another, not to mention between geographic regions. For example, the processes of Chinese subjectivation during the Tang Dynasty vary enormously from those of nineteenth century Latin America. Consequently the rules of such processes are extremely diverse. Second, these processes of subjectivation cannot be said to act on any subject, unless, as Deleuze writes, 'we divest the subject of any interiority and even any identity' (*N*: 98). Thus, as we will see in this chapter, subjectivation has nothing to do with a 'person' or a 'political actor', but is rather tied to the Event and occurs in the process of individuation in the virtual. It is 'a specific or collective individuation relating to an event (a time of day, a river, a wind, a life ...). It is a mode of intensity, not a personal subject' (*N*: 98).

Indeed it is hard to imagine Deleuze's immanent metaphysics being populated by any thing, subject, or sovereign individual, or possessing something else beyond what is in the immanent world or, as he puts it, having interiority. This points precisely to the nature of immanence. If we take it to the limit of its meaning and not as metaphor or worse, hyperbole, there cannot be immanence plus something else, for such a something else would be transcendence. In other words, any appeal to a bounded or interior self or subject must be read as an appeal to transcendence and as such inconsistent with Deleuze's ontology. What is required of Deleuze then is a theory that explains individuals or agents acting in the world and yet avoids sovereign subjects. At the personal level – the register often taken by those concerned with questions of the subject – the question would be, then, what is this thing that I am? What is this feeling of subjectivity that I have? For Deleuze the only answer can be a bubble of perception with memory (see *LS*: 349–50; *ATP*: 262), but consciousness is not a problem in that it is not predicated of an originary and enduring subject, but rather an effect of Events. Likewise for the same reason he is not interested in epistemology because for him there is no such thing as a stable self or subject which is capable of having knowledge of the object or making a truth claim. All claims are in this sense true and differ only in their productivity. For Deleuze epistemology is an aspect of transcendental empiricism. In other words, knowledge is not the collection of facts by a sovereign mind or self, but rather a series of connections to a (virtual) Idea. As we will see below, the subject is not a site of representation but of production (the unconscious being not a theatre but a factory) and thinking is a plugging in, a riding of a wave.

A brief genealogy of subjectivity

Before getting to what sort of 'subject' we are dealing with based on the reading of Deleuze in this book, it would be profitable to briefly sketch the history, or perhaps better, genealogy of the notion of the subject. This implies not the objective analysis of the development of a concept, but mapping the changes over time in the rules of formation of a notion. Put another way, an internal or immanent rather than an external or transcendent account, meaning that variation in the rule and its formation must be distinguished immanently and cannot be taken from outside in the form of a viewpoint, a telos, or God. An excellent source for such a genealogy is Paul Hirst and Penny Woolley's *Social Relations and Human Attributes* (1982), a study that – in a move rare in the English-speaking world at the time – infuses sociology with the contingency of culture (see Stratton 1984). In it they relate how the founding of the autonomous subject is traditionally understood to have taken place during the classical period of Ancient Greece. Here a distinction was made between a specific *persona* and a particular status or role. This means that rather than, or in addition to, fixed social relations with their obligations and responsibilities, a person is developed 'as an independent moral entity, a being whose conduct is self-governed' (1982: 119). It is here that we see the beginnings of the appeal to transcendence in the establishment of the subject. The latter is not irrevocably embedded in, a part, nor a product of its social horizon, but rather is endowed with not only a stand-alone value, but an ability – indeed a moral calling – to take an active role in its own conduct and development. During the European Christian era, this moral entity is further endowed with certain metaphysical attributes. 'It became both an agent and an immortal soul, the well-being of the soul being influenced by the conduct of the agent' (1982: 119). Thus to the extent that Christianity dominated the social landscape of the ancient and medieval European worlds, the unique entity or subject becomes independent of its social relations. Notions of identity and belonging could easily be constructed on such a firm bases of subjectivity.

This identity and belonging was crucial in the development of humanism in Renaissance Italy and its emphasis on the autonomous individual or the constructed self. Writers such as Petrarch (1904) mark the shift from the denial of the self found in medieval thought and mores to the keen interest in the 'inner world' that humanists found fundamentally defines human existence on earth. In the context of the discussion here, it is worth pointing out that such a shift in subjectivity is not a matter of quiet, inward speculation across various eras, for such a view would tacitly assume the presence of an enduring sovereign subjectivity. Rather, this shift brings with it enormous changes in time and space such as were discussed in the last chapter. The shift to the individual entailed nothing less than a move from a highly muted subjectivity within static, medieval time to 'an indeterminate number of possible lives across an open example of narratable time. ... Autonomy of choice and moral responsibility for self-initiated action replaced collectively defined status and social duty.' (Heller and Wellbery 1986: 4). Ultimately the subjectivity of the Renaissance was a major step in human beings coming to view themselves as being in the world, something that Heidegger would later call *die Zeit des Weltbildes* or the Age of the World Picture (1977: 134–5). Another crucial step to the fuller, modern development of the subject according to Hirst and Woolley is the Reformation, where the now-dominant form of individuation 'clearly linked identity with *consciousness*, and made self-consciousness the ground of individual moral existence.' The authors remind us here that in the first volume of *The History of Sexuality* Foucault points out that practices of confession, for example, were important in 'defining and individuating the subject' (1982: 119). Hirst and Woolley go on to point out that it was Hegel who gives us the fully furnished self, that is, mental norms from which individuals deviate or are deficient (1982: 121). For Nietzsche, of course, this development of consciousness with its double burden of slave morality and *ressentiment* was the birth of tragedy – an inversion of psychic and moral progress which formed the basis of the dominant forms of Western ideology.[3]

In the face of the initial appeal of such humanistic values, however, there was a normative problem, namely, what was to stop rampant individualism reverting to a Hobbesian anarchical society? Of course, given the discussion here, it is somewhat ironic that Hobbes inductively posited the existence of such a pre-social order – what he famously called the State of Nature – when in fact it was the individualism recovered by Renaissance humanism which was causing the problem of anarchy in the first place. In this sense what Hobbes in fact did is lay the foundations for a contradiction that we will pick up later with Whitehead: how can the autonomous individual rise up outside itself and collectively create just institutions which would uphold the ideals of the Enlightenment? The task for the individual or subject was to rise above this new 'life history' and, using reason, arrive at an autonomy that was possible within society. The answer to this question and the legacy with which the West lives today, comes, according to Heller and Wellbery, from Kant, whose solution to this dilemma lies in 'the transcendent figure of the subject as a non-individuated potential for actualization', a view which 'still appears repeatedly in our most enshrined collective practices' (1986: 5). That is, despite the interventions of Marx, Nietzsche, and Freud, this idealized type of subjectivity persists as an abstract autonomous individual today. It 'prevails in institutionalized culture despite criticisms of the ontological grounding or the political consequences of this figure' (Heller and Wellbery 1986: 5). It must be stressed that this subject, this kind of subjectivity, is not merely an example of the individual in the world, but rather the abstract form of the subject: the transcendental self. It perhaps reaches its apogee in the unwavering centrality of the stable, sovereign subject which permeates Rawls' *A Theory of Justice* (1972). Liberalism needs such a stable self or 'I' because, somewhat paradoxically, without it identity transformation and therefore human progress would be impossible (see Hopgood 2000: 13–14).

In more recent times the main criticisms of this fully furnished self were made by those caught up in the intellectual revolution (or fashion, depending on one's point of view) of France in the 1960s and 1970s. Writers such as Althusser, Barthes, Derrida, Foucault, and Lacan challenged 'the metaphysics associated with the concept of the "person". Challenged is the notion of the person as a given entity, the author of its acts and centred in a unitary, reflexive, and directive consciousness' (Hirst and Woolley 1982: 131).[4] One of the analogous arguments today (which is for the most part a rearticulation of this 'French invasion') claims that forces of globalization or late capitalism have begun to dissolve the bounded, sovereign subject, exposing the fact that human nature (on which to base sociological need or political mores), far from being innate or given, is in fact fractured, multiple, decentred, and disembedded. With the post-modernist and post-structuralist intervention, the subject on which all of modern theory was based suddenly starts slipping, coming apart at the seams. Of course at the time when these arguments were first articulated there was considerable hostility towards this anti-humanism for many of the same reasons that continue today. The denouncement of the subject as, for example (to take Althusser) an ideological illusion challenges the basis of much of the social and legal codes upon which Western culture and increasingly global jurisprudence and international law is based, namely human rights and civil liberties.

But despite the force of these arguments and their enormous currency within Anglo-American academia, especially in literary theory and cultural studies,[5] on balance this challenge to the notion of the subject, like that of Marx, Nietzsche, and Freud on which it is based, has been ignored by the social sciences. Fields such as political science, IR, sociology, and economics seem committed to taking human subjectivity as a constant by which to analyse ontic modalities. In other words the capacity for sovereign individuals to act autonomously forms the basis or ground from which to analyse all manner of social, political, and economic phenomena. The autonomous subject becomes the independent variable, in effect the standpoint or constant from which to observe, measure, and ultimately engage with the world.

What seems clear is that the autonomous subject as discovered by Descartes and ratified by Kant has formed the basis – or at least is lurking in the background as an unassailable principle or unuttered truth – of the vast majority of social and political thought since the beginning of modern science itself (see for example Heller and Wellbery 1986: 4–6; Žižek 1990: 250; Hacking 2002: 3). This goes some distance to explaining the rather unfortunate way in which political science in general and IR in particular are so committed to behaviouralism, or perhaps better, methodological individualism and modern political concepts such as contract theory. One of the most sustained critiques of what can here be called the typically 'modern' subject is delivered by Žižek who, through is appetite for film, pop-culture, and news media, delivers an unabashed demolition in the form of his self-styled neo-Lacanian intervention. His target is what he calls the default subject: 'a substantial, essential entity, given in advance, dominating the social process' (1990: 250). It is perhaps this subject more than anything that has saddled the study of world politics with the idea of bounded entities (states, governments, leaders, opponents, communities) which act rationally to maximize benefits. Not only does this completely ignore unintended consequence, pathologies, the notion of competing systems of value, but also the history of the critique of the subject, only some of which has found its way into the literature in such forms as structuration and constructivism.

Going back to Hirst and Woolley (1982), they problematize the entire notion of the 'person' and argue that it is not a given entity since notions of person differ drastically in time and space, as well as in practices and institutions. Nor is the existence and currency of words such as 'subject', 'self', and 'individual' evidence of an enduring concept. Simply from a linguistic perspective, for example, there is a difference between naming the individual and the individual itself. In other words the fact that individuals are named does not necessarily entail the same notion of individual subjects. 'Names and statuses specify, but do not "individualize" in our sense'. All this suggests that there is no norm of human conduct. The limits placed on normal behaviours vary widely depending on circumstances and social relations, 'and behaviours which for us are almost by definition pathological or psychopathic have been tolerated, encouraged, and even required' in other contexts (1982: 125).

Hirst and Woolley also question what today would be called discourse, or how people view themselves. It is problematic because people in different regions of the earth – and indeed there is considerable heterogeneity within regions and locales – do not universally possess this will to individuality.

> What can be said of agents who do not consider themselves as unitary and self-possessed consciousness [sic], who consider many of their actions as the products of external forces or of organs not under their control, or who consider components of mental life, such as dreams, as objective and external realities?
>
> (1982: 125)

We cannot conceive of social agents as 'necessarily unitary subjects centred in a determinative consciousness' and take into account ethnography and cultural analysis that reveals other 'modes of conceiving and specifying social agents', and psychoanalysis that challenges notions of self-possessed consciousness (1982: 133).

A further problematization found in the works of authors such as Foucault is the specifically temporal one which states that in order to find a culture with a sense of the individual or self different from the contemporary one based in the

Western tradition one need not go so far as China or Peru. Drawing on Dodds (1973) and Snell (1953), Hirst and Woolley problematize the whole notion of the development of the Western subject that supposedly has its roots in Greek antiquity. In fact, for all of their centrality to Western thought, according to Hirst and Woolley, Homer's works give us a very fractured and disjointed notion of person. Rather than forming the foundation for the great Western hero endowed with singular traits such as courage, feelings of kinship, and desire for glory, they present the body as a collection of parts upon which a number of forces act, including aspects of Zeus, heightened powers granted by the gods, and the intervention of dreams and visions. What is precisely the point here is the supposed unity of this subject. 'The agent on whom these forces act is not presented as a unitary consciousness but as a complex of faculties or organs, neither purely mental nor physical.' In Homer there is also the matter of the *thumos*, an organ of will and feeling in the chest which compels actions not attributed to the character of the individual. Thus conduct 'which deviates from expectations and norms may be required to be compensated for, but this cannot be construed as a demand for consistency in behaviour because the means to systematization of conduct are not at hand.' In terms of social relations and obligations this presents something on a different order from contemporary social responsibility. Agamemnon is king and as such has obligations: he is 'liable for the consequences of but not necessarily responsible for his actions' (1982: 133).

As Peter Dews points out, the post-structuralist attack of the subject rests in part on a straw-man tactic. In a critique aimed specifically at Derrida, Dews states that

> the assumption – central to the whole pattern of post-structuralist thinking – that the concept of the subject implies an immobile, self-identical, and constitutive centre of experience seriously underplays the complexity and subtlety of the way in which subjectivity has been explored within the Western philosophical tradition.
>
> (1987: xv)

However, it is important not to be distracted by such counterclaims. Although it is true, as Dews suggests, that just what the nature of the subject is has been heavily problematized in the pre-post-structuralist era, those whom Dews lumps together as post-structuralist are questioning not the specifics of modern psychology, but a broader trend which began in the West with Descartes and his *res cogito*. This discovery of the modern subject became heavily bound to all aspects of Western thought and imagination including politics, economics, art, and religion. And the urgency with which post-structuralists attack this notion of the subject perhaps stems from the fact that so many aspects of human life – so many assumptions and prejudices – are bound up with this immobile, self-identifying, and constitutive centre of experience: the autonomous modern subject.

Indeed, such an individual subject can be seen as a liability. Although rampant individualism might be the cornerstone of Western-dominated globalization, it need not lead to utopian levels of personal freedom or expression. On the contrary, 'In the West, indeed throughout the world, the subject increasingly appears as the empty, ideological image of mass culture, the legitimating myth of an administrative discourse' (Heller and Wellbery 1986: 9).[6] Thus in recent years many have argued that the liberated, reflexive subjectivity of multicultural, cosmopolitan inclusiveness replicates the kind of subject that in fact corresponds directly to the logic of late-capitalism or globalization.[7] Although on the one hand many see considerable promise in the form of consumer activism (see Micheletti 2003), there is the sinking suspicion that the freedoms won by the West and increasingly being exported or imposed throughout the world in the guise of human rights, rule of law, property rights, and democracy, ultimately amount to the freedom to choose amongst a variety of fashion genres (classic, retro, punk) or professional sports clubs. Thus one of the challenges or liabilities of the AGM remains its adherence to the modern subject insofar as it emulates the liberal, socialist, or Marxist tradition (Juniper and Jose 2008: 12).

In Chapter 2 the discussion of becoming precluded the notion of the doer behind the doing, citing Nietzsche's example of the lightning strike. Such a perspective no doubt sets up the parameters through which Deleuze will be able to talk about the subject itself. For if there are no things as such – that is, with a fixed, transcendent form or essence – a bounded, essential subject seems unlikely. In what appears to be a paradox, Deleuze essentially maintains that there is no subject of the subject in the strictest sense of the word. In other words, for the purposes of the discussion in this chapter, the subject – that which is the bearer of action, usually considered to be endowed with the capacity for thought, free action, and choice – has no subjectivity; or rather, no identity based on a sovereign, transcendent, inner, or internal self.

Such a position is the theme of the first half of *Capitalism and Schizophrenia*, *Anti-Oedipus*, which sees the practice of psychoanalysis, far from the liberator of the oppressed unconscious, as the guarantor of the illusory subjectivity of modernity par excellence. As an anti-Platonist philosopher and anti-establishment psychoanalyst, what Deleuze and Guattari oppose here is what they call the idealism in psychoanalysis that consists of a whole system of projections and reductions derived from the Oedipal Complex. They take issue with a whole host of 'unconscious representations, and to corresponding forms of causation and expression or explanation' (*AO*: 17). In contrast to the Cartesian theatre of representation which Freud, embedded as he was in the processes of modernity, was sure to find in his patients, they propose the unconscious as a factory. It is not a site of representing but of *production*: 'subjectivity has to be produced precisely because there is no subject' (*N*: 113). The subject is not a place for viewing or representing[8] but a space for doing, and 'the unconscious isn't a theatre but a factory, a productive machine, and the unconscious isn't playing around all the time with mummy and daddy but with races, tribes, continents, history and geography, always some social frame' (*N*: 144). This constant deferral to the social frame can be read as analogous to other calls for recognizing the contingency of the embeddedness of human existence in opposition to the human subject. Thus there is no free zone of the free individual 'independent from any "institutional and social system"' (*F*: 85). Just as there are no stable fixed institutional and social systems but rather, as argued in Chapter 3, complex systems in the process of becoming, there is no fixed subject or form of subjectivity navigating these systems.

Subjects then become more like systems in themselves which are connected or plugged into other systems or what Deleuze often calls series. These are not governed by any rule, law, or reason. In the virtual or the plane of immanence, series simply converge or not, depending on their velocity and capability. Deleuze and Guattari submit that a body

> is not defined by the form that determines it nor as a determinate substance or subject nor by the organs it possesses or the functions it fulfils. On the plane of consistency, a body is defined only by a longitude and a latitude: in other words the sum total of the material elements belonging to it under given relations of movement and rest, speed and slowness (longitude); the sum total of the intensive affects it is capable of at a given power or degree of potential (latitude). Nothing but affects and local movements, differential speeds.
>
> (*ATP*: 260)

Actual individuals – that is, discrete, extended, differenciated individuals – are the products of the concentration, accumulation, and the 'coincidence of a number of converging preindividual singularities' (*LB*: 72). So although in Deleuze's metaphysics there are such things as individuals, they are not the masters of their own subjectivity but rather the result of quasi-causes or intensive processes of the virtual. As Alain Badiou points out, there is no theory of the subject to be found here, 'but an attentiveness to, a registering of the point of view that every subject can be resolved into and which is itself the term of a series that is likely to be divergent or without reason' (1994: 53–4). It is a process that Deleuze calls *nomadic* – pre-individual and impersonal, the study of which we referred to in the previous chapter as transcendental empiricism, the nomadic science. This points not to the determination and discrimination of essences or subjects, but rather to these processes of individuation that denote singularities.

> What we're interested in ... are modes of individuation beyond those of things, persons, or subjects: the individuation, say, of a time of day, or a region, a climate, a river or a wind, or an event. ... The title *A Thousand Plateaus* refers to these individuations that don't individuate persons or things.
>
> (*N*: 26)

But precisely what are these subject–systems or points in systems?

Before embarking on a full examination of the subject in Deleuze, it is worth pointing out that, following Foucault, Deleuze argues that the subject is not even the sources of its own statements but rather 'a place or position which varies greatly according to its type and the threshold of the statement, and the "author" himself is merely one of these possible positions in certain cases.' Thus a statement can have several of these positions, which is why Foucault speaks of the 'anonymous murmur': 'the great relentless disordered drone of discourse' (*F*: 47). Deleuze is anti-interiority. In other words there is no interior self juxtaposed to an exterior environment or Other. In a subtle move, Deleuze posits rather the fold or the folding of the outside to make an inside. In an evocative analogy, he claims that from this perspective a ship is not an entity with an interior, but a fold of the sea (*F*: 81).

The fold

Philosophers of the object – Aristotle, Descartes, Newton, for example – devote considerable effort to explaining objects in the world and their relationship to the thinking subject which, particularly in the case of Descartes, is assumed.[9] They tend, however, to have difficulty in explaining these objects' (and subjects') relationship to Being, as we saw with Aristotle in Chapter 2. The main challenge for those who propose a univocal ontology and its corresponding immanent metaphysics is in a way the reverse. These thinkers have little difficulty discussing Being, but face challenges in addressing the analytical distinction between the One and the multiple. What Deleuze proposes, following Leibniz and to a certain extent Foucault, is the figure of the fold. The fold is, in essence, a way of understanding discrete things embedded in the immanent without recourse to the transcendent. As Badiou writes, the fold is an anti-extensional concept of the multiple, an anti-dialectic concept of the event, and 'an anti-Cartesian (or anti-Lacanian) concept of the subject, a "communicating" figure of absolute interiority, equivalent to the world, of which it is a point of view' (1994: 52).

But what can Badiou mean by this? For those embedded in the Western tradition, it can be difficult to think pure immanence. There is the constant danger that the fourfold collars of representation described in Chapter 2 will pull any form of subject that adheres to the demands of univocity back to a fixed, and perhaps arbitrarily adopted, figure. An attentive reader may find similar cause for concern in Deleuze. Of course he is a long way from the Cartesian *cogito* or Kantian faculties of a priori synthesis, but nevertheless it may seem as though in some of his writings that there is something brought in from the outside, something other than pure immanent relations, be they 'principles that constitute a subject' (*ES*: 109) in Hume or 'modes' in Spinoza (*EP*: 217–218). However, nothing could be further from the case, and Deleuze is constantly aware of his self-imposed restrictions. Maintaining a strict adherence to the principle of univocity allows recourse only to what is at hand, namely Being itself. But how to get to a notion of subjectivity under such restraints? How could one explain mind, consciousness, or point of view? Deleuze accomplishes this through the figure of the fold. The fold is a way of arriving at an inside using only a pure outside (the virtual, the immanent). As such it is consistent with the principles of differentiation; indeed it is repetition itself. Within a system of folds there is no such thing as the primitive (or transcendent) interior because

> the double is never a projection of the interior: on the contrary, it is an interiorization of the outside. ... It is not a reproduction of the Same, but a repetition of the Different. ... It resembles exactly the invagination of a tissue in embryology, or the act of doubling in sewing: twist, fold, stop, and so on.
>
> (*F*: 81)

The folding of the One or the World is an infinite process (*LB*: 40) that is the result of purely exterior forces. These forces are not expressed by any agents, indeed it is 'agency' that is the result of these forces. What is primary at all times is the outside; the inside is merely the result (Boundas 1994: 114).

This is where Leibniz's monad comes in, and in relation to the theme of enveloped–enveloping proposed in Chapter 2, it must be seen as that which actualizes the virtual (*LB*: 90). Significantly, and rather ironically given the discussion below, in social science literature dealing with individual actors, the monad is commonly used to refer to a subject that is self-contained or complete, or in other words bounded, autonomous, and generally sovereign.[10] Thus we read generally derogatory postmodern critiques of the monadic subject which is suspected of being completely separate from the rest of the world. Although Leibniz does present the monad as the self-contained entity that has no parts (1898: 217–18), Leibniz and Deleuze clearly point out that it is not at all separated from the world – in fact the very opposite is the case. What Deleuze's Leibniz makes clear through the double usage of the fold and the monad is that this point of perception is in fact the only guarantor of a consistent philosophy of immanence which precludes the very 'centred' subject that is the focus of so much radical critique. In perhaps Leibniz's most well-known contribution to philosophy, the monad, Deleuze sees the ultimate expression of the principle of immanence that provides an excellent account of the relationship between the One-All or world on the one hand, and the discrete individual on the other. The monad for Leibniz–Deleuze is bound up in the world and expresses it from a particular point of view, that is, a specific segment of it. The notion of the fold comes into play here, with the world consisting of an infinite number of folds, each fold in the space between two folds, at once being folded into (enveloped) the world and folding the world within it (enveloping). The monad is this fold that is always between the fold, a cave within a cave, a fold of the sea.

> At the core of every monad there exist singularities that in every case are the requisites of the individual notion. That each individual clearly expresses only a part of the world derives from the real definition: it clearly expresses the region determined by its constituent singularities. That every individual

Subjectivity and political agency 157

expresses the entire world also derives from the real definition: the constitutive singularities of each one are effectively extended in all directions up to the singularities of others, under the condition that the corresponding series converge, such that each individual includes the sum of a compossible world, and excludes only the other worlds incompossible with that world (where the series would diverge).

(*LB*: 72)

The process which ends in an actualized extensity begins when certain ideal Events are condensed into a monad. These Events, recalling the discussion in Chapter 2, are the monad's clear zone of expression which in turn are actualized into a body which is said to 'belong' to the monad as its final cause (see *LB*: 98).

It is worth repeating that the fold takes place primarily in the virtual, but is expressed, through actualization, as a state of affairs. As Badiou reminds us, the virtual is the realm of duration and intensity wherein it must be the differential rather than the point which has the value of a unit of matter (1994: 53). The infinite folds of the world form a sort of labyrinth, and 'the smallest element of the labyrinth, is the fold, not the point' (*LB*: 6). In this way, the 'unilaterality' of the monad, far from keeping it apart from the world and other monads, implies precisely as its condition of closure or inclusiveness

> a torsion of the world, an infinite fold, that can be unwrapped in conformity with the condition only by recovering the other side, not as exterior to the monad, but as the exterior or outside of its own interiority: a partition, a supple and adherent membrane coextensive with the entire inside [*coextensive à tout le dedans*].
>
> (*LB*: 127)[11]

Thus

> We go from the world to the subject, at the cost of a torsion that causes the monad to exist in the actual [*actuellement*] only in subjects, but that also makes subjects all relate to this world, like to the virtuality that they actualize. ... The world must be placed in the subject in order that the subject can be for the world. This is the torsion that constitutes the fold of the world and of the soul. And it is what gives to expression its fundamental character: the soul is the expression of the world (actuality), but because the world is the expressed of the soul (virtuality).
>
> (*LB*: 28)[12]

But although the world is expressed in the monad or the soul, it is not expressed in its entirety. Returning again to the discussion of enveloping/enveloped, it is only the enveloping series that are expressed clearly, in this case in terms of a segment or a point of view that corresponds to the individual which is differenciated into an actual state of affairs. In this way the continuum between the One and the multiple is preserved. 'The world is an infinite series of curvatures or inflections, and the entire world is enclosed in the soul from one point of view'. It is 'the infinite curve that touches at an infinity of points an infinity of curves, the curve with a unique variable, the convergent series of all series' (*LB*: 26).

Following Foucault, Deleuze argues that it was the Greeks of the Classical Era who located the self as a fold, in an inside of an outside. They made the force of the outside relate back to itself, 'they invented the subject, but only as a derivative or the product of a "subjectivation"' (*F*: 84). This is much more than mere self-government – that a free individual must rule herself before she can rule others. It allows for the relationship with oneself to exist, precisely due to this hollow space or fold between the folds of the outside which develops into a 'unique dimension'. It is thus not merely the relation to oneself that is novel in the Greeks, but the way in which this 'assumes an independent status' (*F*: 83).

Thinking about the role of the political subject, one can make at least two observations about Deleuze's fold at this point. First, this fold of the self is primary and the lack of a science of this fold keeps thought about the subject focused merely on the actual, that is, as a simple given. Second, this Greek discovery can be seen as an eruption of subjectivity that had perhaps not taken place previously nor was necessarily to occur in other places at other times. What is key here is that these folds are the results of variable and non-necessary forces of the outside. Thus the Greek relation to oneself was not simply dropped and then replaced by a Christian morality. Rather, the relation to oneself is continually reconfigured and reborn in other places and times, each according to its own circumstances of – to stay in the Foucauldian register – power and knowledge (*F*: 86). Thus the history of the relation to oneself (in the West since the Greeks, at least) is the transmutation of these circumstances. The question that people must ask themselves, according to Deleuze, is how do power and knowledge fold the subject today. The problem, argues Deleuze, is that we still act as if old powers and sciences are still functioning, and 'in moral matters we are still weighed down with old beliefs which we no longer even believe, and we continue to produce ourselves as a subject on the basis of old modes which do not correspond to our problems' (*F*: 87). In this sense, speaking of liberal values in the West, for example, Western liberals continue to believe they are Greeks and Christians, failing to see the fact that they have become something different altogether.

In *The Fold* Deleuze likens the process of actualization as an unfolding, which is not the opposite of folding as one might expect. Unfolding is the movement from the fold to extensity, or from the inflected line to the point. It is the move from enveloping to developing; from involution to evolution. For example, an organism is twice defined by this double process. In the first place by its ability to fold its own parts as a pre-individual singularity, in the second place to unfold these parts in extensity, not to infinity but to a degree which defines what we generally call a species. For this reason there is considerable overlap amongst species depending on these processes of folding and unfolding. 'Thus an organism is enveloped by organisms, one within another (interlocking germinal matter), like Russian dolls' (*LB*: 9). As Badiou puts it, the One can be 'folded according to eventful declensions with nomadic significance' and likewise, be 'unfolded according to strongly sedentary closed sets' (1997: 96). Like all the figures that populate Deleuze's metaphysics, due to the lack of a transcendent vantage point there can be only relative, differential relations in the folding/ unfolding process, making it inherently dynamic. One might distinguish between such a process on the immanent field characterized by intensity and that of the actual field characterized by extensity. Though of course dynamism is possible in the latter field, there is always an element of fixidity, as space is metricized in one way or another corresponding to Euclidean geometry and time is measured in units. Here one can measure speeds from fixed coordinates. In the virtual there is no such fixed coordinates, but only intensive ordinates that are characterized as differentials that, just as in calculus, are only related to each other as part of a curve. Indeed, they take place at infinite speed (*WP*: 21). In this manner the fold is a continuous process; making subjectivity likewise a dynamic motion, as Negri notes, the boundary of a continuous movement between the outside and the inside (*N*: 175–6).

Specifically in terms of the subject as agent, such an approach has the advantage of being fully consistent with Deleuze's metaphysics. Subjectivity is the fold of the outside: the inside of the outside – nothing innate (*F*: 80). There is no interior, only the inside of the outside, which is the fold or anti-interiority itself. This subject, this fold within the fold, when rigorously analysed and adhered to, is unlikely to slide back to modern formulations as mentioned above. 'Deleuze is searching for a figure of interiority (or of the subject) that is neither reflection (of the *cogito*), nor the relation-to, the focus (of intentionality), nor the pure empty point (of eclipse). Neither Descartes, nor Husserl, nor Lacan' (Badiou 1994: 61). As such, it stands a very good chance of making a clean break with other, sometimes adjacent – for example, post-Marxist, as we will see below – versions of the subject, enforcing different ways of thinking about the subject in the world.

Recalling the discussion in Chapter 2, inflection would be the enveloping intensities which from the perspective of a series – or in this case a fold – express the world confusedly, whereas what is enveloped by the series expresses the world clearly. Looking at subjects in the actual world (the actual) here, the process of differenciation into extended individuals in the world is the action of the soul:[13]

> Inflection is an ideal condition or a virtuality that exists in the actual [*actuellement*[14]] only in the soul that envelops it. Thus the soul is what has folds and is full of folds. Folds are in the soul, exist in the actual [*actuellement*] only in the soul. That is already true for 'innate ideas': they are pure virtualities, pure powers whose act consists in habitus or dispositions (folds) in the soul, and whose completed act consists of an inner action of the soul (an internal deployment). But this is no less true for the world: the whole world is only a virtuality that exists in the actual [*actuellement*] only in the folds of the soul which convey it, the soul implementing inner pleats through which

> it endows itself with representation of the closed [*inclus*] world. We are moving from inflection to inclusion in a subject, as if from the virtual to the actual [*actuel*], inflection defining the fold, but inclusion defining the soul or the subject, that is, what envelops the fold, its final cause and its complete act.
>
> (*LB*: 24)[15]

Again, with the fold it is as if the world is infinitely folded – caves within caves, spaces within spaces – and the subject occurs at a point of perception, and is at once an expression of the entire world and envelopes the entire world. As Badiou so succinctly puts it 'Deleuze's subject, the subject-as-fold, has as its numeric formula $1/\infty$, which is the formula for the monad, even if its clear part is $1/n$. It articulates the One with the infinite.' (1994: 68). Through this process the soul or subject is what becomes actual, not the entire world at once.

But there is still the problem of individuals (subjects) with characteristics. Are not these characteristics essences, especially when we move to the species level? In fact, no. Because of the special relationship between the world and the individual Deleuze can avoid talking about predicates of subjects (or species) with the notion of attributes, borrowed from Spinoza (1992: 34ff.). 'Attributes are like points of view of substance; but in the absolute limit these points of view are no longer external, and substance contains within itself the infinity of its points of view upon itself' (*EP*: 22). Thus Deleuze's subjects have no predicates, but rather attributes which come from the Event and which are more like verbs that express an action or passion. From a logical standpoint a predicate '*is the proposition itself* and I can no more reduce "I travel" to "I am a travelling being" than I can reduce "I think" to "I am a thinking being."' (*LB*: 60).[16] Thus there is no list of predicates attached to an individual's subjectivity that would describe an essence. This is a very clear distinction in Deleuze, and his use of the virtual Event here leads to more precision than other approaches generally found in the post-structuralist or post-Marxist register. This precision, according to Deleuze, comes from Leibniz's genius in dealing with the Event.

> Then Leibniz implemented the second great logic of the event: the world itself is an event and, as an incorporeal (= virtual) predicate, the world must be included in every subject as a basis from which each one extracts the manners that correspond to its point of view (aspects). The world is predication itself, manners being the particular predicates, and the subject, what goes from one predicate to another as if from one aspect of the world to another.
>
> (*LB*: 60–1)

This is in strict opposition to essences or form, avoiding the essentialism of first Aristotle and then Descartes.

The entire notion of the subject-as-fold in Deleuze is bound up with what thinking is. To the public teacher (Socrates) or State philosopher (Hegel) as well as to the 'private' thinker (Descartes), Deleuze proposes a folding of exteriority. Thinking then becomes less something engaged from within, but rather what 'happens' from without. Thought is provoked by forces from the outside, the inside of which is merely the inflection of immanent relations. In some places Deleuze describes this kind of thought as being a foreigner in one's own language, best embodied for him in the works of Franz Kafka (see Deleuze and Guattari 1986): to be taken hold of (*N*: 100), to bring something new and incomprehensible into the world. The reason for this is basically that with no autonomous self-same subjectivity there can be no spontaneous, individualized thinking. If subjectivity is a fold, then thinking must come from without by engaging with external forces. Thought from the inside could therefore only consist of the reproduction or interpretation of the internal, the stratified. This shows Deleuze's distance from phenomenology and Heidegger, even though the two philosophers often address similar questions. Unlike Heidegger, for Deleuze consciousness cannot be the beginning of thought and thought cannot be presented by 'intentionality dependent on an internalized relation: between consciousness and its object, ideation and the ideatum, the neotic pole and the noematic pole, or, in Sartrean variant, the for-itself and the in-itself.' (Badiou 1997: 21). In so far as thought is an immanent process, Deleuze calls it nomadic thought. This is in no way to deny the reality of the public teacher, the state thinker, or the private thinker, only that such modes of thought are not primary, but rather the effects of immanent, incorporeal encounters on the plane of immanence.

It is important to specifically seize on just what distinction Deleuze is proposing here. It is not just that thought–thinking–thinker as fold is the polar opposite of the private, interior thinker–thinking–thought of Descartes. The two-poles approach adopted in Chapter 2 is a means to illustrate the movement of the virtual. Here we are seizing upon the primary differences between various kinds of thinking. But exteriority of thought – thought from the outside as it is often referred to – is not simply *another* image of thought, that is, thought as a transcendent function from an interior space. Exteriority of thought denies the possibility of such images, it is incommensurable with images – it is in fact 'a force that destroys both the image *and* its copies, the model *and* its reproductions, every possibility of subordinating thought to a model of the True, the Just, or the Right (Cartesian truth, Kantian just, Hegelian right, etc.)' (*ATP*: 377).

Badiou provides a nice summary of the subject-as-fold in Deleuze by means of three qualifications. The first is that the subject is not a cause but a result of a topological immanence. It is not the originator of itself but is rather *what happens* when the outside is folded to make an inside. Second, as such it is not at all separate from the outside, but rather forms a part of it as fold. Third, the subject only exists as thought, but again this is thought in a special sense, not the original thought of the *cogito*, but thought as inflection or reflection. Badiou characterizes the subject as what happens when 'Being coincides with thinking' or, put another way, '*the subject (the inside) is the identity of thinking and being ... to think is to fold*' (1997: 89).

Deleuzian subjects

Thinking about world politics in general and the case of the AGM in particular, what then *is* the subject based on the preceding discussion of Deleuze? In a very weak reading of Deleuze's formulation one could detect an overlap with reflexive modernity literature such as Bauman's model of individualization (2002), namely that the life of the individual is not a thing with a stable origin that extends this stability through time, but is rather something embedded within and swept away by a broader social milieu. We can see this, says Deleuze, in that new sports (surfing, hang-gliding, windsurfing – to which could be added snowboarding, paragliding, parkours, among others) do not revolve around stable origins,

> they take the form of entering into an existing wave. There's no longer an origin as starting point, but a sort of putting-into-orbit. The key thing is how to be taken up in the motion of a big wave, a column of rising air, to 'get into something' instead of being the origin of an effort.
>
> (*N*: 121)[17]

The difference here with Bauman is that for Deleuze there are no originary subjects which choose their own varied, decentred life course, but a literal and primary being swept away. As such the illusion of interiority is dispersed amongst the many ways in which one is taken hold of from the outside, making the 'subject' itself a surfer (or more accurately a being-surfed) of individualizing intensities (*WP*: 71) or what Deleuze and Guattari refer to as 'conceptual personae' (*WP*: 61ff.). As for the construction of a particular human subjectivity, it is memory that makes the difference among animals. It is the capacity to remember, or more accurately to take part in memory, that forms the particular foundation of actualized human beings. It is decidedly not some capacity of reason or autonomous nature. The latter, as shown above, is rendered impossible by Deleuze's dedication to an immanent metaphysics. The former, as will become clear below, is only an effect of the illusion of autonomy.

It is at this point we begin to understand that this subject-as-fold must exist in the virtual (or construct a plane of immanence) as a 'self-referential territory' (Bains 2002: 104).[18] Indeed, self-reference is only possible in the virtual, or put another way, can only be understood as Bergson's duration. In a numerical or actual multiplicity such self-reference is simply not possible, for folded extensive space always implies a metric relation. Infinitely divisible extensive space simply cannot relate to itself in the same way as intensive duration. Such a folded space is not immanent in-itself, but is a result of immanent connections. It is for this reason that Deleuze and Guattari argue for the virtual nature of the brain. The latter is

> *form in itself* that does not refer to any external point of view ... it is an absolute consistent form that surveys *itself* independently of any

supplementary dimension, which does not appeal therefore to any transcendence, which has only a single side whatever the number of its dimensions, which remains copresent to all its determinations without proximity or distance, traverses them at infinite speed, without limit-speed, and which makes of them so many inseparable *variations* on which it confers an equipotentiality without confusion. We have seen that this was the status of the concept as pure event or reality of the virtual.

(*WP*: 210)

Organisms are virtual production machines (again, Leibniz calls this the monad); they actualize the virtual. The brain or (organic) subject is thus the 'faculty of concepts' which creates them as infinitely variable virtual relations. Thus primacy is not given to the Kantian subject in its receptive capacity, but to 'the contractile power of contemplation' that is the organism (Ansell Pearson 1999: 101). It is here that Deleuze's special view of time, as distinct from the numerical multiplicity of Newtonian time, plays a role. This contemplation contracts the virtual relations that ultimately make up the subject (*DR*: 95). Indeed, the notion of the subject is not necessarily bound to human consciousness in so far as all things contemplate through contraction, 'the plant contemplates by contracting the elements from which it originates' (*WP*: 211). Of course plants here have no fully-fledged nervous system, but there is a faculty of 'feeling' that appears in the species, thus eradicating the distinction between thought, concept, life, and death, and evoking the way that species are contained within each other, as noted above. 'Not every organism has a brain, and not all life is organic, but everywhere there are forces that constitute microbrains, or an inorganic life of things' (*WP*: 213). In this way there are two kinds of contraction: on the one hand intensive contraction of the virtual pasts which coexists (first synthesis of habit), and then subject-related contraction which takes each of these levels and actualizes it into a state of affairs or an image of recollection (second synthesis of memory) (*B*: 65; *DR:* 100–1). Humans are both a form of habit and memory, as pointed out in Chapter 2. But again this is not the same as positing an interiority or ego. We are not, as Nietzsche reminds us (1990: 60ff.), the cause of our actions.

In this context it is worthwhile going back to a distinction made in the last chapter, that of between pluralism and multiplicity. The latter term is often used in postmodern renditions of political theory in particular. Most of the time its import is left unexplained, but contextually it seems to be a hyperbolic form of pluralism meaning essentially, a 'very great many' (see Bains 2002: 104). It is hard to know how much of its usage originated in the works of Deleuze, but in any case Deleuze has a very special sense of the term which he borrows from Georg Riemann. The French version (*multiplicité*) has an unfortunately distant connection to the English translations of Riemann, where his original term *Mannigfaltigkeit* is traditionally rendered as 'manifold'. Thus in English the usage of the Deleuzo–Guattarian term – multiplicity – becomes uncomfortably close to multiple-ness, or worse, plurality. However, what Deleuze is pointing to with multiplicity is the non-denumerable set.[19] This is a set – a group of things – but one cannot arrive at the number of elements by counting from one. At first this appears to be a paradox, but recalling the distinction in Chapter 2 between intensity and extensity, non-denumerable sets are things grouped not according to their quantitative and extended coordinates, but by their intensive ordinates. Thus the relationship between elements and entities can be seen as virtual and infinite. Since there are no quantitative expressions here, it only makes sense to speak of Events and processes rather than forms and essences, making a virtual multiplicity a zone of becoming. This somewhat counter-intuitively leads Deleuze to favour the concrete over the abstract, for the concrete is what is linked to the Event and therefore has specificity and haecceity:

> Abstractions explain nothing, they themselves have to be explained: there are no such things as universals, there's nothing transcendent, no Unity, subject (or object), Reason; there are only processes, sometimes unifying, subjectifying, rationalizing, but just processes all the same. These processes are at work in concrete 'multiplicities,' multiplicity is the real element in which things happen. It's multiplicities that fill the field of immanence, rather as tribes fill the desert without it ceasing to be a desert.
>
> (*N*: 145–6)

In the literature dealing with the AGM, most of the time there is little effort to explain in what sense a multiplicity might be significant. Chesters and Welsh, for example, do mention the difference between denumerable and non-denumerable sets in passing (2005: 190), but they do not adequately clarify what this might mean for an analysis of the AGM.[20] But in the vast majority of cases no effort is made to get even that far. One can take, for example, the back cover of *Another World is Possible* (Fisher and Ponniah 2003): 'Its [the global movement for justice and solidarity] power emerges from the multiplicity of activists and organizations that make it up.' A multiplicity of activists and organizations is indeed compelling, but distinguishing between plurality and multiplicity problematizes, hopefully constructively, such assertions. The author of such a text probably refers to a great number (a plurality), when in effect, treating it as a Deleuzian *multiplicity* would be quite profitable – but needs considerable explanation. The problem is that a shifting plurality with its variety of identities and cultural artefacts in fact corresponds perfectly not only to the actual, but ultimately to the form of neoliberal globalization that the AGM claims to combat, as will be explored in further detail below.[21]

Hopefully by this point it is clear why one must heavily associate the notion of becoming with the subject in Deleuze. Subjectivity or the fold of subjectivation has everything to do with the virtual or the plane of immanence which, far from being bounded or static, is, rather, creativeness itself. Deleuze sees political subjectivity 'in terms of new becomings and the creation of new assemblages that emerge within the plane of immanence rather than in obedience to a transcendent ideal' (Schrift 2006: 192). But this does not mean that it is impossible or somehow logically suspect to speak about distinct and even material entities such as people, political actors, groups, or communities. It just precludes references to general essences, either in singular (individual) or specific (group) terms. Again, going back to Delanda, a commitment to entities need not mean a commitment to essences (2006: 132). What we are after here is an analysis of the processes of actualization and counteractualization; in other words, becoming. The political impulse in Deleuze – what he calls becoming-minoritarian – has nothing to do with numbers – in fact it is opposed to the minority and the majority – it has no model, it is a virtuality. Moreover, it is the primary mode of reality, including for human subjects.

> Everybody's caught, one way or another, in a minority becoming that would lead them into unknown paths if they opted to follow it through. When a minority creates models for itself, it's because it wants to become a majority, and probably has to, to survive or prosper (to have a state, be recognized, establish its right, for example)
>
> (N: 173).

This 'opting' is the act of the *Übermensch*, she who can enact the third synthesis of time, or in other words who wills the eternal return.

But we must remember that the process of becoming is not *determined* per se by forces of the outside. What is on offer here is not a bounded subject of becoming under various determined or structured social regimes, as some commentators might be tempted – especially in view of other 'post-structuralist' deployments as will be discussed directly – to insist. As Bains argues, Deleuze and Guattari's (and Foucault's) 'fascination with the creative generation of subjectivity seems to have been ignored in over-emphasizing the deterministic construction of subjectivity and the subject by the symbolic order and power relations.' (2002: 103). Again, in a strong reading of Deleuze the distinction between structure and agency breaks down: they relate to each other on the plane of immanence (that is, virtually) and neither are primary or determined.

Post-Marxism

Chapter 1 pointed out that post-Marxist approaches are better suited to understanding some contemporary political phenomena such as manifestations of the AGM because of the special way in which these approaches tend to view identity, a notion fundamentally based on the subject. Because post-Marxist approaches are the ones which explicitly problematize the subject, it is worth taking a little time to distinguish such approaches from the Deleuzian subject-as-fold proposed here. This is necessary, for their similarities are bound to cause confusion, especially in so far as both approaches generally fall under the rubric of post-structuralism, which too often is treated as a stable field of critique and practice. A look at a recent book by Jason Glynos and David Howarth, *Logics of Critical Explanation in Social and Political Theory* (2007) will serve to illustrate these differences. There are two main differences at the outset, the notion of lack as a source of movement (versus differentiation in Deleuze) and difference as a function of representation (as opposed to Deleuze's difference in itself).

Without going into a full rehearsal of Glynos and Howarth's book, one can state that drawing heavily on Laclau and Mouffe (1985) and Laclau (1990) they present a compelling account of political struggle and social change. In an admittedly crude simplification, ontologically they rely on the distinction between the political and the social, of which the latter is the 'entire regime of practices' (2007: 105) and the former those practices which challenge that regime. These political practices succeed when they become hegemonic – that is, 'link various demands together across a variety of social spaces and sites of struggle' – resulting in 'a new regime and the social practices that comprise it' (2007: 105). Thus the political constitutes 'the way a social practice or regime *was* instituted or *is being* contested or instituted' (2007: 106). The logic of equivalence (see Laclau and Mouffe 1985: 130) is then the drawing up of new frontiers of inclusion and exclusion under some new ideal, while the logic of difference is the maintenance of old frontiers of inclusion and exclusion. In thinking about actual intellectual struggle they distinguish between the ethical (acknowledgement of social reality) and the ideological (the concealment of this reality). As to the question of what drives this political change or struggle they add the fantasmatic dimension. Thus in positing three logics (social, political, and fantasmatic) they address the what, how, and why questions respectively.[22] Such a political ontology is concise, often parsimonious, and ultimately productive in so far that it compartmentalizes the world into very non-ambiguous and therefore workable or operationalizable aspects. The pertinent question for the purpose of this book is by what means these authors – on their own and as representatives of the broader post-Marxist approach – justify such ontological and logical distinctions.

The central assumption in general in post-Marxism is that 'all practices and regimes are discursive entities' (2007: 109).[23] Moreover, 'every subject is a discursive construct or entity' (127). The implications of this for social and political analysis and practice are considerable, and their fullest expression can be found in *Hegemony and Socialist Strategy* (1985). Here Laclau and Mouffe describe how society is not united by necessary laws. Moreover, not only are the relations between elements non-necessary, but the identities of the elements themselves are non-necessary. 'A conception which denies any essentialist approach to social relations, must also state the precarious character of every identity and the impossibility of fixing the sense of the "elements" in any ultimate literality' (1985: 96). Here the broad differences between Laclau and Mouffe and Deleuze come to the fore, for example, in terms of difference, necessity, and society. Both approaches strive for non-essentialist, non-fixed notions of society and subjectivity (individual elements) – and thus to a certain extent can be hesitantly called post-structuralists. However, whereas Laclau and Mouffe affirm the indeterminacy of identity (or the essence of, say, society), necessitating their move to hegemony, Deleuze will instead focus on the becoming of any given element, thereby in a sense being able to determine it (this is why it is a materialism), though this is far from identifying fixed individuals, elements, and subjects. As Deleuze writes, he is interested in haecceity: the hour of the day, the direction of the breeze, etc. (*N*: 26)[24] – in short, specificity. His methodology is mapping the

Subjectivity and political agency   167

lines of flight of these haecceities. This would mirror the distinction Deleuze makes between himself and Foucault, namely, the addition of the virtual–actual dimension to the relative opposition of forms of content and forms of expression, as discussed in Chapter 2. In short, the difference is that rather than shifting elements on a uni-dimensional plane of discursive power relations, Deleuze introduces the virtual. He posits a virtual field of pre-individualizing singularities which opens up considerable possibilities especially in terms of emergence and change, or in other words, dynamism. In Deleuzian terms, the hegemonic struggle with which Laclau and Mouffe and their post-Marxist adherents concern themselves would be at the level of the actual.

The dynamic impulse in post-Marxism comes from the very special treatment of the subject, which, it must be said, is remarkably homogeneous across the spectrum of post-Marxist authors to the point where one could call it *the* defining characteristic. The basis of this approach is found in negative theology or what became solidified in Jacques Lacan as lack. 'The irreducible presence of negativity means that any social edifice suffers from an inherent flaw or crack which may become visible in moments of dislocation' (Glynos and Howarth 2007: 105). Basically when such a crack occurs, a subject can identify itself differently. Thus 'dislocation of social practices can provoke *political practices*.' This is analogous to the line of flight in Deleuze with the big exception that there is nothing negative or lacking about the line of flight. For post-Marxists the inherent crack is the trigger; whereas in Deleuze it is primary – the line of flight is creative and positive. This is particularly interesting in that it suggests in fact that the post-Marxist subject must be more stable than Deleuze's broader notion of subjectivation: it has to be in order to have a crack in the first place.

Thus the central role played by lack generally in the post-Marxist register lies in supplying the impetus for movement within the ontology. Subjects essentially engage in order to overcome their lack, which of course is never fulfilled. 'It is because the master signifier simultaneously promises a meaning, and yet withholds it, that subjects can be politically engaged. They are engaged in a search for identity and a struggle over meaning' (Glynos and Howarth 2007: 131).[25] Because these subjects are characterized by an 'identity which is impossible to suture' they are periodically 'compelled to engage in identification' (129). In Laclau's words, the subject 'is merely the distance between the undecidable structure and the decision' (1990: 31). It is enjoyment that supplements a subject's lack by 'providing an image of fullness, wholeness, or harmony' while at the same time an outside Other (Glynos and Howarth 2007: 130). Deleuze has a similar notion in his usage of desire, but it 'implies no lack; neither is it a natural given. It is an *agencement* of heterogeneous elements that function; it is process as opposed to structure or genesis; it is affect as opposed to sentiment' (*DP*: 189).

Such an account of movement in post-Marxism in general highlights the inherent emphasis on struggle and conflict that is synonymous with political change. As such the metaphysical approach here can only be described – in Deleuze's terms, admittedly – as representational. A definition of opposition – in fact, the whole idea of Other in general – relies on a difference from a standard, even if it is a mobile and non-sutured one. This is difference within the concept as was described in some detail in Chapter 2 of this book. For Deleuze, the impetus for change is always immanent and thereby irreducible to various actual (as opposed to virtual) causes; change always comes from the Event which acts as a quasi-cause. Thus he questions the stages in between regime changes that are immanent, referring to a starting in the middle, that is, understanding changing patterns in their immanence and not the product of some originary cause or push towards some future endstate. The regimes themselves are primarily virtual multiplicities that differenciate into states of affairs

Relying heavily on Gramsci, Glynos and Howarth deploy the distinction between the ethical and the ideological to considerable effect, as noted above. The former (the authentic response) is when the 'radical contingency of social reality and identity can be acknowledged and tarried with'. It is inauthentic (ideological) when it 'can be denied or concealed'. The question then becomes: 'To what extent do subjects engage authentically with the radical contingency of social relations (where the ethical dimension is foregrounded), or to what extent are they complicit in concealing it (where the ideological dimension is foregrounded)?' (2007: 111). One legitimate question, however, must be, how do we know whether any given engagement or struggle is ethical or ideological? How can we possibly know? Who decides? In Deleuze's terminology the ethical would be the philosophical: the identification of the immanent and the creation of concepts. The ideological would only entail engaging the actual – 'science' as defined in *What is Philosophy?* One could of course put the same question to Deleuze, that is, how do we know when a deterritorialization is absolute? But as far as the subject is concerned, in Deleuze's case such a question has more to do with the eternal return. The ethical is the one who wills the eternal return as will be discussed below, *not* the one who engages with radical contingency. In *Hegemony*, for example, there is no way of identifying *in the moment* (or perhaps ever) whether one's struggle is ideological or ethical. In Deleuze the ethical moment is never one of struggle, it is not a matter of landing on new forms of exclusion and inclusion.

In the context of this chapter one can read in post-Marxists a stronger commitment to a modernist form of subjectivity than can be found in Deleuze. Although in general they are purveyors of contingency and often prefix various notions with 'radical', they are nonetheless committed to essentially modernist political categories such as democracy and power in what can be seen as an extension of the basic tenets of the French Revolution – liberty, equality, and community. It is for this reason that their critics accuse them of being reformists at heart, interested more with seizing (state) power in their strive for inclusiveness than engendering a new system altogether (see for example Day 2004: 727). Politics for post-Marxists in this light is a relatively narrowly defined, closed affair determined by a kind of hegemonic critical mass. All of this relies on a subject that must be interested in its own welfare in terms of these modernist ideals. Sentences such as 'dislocations are those occasions when a subject is called upon to confront the contingency of social relations more directly than at other times'

(Glynos and Howarth 2007: 110) presume not only the conflictual nature of society in general, but also a kernel of subjectivity, in other words, a transcendent element. It is a thing standing outside or distinct from social relations. There is nothing wrong with this, of course – post-structuralist theory is not a competition to see who can devise the least transcendent notion of subjectivity. But from the perspective of an immanent philosophy such as Deleuze's, it is difficult to see what justification there is for such a move, and furthermore it is, especially given the conflictual nature of their political ontology, a small step to affirming if not a rational then at least a subject capable of the (rational) selection of different options, in other words, the bounded, rational subject of modern theory. Of course for many it may be difficult to imagine how notions of struggle or conflict could exist without the kind of numerical, quantitative coordinates (of a subject, of a moral being) that Deleuze associates with the actual; in other words without fixed units within what could broadly be defined as a Euclidean/Cartesian space – even if characterized by lack. This indeed possibly explains the appeal of post-Marxist theory. In any case this is not the place for a sustained critique of post-Marxism through a Deleuzian deployment; it is only important to note the difference between two 'camps' that all too often are lumped together as 'post-structuralist', and in the present case to illustrate to a greater extent what is at stake with the Deleuzian nature of the subject as presented in this book.

Deleuze and consequences

We can summarize the above discussion of the subject in Deleuze by saying that an individual is the point of perception between the enveloping and enveloped that was described in Chapter 2. Everything contains the world, but the individual is a point of perception that only expresses a particular segment of the world. Of course the question of prime importance is, what does this do for the present study of world politics and the case of the AGM? And furthermore, what is the horizon of action for such a political subject? What can it do? What ought it to do?

The implications of Deleuze's treatment of subjectivity are part of what is known as the death of the subject, or 'the end of the autonomous bourgeois monad or ego or individual' (Jameson 1991: 15). Of course such a formation of subjectivity has enormous consequences for humanism in the broadest terms, which explains, in part at least, what is sometimes referred to as the recent reversion to pre-modern formulations of subjectivity – namely, non-humanist ones. The evidence for this death of the subject is found in, for example, the postmodern figure of the character in the novel or cinema. 'Drained of its distinctive substance, character returns as a ghost – a mannered replication of the pre-modern allegorical form left behind in the Renaissance' (Heller and Wellbery 1986: 4). Such characters lack the quality of a grounded centre from which their actions are (rationally) chosen, instead consisting of a criss-cross or patchwork of personalities and influences. Of course if we get rid of the subject – if, in fact, we get rid of humans – then humanism, and the project of modernity in general, becomes a rather moot point. What this describes, in effect, is the end of *homo sapiens*, the end of human beings as thinking subjects, 'the disappearance of human discourse (*Logos*) in the strict sense' (Pefanis 1991: 2).

We can temper this immediately by saying that although this implies the end of *homo sapiens* and the end of human history in the narrow Hegelian sense of the word, it need not entail the end of freedom as a concept – indeed, perhaps it offers a way towards a different notion of freedom altogether. Additionally such a position does not necessary involve the rejection of values per se. In fact, Deleuze argues explicitly and extensively for the contrary in *Nietzsche and Philosophy*. The point is to create new, as-of-yet unheard of values rather than struggling for a certain set of values which modernity has proposed such as autonomy, justice, and truth. Deleuze notes, echoing Nietzsche (echoing Spinoza) that we do not know what the individual is capable of (*NP*: 36).

In dealing with the significance of the preceding analysis, an important distinction to maintain here lies between subjectivity and identity. For most theorists, the latter is a predicate of the former, that is, the subject is the bearer of an identity, or identity is found in a subject. In this sense the subject or subjectivity in general is logically prior to identity. Different approaches to the political actor illustrate the relationship between the two (see Table 4.1 below). In very broad terms, most sociological and political approaches adopt the rational actor model of subjectivity and identity wherein the subject is an autonomous agent capable of rational choice based on self-benefit. This is the quintessential modernist perspective and includes (with caveats, of course, which will not be addressed here) both liberalism and Marxism and their sub-variants such as neoliberalism and socialism. Curiously, identity here is usually understood as given and rather static at best, and at worst ignored as irrelevant and underproblematized. The unfortunate consequence is the conclusion that divested of all social embedding and identity, rational minds will all choose the same benefits; that humans are, in essence, the same.

Reflexive modernity literature tends towards a slightly more restricted notion of the subject in that although the latter possesses autonomy, it is nevertheless more beholden to its environment from which it chooses its identity. Post-Marxists, again to generalize, view the subject as fractured, incomplete, and above all characterized by lack as described above. Here identity is never given but is contingent and largely imposed by external powers such as the family, society, and state. It is worth remembering that insofar as this rendition is not a purely immanent one, it has the character of the transcendent to some degree. In

Table 4.1 Subject and identity

	Subject	*Identity*
Rational actor	autonomous	given
Reflexive modernity	bounded	*homo optionis*
Post-Marxist	fractured	contingent, imposed
Deleuze	folded exterior	actualized

other words, even though the subject is fractured, there still must be an 'it' in the first place, and this is the kernel of the sovereign self, as previously discussed. In Deleuze, by contrast, identity is the effect of virtual Events as actualizations. More specifically, they are very much real, indeed they have a material and not merely discursive basis. However, as ontological effects – Deleuze sometimes likens these to sound or visual effects – they are the very antithesis of given, and yet without an underlying subject they are also far from selected or chosen. The cause – or rather quasi-cause – of them is the differentiation of virtual series determined by speeds and slowness.

This is another way of saying that identity is not fixed or essential. And those keen to hold onto the notion of primacy of culture (being, belonging, identity) will find little of value in Deleuze's model of folded multiplicities actualized through individuation. Indeed, Deleuze's 'subject' is inimical to the research agendas of some feminist and post-colonialist interventions (see for example Wuthnow 2002: 192–4) that remain hostile to any theory that appears to dismiss sentiments of location, experience, and belonging. Thus in terms of AGM participants, one might reasonably be sceptical of a theory that rejects the primacy of a peasant's connection (and desire for stewardship) of the land, or the protection of indigenous rights in the post-colonial word. But there is a big difference between recognizing the actualized or secondary nature of identity and dismissing it altogether. A more nuanced reading of Deleuze would simply call for the recognition that no identity is a fixed, closed system; that all cultures, societies, experiences, and sentiments of location are complex and in constant motion. The political significance of such a recognition might ultimately be a source of political strength and stability for groups that struggle to cope with their environments and redefine their futures. As Appadurai reminds us

> [m]uch that has been considered local knowledge is actually knowledge of how to produce and reproduce locality under conditions of anxiety and entropy, social wear and flux, ecological uncertainty and cosmic volatility, and the always present quirkiness of kinsmen, enemies, spirits, and quarks of all sorts.
>
> (1996b: 191)

In any case, such a version of identity in fact accounts for the 'merging rivulets' of the AGM itself quite nicely, as culturally and geographically disparate groups acknowledge the commonalities of their becoming. Furthermore there are advantages to an approach which successfully locates the individual in what is more commonly called its contingency but is probably closer to what Heidegger called *Geworfenheit* or 'thrown-ness' (1962: 174). Jettisoning the despotic signifier of given or essential communities reveals a truly free relation between the individual and its environment. Recognizing identity as the result of 'deeper physical properties, and not as fundamental categories on which to base an ontology' (Delanda 2002: 42) defuses an all-too common basis for aggression. As Patomäki notes,

The preparedness to use violence is typically based on the necessitarian assumption about the unchangeable essence of both oneself and the others (perhaps seen as enemies). In Manichean understandings, evil must be eliminated. Violent threats and sanctions presuppose something similar. Only simple and unchangeable – essentially atom-like – beings can be treated unproblematically in utilitarian terms by teaching them lessons of obedience by means of sanctions and painful experiences.

(2003: 366)

Another important consequence of Deleuze's rendition of the subject concerns human free will. Is free will possible with such a folded subjectivity? The answer to this question depends on what freedom actually is. Predictably perhaps, the argument turns back to the humanistic principles that were philosophically, psychologically, and finally sociologically solidified during the European Enlightenment, namely the autonomy of the subject and its ability and moreover its sovereign nature to command itself in the form of decision making. Such a principle of free choice had already become one of the basic theo-ontological principles of Christianity. Human beings' freedom to choose good over evil explained their relationship with God and also why there must be evil in the world. Without over-emphasizing a causal link, such personal freedom became inherent in the socio-political thought of Locke, Rousseau, and Smith, forming the basis of Western notions of government and democracy. During the twentieth century and possibly even more so in the twenty-first, human freedom of the sovereign, rational individual variety is almost an unassailable principle of political theory. Not only has it since the mid-1990s served – inconsistently, it must be stressed – as the justification of interstate aggression and to propagate human rights worldwide, but it turns up in almost comedic proportions in popular representations of cultures other than the Western cosmopolitan one. If one were to believe media accounts and a great deal of academic analysis, it seems that the motivation of all people everywhere from Columbia to Iraq to China has been the attainment and maintenance of this principle of freedom, to the point of obscuring other motivations such as subsistence, peace, social justice, and effective governance.

In the face of this many agree that such a concept of freedom is not a universal given and was only discovered and subsequently propagated in the modern era. Actually it is a rather heterogeneous notion that developed over time and has always been far from evenly distributed, even in regions influenced by modern, liberal thought. Despite these counterclaims, the justification of freedom all too easily becomes an end in itself in political theory, necessitating ever more baroque philosophies. Frederick Turner (writing within the perspective of a Western cultural experience) puts it thus:

Freedom felt so simple and homogeneous a thing to us that we could not but ascribe to it an uncomposite, unique, indescribable, and irreducible essence, and thus we were persuaded to construct systems of metaphysics to house it and position it within the world: hence centuries of mind-body problems, and tortured issues of reference and ethical philosophy.

(1997: xvi)

However, this unassailable assumption regarding human freedom was and continues to be a problem for both philosophy and the social sciences. According to Whitehead, it posits a blatant contradiction between a mechanistic, scientific realism on the one hand and 'the unwavering belief in the world of men and of the higher animals as being composed of self-determining organisms' on the other. He continues: 'This radical inconsistency at the basis of modern thought accounts for much that is half-hearted and wavering in our civilisation. ... It enfeebles it, by reason of the inconsistency lurking in the background.' Unlike the Scholastics who strove for harmony of understanding,

> We [of the modern era] are content with superficial orderings from diverse arbitrary starting points. For instance, the enterprises produced by the individualistic energy of the European peoples presupposes physical actions directed to final causes. But the science which is employed in their development is based on a philosophy which asserts that physical causation is supreme, and which disjoins the physical cause from the final end.
>
> (1925: 76)

Whitehead notes that it is not popular to dwell on this point. This contradiction at the very foundation of social science continues to this day in the structure–agency debate[26] and its most promising solutions, structuration theory (Giddens 1984) and constructivism.[27] From the perspective of the present analysis, these solutions, as if with two oppositely charged magnets, force two incompatible views of the world together: a natural one of systems and structures, and the extra-natural one of human (and, problematically, animals to various degrees as well) autonomy. Again, in the absence of any proof or a priori principle, the impetus of such an effort can only rest on this unwavering and in effect cultural–ideological belief in the essential freedom of humans.

At this point we once again see the application of complexity theory that in fact proposes an immanent account of reality in its entirety, that is, without the problem of the transcendent subject colliding with what is essentially a deterministic, clockwork universe. The first step in such an approach is to problematize the very notion of freedom – 'if the apparent simplicity of freedom is the "operating system" of a highly complex, but common, phenomenon of turbulent self-organizing feedback, many of the old problems simply go away' (Turner 1997: xvi). Problematizing freedom and denying the essential way that it is natural to humans, however, demands another explanation. 'Freedom implies discoverable meaning in an act – indeed, it distinguishes an act from an event. A free act is one that may be unpredictable but that, after it has occurred, is retrodictable in that it "makes sense."' Predictable events are symmetrical with regards to past and future whereas free events or acts are not. In other words, 'What can be known about them before they happen is fundamentally different from what can be shown about them afterward' (1997: xiv). A corollary of this, which some might find unpalatable, is that it precludes meaning in the traditional sense. Indeed, thinkers like Deleuze and Foucault can be seen as dismantling hermeneutics altogether. Since there is no bounded, autonomous subject, there can be no meaning per se, that is, in the sense in which it is normally referred. Again, what humans experience as meaning is the retroactive effect of a surveying memory. This is reflected in practical life on a number of levels. As mentioned in the last chapter, the Deleuzian notion of the singularity of Events – how they are not dependent on actors, conscious or otherwise – can be felt in the notion of risk society and chance in the form, for example, of life pathway success as a function of being at the right place at the right time. This very 'weak' version of freedom brings us to the notion of ethics in Deleuze. The main question for the purposes of this book is, ultimately, when pushed, does Deleuze's philosophy of the subject commit us to an anti-humanist taxonomy of social organization devoid of any normative concerns, only interested in explanation and prediction?

The clearest ethical position in Deleuze is the Nietzschean one[28] found in the figure of the eternal return. Deleuze attacks any use of the eternal return as a blank repetition or circular motion, as well as any suggestion of continuance or monotony. In fact, eternal return implies the opposite. Eternal return is 'the reproduction of diversity as such, of the repetition of difference' (*NP*: 43). This is the complex repetition of the virtual as opposed to the material repetition of the actual (*DR*: 106). The eternal return is 'the expression of a principle which serves as an explanation of diversity and its reproduction, of difference and its repetition' (*NP*: 45). This principle is the will to power, an active state or a becoming-active and for Deleuze as for Nietzsche it is only such activity that really returns (*NP*: 66). Reactive forces, *ressentiment*, and bad conscience do not return, that is, they do not advance, change, vary, or grow – they do not pass to the next level, whatever that may be. The ethic distilled from the eternal return amounts to this: '*whatever you will, will it in such a way that you also will its eternal return*' (*NP*: 63). This is not an ethic of producing judgement by synthesizing an array of true propositions, but of determining good values from bad values. As Nietzsche says, going beyond good and evil does not mean going beyond good and bad (1989: 55). The good here, or what has value, is the position which best embodies the Event. Deleuze and Guattari characterize the dignity of the Event as the *amor fati* of philosophy, of 'being equal to the event, or becoming the offspring of one's own events' (*WP*: 159). Or as Deleuze writes in the *Logic of Sense*,

> To the extent that events are actualized in us, they wait for us and invite us in. They signal us: 'My wound existed before me, I was born to embody it.' It is a question of attaining this will that the event creates in us; of becoming the quasi-cause of what is produced within us, the Operator.

In short, 'Either ethics makes no sense at all, or this is what it means and has nothing else to say: not to be unworthy of what happens to us' (169).

Of course this is little source of guidance to someone facing a moral dilemma or an ethical crisis – or, of particular relevance for this book, those promoting global social justice. But with Deleuze's emphasis on the will to power as capacity, in a practical sense an individual will carries out what is in her power to do. Ultimately from such a perspective there can be no universal moral standard by which to justify any action. And this cannot be stressed enough: those who would feel uncomfortable with the adoption of such a position cannot deploy Deleuze to any consistent degree. His principles, as has been shown at some length over the last two chapters, are the necessary conclusion drawn from his ontology and metaphysics. However, this need not be inconsistent with political struggle; it is not a position of ambivalence. As Foucault once said, invoking Spinoza, the proletariat wage war against the ruling class not because it believes itself to be just, it does so because it wants to take power. 'And because it will overthrow the power of the ruling class it considers such a war to be just' (1997: 136). The point is that if one truly rejects, as Deleuze does, appeals to the transcendent principles of European modernity such as justice grounded in a freedom based on the autonomous subject, one cannot simultaneously justify one's position (on, for example, social justice) on the basis of such principles. In a truly immanent philosophy it is impossible to justify actions in the name of something else such as right, truth, or justice. Actions can only have immanent causes and rules of evaluation.

In order to clear up any confusion, it is important to emphasize that the ethical question in Deleuze's philosophy is not a matter of *choosing* to become minoritarian – as if one was stratified or captured, but managed via some internal movement to become minoritarian. It is not a matter of the individual selecting an Other to become, or some kind of conscious identity slippage. It is rather the recognition that becoming minoritarian is the basic state of being human. The Übermensch in Nietzsche is the one who is capable of allowing herself to be open to the external forces; of letting herself be chosen. The ethical challenge is to reject any sort of neo-Platonist ontology or any Kantian moral order.

In terms of morality, Deleuze is, not surprisingly, highly critical of any kind of moral code (*NP*: 91) or of any legal code founded on transcendent principles such as natural rights. In fact, in Deleuze ethical determination is opposed to moral judgement (see Schrift 2006: 188). For this reason he tends to be more interested in questions of jurisprudence than questions of law. However, writers such as Villani must be wary of placing too high expectations on the power of jurisprudence as a method of resolving conflicts in their specificity or 'case after case' (2006: 206), though Villani is correct to call Deleuze a pragmatist. After all, Deleuze, especially when one moves away from the more peripheral works (*Dialogues, Negotiations*) to the core texts, is rather silent on the question of jurisprudence or more specifically, by what means one should approach conflict and legality. Although it is safe to say that Deleuze sees society as the reflection of interests rather than their protector (*ES*: 43–6), his fascination with common law, for example, reflects the intellectual frustration with approaches to morality and values in France in the 1960s. As we will discuss below, Anglo-American thought, literature, pragmatism, and law, which Deleuze sometimes cites as truly forward looking, turned out to be just as susceptible to apparatuses of capture (that is, reterritorializations) as 1960s French middle-class conservatism.

In terms of the AGM, from this discussion we can conclude that challenging globalization on the grounds of human rights or individual liberty is problematic in several senses. First, the principles of autonomy and individuality which serve as the fabric for such rights are precisely those which reinforce power structures that perpetuate inequality and asymmetrical relations, such as the status quo liberal values of economic liberty and property. To take but one example, the United Nations Declaration of Human Rights secures, after all, property rights in article 17 (United Nations 1948) and is a document inherently Western in fabric, ignoring so-called second and third generation rights. The second problem, as mentioned in Chapter 1, is that human rights become a matter of enforcement. The point to be made here does not merit a long discussion, but we can say that the inconstancies in the application of the principle of human rights as defined by the UN Charter or the Stockholm Declaration, for example, underline the problems with a system based on modernist principles of subjectivity and legality. This in turn highlights, third, the largest problem of human rights in the context of this book, namely that of the state of exception. As Agamben so persuasively argues, if human rights is accepted as a universal principle, then power finds expression in the exception (1998: 126–35). In other words, asymmetrical power relations become articulated through exclusion and definition. Such forms of exclusion form the ideological basis for genocides, renditions, and extra-territoriality,[29] and in general actions which otherwise would be called human rights violations. According to Agamben, this 'state of exception' has become a 'paradigm of government' (Agamben and Raulff 2004: 609). For these reasons the association of Deleuze as presented in this book with struggles for any liberal version of global social justice is problematic at best and very probably completely inconsistent.

In this and only this sense we have to say that Deleuze is, as Badiou and Žižek argue, a quintessentially elitist and ascetic philosopher. If we wish to use his theories to their full measure and effectiveness to understand world politics and phenomena such as the AGM it is necessary to commit to their principles in full. In this case it makes sense to separate Deleuze the individual who in writings and various other media has expressed his personal views on political issues from Deleuze's exacting philosophy. Confusing Deleuze's politics and his philosophy risks overlooking the latter with the result of undermining the value of the former. Take, for example, Deleuze and Guattari writing that the problem of democratic states is that such a 'society of friends' nonetheless tolerates shanty towns and will always give the order to fire when the poor come out of them (*WP*: 107). This should be read less as a normative challenge than as a critique of a Western liberalism that cannot live up to its own standards of human rights. Their point here is not that poverty is bad, but that modern foundationalist thinking – here played by Habermas – has never and cannot live up to its own principles. Their anti-capitalism stance should also be read in a similar way: It is not capitalism's destructive force per se that is reprehensible, but its power as an axiomatic to de- and re-territorialize flows. In this way it is possible to preserve a consistency between the two Deleuzes: one concerned that capitalism leaves three-quarters of the world's population in 'extreme poverty' (*N*: 179) for whom philosophy is about exploring the shame of being human *(NP*: 99), and the other who notes the 'suicidal' nature of lines of flight (*ATP*: 503) and urges us to be worthy of what happens to us.

Globalization/alter-globalization

Given Deleuze's notion of the subject-as-fold and the consequences this poses for thinking about agency and ethics, the next step to a comprehensive and consistent approach to world politics is to describe political action in general and processes of globalization and alter-globalization in particular. More specifically, how are we to understand this challenge to theory, the AGM? In a broad sense, the AGM stands in opposition to neoliberalism, for which David Harvey offers the following definition:

> Neoliberalism is a theory of political economic practices proposing that human well-being can best be advanced by the maximization of entrepreneurial freedoms within an institutional framework characterized by private property rights, individual liberty, unencumbered markets, and free trade. The role of the state is to create and preserve an institutional framework appropriate to such practices.
>
> (2007: 22)

There is little need here to survey the literature on what activists and academics find problematic and reprehensible in neoliberalism. The point of concern is to locate world politics and the AGM within the above assessment of world order. In order to so some time must be spent analysing how neoliberalism fits into Deleuze's political metaphysics as presented in this book. Although Deleuze and Guattari naturally never use the world neoliberalism, it is clear from *A Thousand Plateaus* with its treatment of capital accumulation, finance, and the individual and societal effects of these, that neoliberalism is a form or a (heightened) stage of capitalism. This is immediately significant because, in a Foucauldian way they will therefore not talk about ideology. Indeed, from the above discussion there simply is no self to be subject to ideology. Again, to distinguish Deleuze from post-Marxists, and contrary to much rhetoric on the subject, from a Deleuzian perspective there can be no neoliberal ideology.[30]

Capitalism for Deleuze and Guattari – drawing here explicitly on Marx (*N*: 171) – is a system that constantly adjusts its frontiers seeking ever-new means of profit. This is not accidental, but the fundamental characteristic of the system itself. In understanding this, they distinguish between an axiomatic and a code.

An axiomatic directly relates purely functional elements of an unspecified nature and can be immediately realized in various domains of the system itself, in this case the world. An axiomatic is thus not a thing but a description of relations. A code, on the other hand, is always relative to a specific domain and describes definite relations between specified elements (*ATP*: 454). In other words codes operate wherever there is specific reference to qualified things. 'Capitalism is the only social machine that is constructed on the basis of decoded flows, substituting for intrinsic codes an axiomatic of abstract quantities in the form of money' (*AO*: 139). Thus capitalism for Deleuze and Guattari is an immanent system that is 'constantly overcoming its own limitations, and then coming up against them once more in a broader form, because its fundamental limit is capitalism itself' (*N*: 171). They base this on the principles of the falling rate of profit (*ATP*: 463) by which capital demands ever-new frontiers to be opened for exploitation, frontiers that today include intellectual property, government-run social services such as public transportation, health care, and education, and the production and reproduction of culture in general. This implies that any temporary receding of capitalism's boundaries will be compensated in other ways (to compensate for the problem of diminishing profits) and is in all likelihood to be reabsorbed into the system at a later time. Likewise incremental reform of the system is impossible – it is an immanent system that has no parts to reform – it cannot be divided without changing its nature. To choose a more directly economic example one could point to tightened financial regulations in US trading in the 1990s which were only to be undermined as new loopholes to these regulations were exploited, and then eventually to be in essence supported by the US Federal Reserve from 1998 onward (Brenner 2002: 268). Following this argument a politics of concession towards neoliberalism, for example, is deeply flawed in principle. The implications of this analysis is that no amount of reform, regulation, or 'good capitalism' will rectify the destructive aspects of capitalism when understood as an immanent system.

A Deleuzian approach to globalization must not just be anti-capitalist in the sense of being against post-industrial capitalism or 'bad' capitalism, but must seek to circumnavigate, destroy, disrupt, or flee from capitalism itself. This exposes the problematic nature of elements of the AGM arguing for 'good' capitalism, which by and large amount to mainstream liberal arguments that ultimately rest on Keynesian economics: a call for market economies tempered by socially responsive political systems. Likewise from this perspective the problem with the condemnation of the international economic regime such as trade agreements and structural adjustment programmes is that they do not confront the nature of capitalism itself. Thus the policies are not the problem but rather the system itself. As Samir Amin argues, 'The policies are accused of fostering poverty, as if the logic of the system had nothing to do with it. Poverty is thus seen as the product of "errors" which could be "corrected"' (2000: 13).

One of the secondary effects of neoliberalism – but perhaps much overlooked and suggestive of further research – is the focus on the individual as the core of social, political, and perhaps especially economic engagement in the form of consumerism, free-market competition, democracy, and civil society. The individual, write Beck and Beck-Gernsheim, 'is becoming the basic unit of social reproduction for the first time in history' (2002: xii). Besides the argument from many participants of the AGM that placing so much emphasis on the individual destroys the very social fabric that has kept families, communities, and nations together for centuries, such a process of individualization is particularly insidious when viewed as a sort of discursive colonialism. Heller and Wellbery compare the discursive segregation between the culturally determined native social orders which were being administered as colonies in the previous centuries, and the worldwide promotion of the autonomous individuals of the global centre's or global North's metropolises today. Such promotion

> imagined the natural evolution of a full, free adult subject from a child in need of administration. In a like manner, the development of societies from the pre-modern to the contemporary would transfigure those describable as objective cultural orders to those composed by the agreement of autonomous individuals.
>
> (1986: 8)

Of course from the above analysis of the subject in Deleuze this cannot mean an intensification of the role of the autonomous agent in a global society, but rather reflects the sense in which relations between individuals are increasingly abstracted. In other words this sense of increasing choice is an illusion – indeed, it has to be. What is at play here is the effect of relations that are no longer founded on codes such as family, culture, identity, and traditional roles, and in this way the individual comes into unmediated contact with the global axiomatic of capitalism, and thus the process of neoliberalism or late capitalism actually instils the concept of the bounded subject that serves to reinforce the system itself. As Žižek writes,

> We are here at the very nerve-centre of liberal ideology: freedom of choice, grounded in the notion of the 'psychological' subject, endowed with propensities which he or she strives to realize. And this especially holds today, in the era of a 'risk society' in which the ruling ideology endeavours to sell us the very insecurities caused by the dismantling of the welfare state as the opportunity for new freedoms.
>
> (2005: 18)

Thus the unparalleled emphasis (in politics, ethics, law, international relations) on the bounded, essential subject becomes the sine qua non of contemporary social, economic, and political relations themselves. Nevertheless, from the perspective of the Deleuzian political metaphysics and treatment of the subject, this must be understood as an unintended consequence. The promotion of the subject as the basis for social, political, and especially economic and legal relations is not the work of a cabal of malevolent geniuses or global elites as some might argue (see for example Saul 2005: 46), but rather the unfolding, among other things, of the capitalism axiomatic and liberal democracy. In a case of global serendipity, the triad of capitalism, liberal democracy, and the essential subject actualize themselves in a reinforcing system or stratification which is highly flexible and extremely accommodating.

On this last point it is interesting how strands of alter-globalizations react to neoliberalism's double imperative on the one hand to circulate identities and on the other hand to define the individual. We have to be clear here: neoliberalism is pro-identity, pro-minority. It has come to embrace diversity as part of the logic of its ever-expanding system of inclusiveness. It not only tolerates but actually needs a variety of identities, provided they circulate in the axiomatic as abstract quantities. The problem from the perspective of platforms of resistance is the commodification of these identities. For example, in many Western countries one witnesses the move from homophobia to the tolerance of 'homosexual activity' (the so-called 'don't ask don't tell approach') to 'Queer Eye for the Straight Guy'. The latter, a television programme aired by the National Broadcasting Corporation in the US and other countries, is but one example of an identity (a minority one) being repackaged to sell as a lifestyle-as-commodity in the name of inclusiveness and diversity. Similar examples of identity circulating as abstract quantities of consumption are literally countless, from Ché Guevara T-shirts, to 'alternative rock' becoming a music genre, to threadbare and faded nostalgic patches on clothing commemorating communities that never existed and events that never took place. This extreme form of distance or pure simulacra is what Baudrillard refers to when he writes that ethnology, free from its object, is 'no longer circumscribed as an objective science' but comes to be applied to everything, like a fourth dimension (1983b: 16). Consequently, adhering closely to the Deleuzian approach to world politics presented here would involve reformulating any alter-globalization challenge framed in terms of individual freedom and civil society. Ironically, most groups push for more individual autonomy from the forces of globalization – they want neoliberal globalization out of their lives – but this ignores the problem of recirculation which is precisely what makes globalization a 'postmodern' process. As Hardt and Negri put it, even postmodern and post-structuralist thinkers, focused as they are on attacking modern forms of authority and control, have been outflanked: 'Power has evacuated the bastion they are attacking and has circled around to their rear to join them in the assault in the name of difference' (2000: 138).[31] Thus somewhat paradoxically and certainly counter-intuitively, the challenge from the AGM following the present analysis should be the call for *less* autonomy, less individuality, less freedom framed from a liberal perspective. In other words the goal must be to develop a subjectless subjectivity free from the illusion of the stable, static, sovereign self.

Another common means of redress against neoliberalism is sought in a rights discourse. But today, if there is a renewed emphasis on natural rights it is because the economic and cultural environment put these rights gravely at risk in the first place. As Gray argues (1995: 45–6), natural rights depend on a teleologically based order such as the will of God for Locke or the propensity for perfection in Aristotle. In a reformulation of Nietzsche's 'God is dead', the problem with any political order today is that the modern scientific world view has expelled all accounts of teleology. The Enlightenment project was founded on natural rights – but these were eventually dismantled by the scientific (in the broadest sense) models that shaped the contemporary Western world view. This seems to outline the ironic limit of modernism where its logically inevitable consequences undermine the very foundations upon which it rested. But Gray argues that this has not been understood. 'The intellectual foundations of the Enlightenment project have fallen away; but liberal theory, for the most part, proceeds as if nothing has happened' (1995: 85). The hope of resolving the problem of liberalism

> by refounding morality on a universal compelling basis of reason, which animated Hobbes's project of a moral geometry, his individualist philosophical anthropology and the conception of rational choice as the generator of political order which these Enlightenment beliefs supported, has faded irrecoverably.
>
> (1995: 86)[32]

The problem with liberalism today is that it cannot have it both ways: having undermined natural (moral) foundations (in order to prosper economically), liberals cannot now turn to those foundations (as in natural rights) in an attempt to mitigate the problems of globalization. From Deleuze's perspective, a rights discourse actually detracts from the human emancipation found in lines of flight and the eternal return.

> These days [1985] it's the rights of man that provide our eternal values. It's the constitutional state and other notions everyone recognizes as very abstract. And it's in the name of all this that thinking's fettered, that any analysis in terms of movements is blocked. But if we're so oppressed, it's because our movement's being restricted, not because our eternal values are being violated.
>
> (N: 122)

From this standpoint the strategic task for Deleuze consists not in the challenge – hegemonic or otherwise – to the status quo or the powers that be, but a sensitivity to the reworking of immanent relationships that permeate the social horizon and effect new subjectivations (and not subjectivities). Politically this involves recognizing the forms of content and forms of expression that are actualized today: 'What is our light and what is our language, that is to say, or "truth" today? What powers must we confront, and what is our capacity for resistance?' (F: 95). And crucially the task of the individual is to understand her own role in subjectivation and to capitalize on the inherent opportunities for becoming therein:

And do we not perhaps above all bear witness to and participate in the 'production of a new subjectivity'? Do not the changes in capitalism find an unexpected 'encounter' in the slow emergence of a new Self as a centre of resistance? Each time there is social change, is there not a movement of subjective conversion, with its ambiguities but also its potential? These questions may be considered more important than a reference to man's universal rights, including the realm of pure law.

(*F*: 95)

To put it into the language of the foregoing analysis, resistance to power is a matter of willing the eternal return in the form of being open and ready for the new possibilities brought about by deterritorialization. Power is actualized and circulates in the stratifications, but the virtual is primary. Now surely this is not a recipe for immediate political success; it does not ensure the putative practical goals of something called the AGM. But what it does suggest is a resistance towards any kind of subjectivation that reinforces representational thought through an adherence to elements actualized in states of affairs. It cautions against replacing one hierarchical, dogmatic regime with another, however seemingly just, worthy, or benign. It is not a matter of choosing a good kind of capitalism over a bad kind of capitalism, for both are inferior in value insofar as they reterritorialize. But – and this is the crucial thing to take away from Deleuze's philosophy – it is not only the human misery that results from this reterritorialization that is reprehensible, but the very process itself is of a lesser value in its restrictiveness. Likewise with stratified regimes. For Deleuze it is never a matter of deciding which regime is better (disciplinary or control societies, the institutionalized restrictions of the Chinese State or the *Denkverbot*[33] of European ones) because they are both at once liberating and enslaving (*N*: 178). The main point here for Deleuze is that political resistance will never take the same form; there is no model of alter-globalization. In terms of the individual, Alan Schrift draws Deleuze closer to Foucault when considering what a subject is to do (2000: 157). If the subject-as-fold is always actualized or territorialized in stratifications of power – if an individual's line of flight is always relative – then the individual goal must be to attain self-government[34] and minimize the domination of power forms. Lest willing the eternal return be understood as defeatist and nihilistic, it must be stressed that this self-government is precisely the opposite of quietly accepting oppression.

In the strongest reading of Deleuze as proposed here, active resistance to neoliberalism in terms of countering points of contact with an opposite force is not possible and moreover illusory, for the subject-as-fold is not capable of such active participation. Such a subject can only participate in the eternal return and 'direct' her will accordingly. In a somewhat softer reading that treats the illusion of free will as nevertheless a political operative, calls for more autonomy and freedom would be paradoxically counterproductive. Again, the problem with neoliberal globalization is not that rights are being infringed upon, but rather that movement is being restricted. What this calls for is not a push for better

Subjectivity and political agency

governance, still less activities aimed at mitigating the negative effects of neo-liberalism, but rather a flight from the axiomatic of capital itself. This would certainly involve a micro-politics of immanent engagement (line of flight, eternal return) in the form of non-hierarchical, non-identitarian, and anti-power political practices. This is precisely the strongly *alter* aspect of the AGM that was addressed in Chapter 1 found in social experiments such as social centres or networks like Reclaim the Streets. From the reading of Deleuze given here, the value of any given political practice is the extent that it corresponds most to its virtual pole. Thus true transformation of political, social, and economic relations do not come about, according to Deleuze, through the discovery of a new identity, global or otherwise, nor through a new structure of power embedded in institutional arrangements. True revolution comes only through the circumvention of the power structure of the actual. Here Deleuze and Guattari distinguish between 'the majoritarian as a constant and homogeneous system; minorities as subsystems; and the minoritarian as a potential, creative and created, becoming' (*ATP*: 105–6). This last has the most value, but minorities are superior to majorities in that it is here where the seeds of becoming minoritarian can be found – what Nick Thoburn calls 'cramped space' (see 2003: 18ff.). Thus the minorities of the world who are excluded from the benefits of globalization must not try to become a majority (seize power, become the model) but rather

> bring to bear the force of the non-denumerable set. The issue is not at all anarchy versus organisation, nor even centralism versus decentralization, but a calculus or conception of the problems of nondenumerable sets, against the axiomatic of denumerable sets. Such a calculus may have its own compositions, organizations, even centralizations; nevertheless, it proceeds not via the States or the axiomatic process, but via a pure becoming of minorities.
>
> (*ATP*: 471)

Of course, such a project, in addition to being completely inappropriate for an institutionalized approach – the central method of contemporary thinking – is fraught with difficulties. The main one, to be addressed in the next section is, do not these lines of flight, this deterritorialization of relations, make the perfect materials for the axiomatic of capital, a system which operates on the basis of decoded elements?

The 'catch'

The typical 'Deleuzian politics', largely in the form of resistance to the powers of the status quo, found its best expression in the early 1970s. During this period

> he was the mentor of that fraction of leftism for which all that mattered was desiring machines and nomadism, the sexual and the festive, free flux and the freedom of expression, the so-called free radio stations along with all the

other spaces of freedom, the rainbow of minuscule differences, and the molecular protestation fascinated by the powerful moral configurations of Capital.

(Badiou 1997: 94–5)

But as some commentators point out (Plant 1993: 100; Patton 2000: 6), this revolutionary desire is all too easily co-opted back into the system which it purports to challenge, in a similar manner as the decentred subject as discussed above. Thus great care must be taken when deploying the 'revolutionary nature' of Deleuze's philosophy. As Day notes,

> postmodern societies of control are becoming increasingly dependent upon decentred multiplicities that are, none the less, hierarchical and authoritarian in nature. It is crucial to mark the distinction Deleuze and Guattari make between these *radicle* rhizomatic forms that have significant arborescent effects, and those *radical* rhizomatic systems that are anti-hierarchical and preserve local autonomy to the greatest possible extent. Without keeping this distinction in mind, it would indeed be Utopian to believe, as many theorists and activists seem to, that *decentralization means autonomy*. It means no such thing, necessarily. Rather, decentralization just as easily, and much more likely under current conditions, means a shift from modern discipline to post-modern control.

(2005: 216)

A case illustrating this danger is again Chesters and Welsh's *Complexity and Social Movements*. In it they point out that contemporary life is marked by a nomadism, both in terms of 'life style' and 'work force'. In their view everything today is mobile, long distance, and open, in contrast to the '"closed" national systems (of signification)' (2006: 5). Unfortunately by placing so much emphasis on the nomadic nature of Deleuze and Guattari's philosophy they commit what one could call the 'voyage to the South Seas' fallacy (*ATP*: 158ff.) wherein 'pseudobreaks' are mistaken for 'ruptures' or 'clean breaks' (see *ATP*: 199). In terms of the present book, the simplest way to put it is that they confuse nomadic (or virtual) movement and nomadic science. In a sense the world *is* defined by a nomadic movement (virtual, immanent relations) for which we need a nomad science and the method of transcendental empiricism. But a nomad science, crucially, also deals with the actual, with states of affairs and stratification that characterize actualized, quantifiable existence. Perhaps through their explicit reluctance to define Deleuzian terminology (2006: 4) Chesters and Welsh overlook the other (actual) half of political activity and neglect the way that summit protest participants are constantly 'reterritorialized' by, for example, 'flexible worktime', Blackberries, and implicit identity distinctions that rely on individuals being different in relation to something else or an Other, as opposed to being different in themselves. By so doing they miss the dangers inherent in the AGM: that all the aspects and expressions of this movement will be reterritorialized into political parties, consumer culture, in short, 'fascisms' (see Foucault 1983) of all kinds. As Thoburn rightly points out, Deleuze is misrepresented as a theorist of strictly abstract becoming or pure deterritorializations. Although different political strategies (or perhaps better, 'anti-strategies') for entities which make up aspects of the AGM may be non-denumerable minorities in the face of molar identities, 'one does not easily leave identity behind, and the composition of territory is a necessity for life ... the minor and the molar exists in continuous interrelation as two tendencies in matter' (2003: 15). The great danger here is a complacency, a neglect of Foucault's self-governance, which can be found in the energy and hype surrounding rallies and participatory experiments, or the emancipatory expectations placed in networks or newest social movements. As Holloway points out in reference to Negri's autonomism, but in a way that could equally be applied here as well, the danger is much the same as the one faced by the prisoner in the cell who imagines she is already free. It is 'an attractive and stimulating idea, but a fiction, a fiction that easily leads on to other fictions, to the construction of a whole fictional world' (2002: 167).

Further clarification of this 'catch' can be attained through a brief analysis of a Deleuze interview by Antonio Negri in 1990. Negri puts the following question to Deleuze: 'How can we conceive a community that has real force but no base, that isn't a totality but is, as in Spinoza, absolute?' to which Deleuze answers:

> It definitely makes sense to look at the various ways individuals and groups constitute themselves as subjects through processes of subjectification: what counts in such processes is the extent to which, as they take shape, they elude both established forms of knowledge and the dominant forms of power. Even if they in turn engender new forms of power or become assimilated into new forms of knowledge. For a while, though, they have a real rebellious spontaneity. This is nothing to do with going back to 'the subject', that is, to something invested with duties, power, and knowledge. One might equally well speak of new kinds of events, rather than processes of subjectification: events that can't be explained by the situations that give rise to them, or into which they lead. They appear for a moment, and it's that moment that matters, it's the chance we must seize. ... I think subjectification, events and brains are more or less the same thing. What we most lack is a belief in the world, we've quite lost the world, it's been taken from us. If you believe in the world you participate in events, however inconspicuous, that elude control, you engender new space–times, however small their surface volume. It's what you [Negri] call *peitas*. Our ability to resist control, or our submission to it, has to be assessed at the level of our every move. We need both creativity *and* a people.
>
> (*N*: 176)

On face value and without a broad consideration of his political metaphysics, it is difficult to see what Deleuze might be getting at here when he talks about seizing such chances. And it might be tempting to read his comments about 'the world' and 'a people' in the context of political resistance, May 1968, the AGM, and so on – that the world has been taken from 'the people' (possibly by malevolent elites) and that a new subjectivity must reclaim it. The final incitement, the final advice – which is almost never offered in Deleuze – is to seize the world, to act, to create new things, however small, which seems rather straightforward. But perhaps Deleuze is saying more than that we have merely to elude control and act in creative ways. In the context of the main argument of this book, what makes the difference in terms of political efficacy is what one believes the world is made of; how it operates, how it develops, how things emerge. As Žižek might say (see 1999: 324ff.), everyone *knows* that people are oppressed, that they live under the yolk of external powers. The question is how one imagines these relationships to work and how change takes place. In a like manner Deleuze's reference to 'space–times' need not refer to some outside space or some creative arena that awaits the actions of an enlightened citizenry. One may read Deleuze as being quite literal here: the virtual has been taken away from us not by corporations or transnational masters, but simply by representational thought. So 'thinking the world' refers to the plane of immanence; virtual connections, becoming, and lines of flight. What Deleuze is picking up on in the above quote is that we only seem to deal with the actual half: representations of individuals and states of affairs in general. His point is this: political liberation is not just about recapturing the world but recapturing the virtual, thinking a politics of the event.

The problem with (or for) Deleuze is that so many of his readers and apologists respond so profoundly to that which is embodied in his own attraction in the 1970s to Anglo-American literature, what he calls thought bent on becoming (see *D*: 27ff.). This attraction in itself may not necessarily be problematic, but deploying it without investigating its very problematic implications for culture, capitalism, and politics leads to conclusions that are inconsistent with Deleuze's philosophy as a whole. This is because the very attraction to Anglo-American literature and ways of thought/expression (starting in the middle, etc.) are the very engines of the smooth-space capitalism that virtually all of Deleuze's readers, not to mention Deleuze himself, abhor. The 'catch' here is perhaps best described in the observation by Žižek, in reference to the disturbing irony of the yuppie reading *What is Philosophy?* on the Paris metro,[35] that Deleuze, with his reliance on desire, becoming, and event, *could* be thought of as the 'ideologist of late capitalism' (2003: 184). Indeed, some of the goals and tactics of the AGM mirror new managerial styles and organization theories of international corporations and finance including less vertical hierarchy, fewer people giving and receiving orders, as well as networked relations. There are obvious strategic dangers here. Because of their isomorphism, the supposedly new forms of organization and identity of the AGM will become subsumed by the increasingly flexible and open organizations which are the target of protests. For example, there is the real risk that the new era of corporate citizenship and the fact that most transnational institutions have stakeholder consultancy sessions with NGOs and activists subvert the revolutionary potential of the AGM. At the end of *A Thousand Plateaus*, Deleuze and Guattari warn the reader: 'Never believe that a smooth space will save us' (500), in effect, qualifying the entire political philosophy laid out in the book. It does remain possible, however, for his thought to act as tools in understanding the contemporary world without becoming 'fascinated' and 'mystified', that is, without using chic Deleuzian terminology in an evocative but ultimately unproductive way. The most important thing about Deleuze's thought is that virtual and the actual are relative expressions of the same thing: a relation between the whole and its expression or attributes. The 'catch' here is resolved by this emphasis on the two-poled metaphysics. Thus *A Thousand Plateaus* should be read as a playing out of cases of this tension on a variety of fields including psychology, architecture, history, technology, linguistics, war and politics. What must be remembered, ultimately, is that both appeals to the liberating rhizomes and suggestions that Deleuze is a capitalist apologist neglect the two-poled nature of his metaphysics. When we take into account the breadth of Deleuze's philosophical writings as a whole (in contrast to the few fragments, usually quite off-handed, of political or normative posturing) we come to the conclusion that the error of Western thought has not only been the emphasis on the actual over the virtual, but that it has, with few exceptions, ignored the latter completely. It does not even know how to think the virtual – in Deleuze's terms it is not thinking at all. In short, Western and increasingly globalized thought is not aware of the illusory nature of its own obsession with the actual (closed systems) over the virtual (immanent relations). And it is in this sense, which remains especially all the more pertinent now in our heightened era of globalization, that the world has been taken from us.

Conclusion
World politics as nomad science

World politics is characterized today, at least in part, by open-ended processes so well exemplified by what has been described here as the AGM. And yet all theories which would deal in one way or another with world politics fall short in at least some aspects of accounting for the AGM. This is a signal that theoretical apparatuses and models need expansion, readjustment, or revision. The argument of this book is that Deleuze's philosophy provides one productive way of incorporating the anomalies of the various aspects of the AGM into a comprehensive approach to world politics, a world politics characterized by fluctuating systems of de- and re-territorialization. Fundamentally and principally it exists as a purely immanent form, outside of time in undifferentiated space characterized by intensive relations. This plane of immanence is differenciated, through quasi-causal operators, into historical time and metricized space, actualizing the human beings and communities, the rise and fall of empires, as well as the history of the international system. These actualized entities are constantly changing and morphing through the process of becoming whereby they counteractualize to the virtual realm, to be reactualized as different extensions in time and space. From this perspective there have always been, or perhaps more accurately (from the perspective of the Aion) always *are* lines of flight: the barbarians outside the Empire, the Silk Road, or the trade winds, a new scientific or technological discovery that deterritorializes governments and economic relations. Some of these have had wide-reaching system effects (global climatic change, twentieth century Communism, the railroad in the nineteenth century), some more local. The AGM is a deterritorialization with a near global effect, and it has aspects that both reterritorialize as strengthened forms of civil society or local governance, as well as those that continue on their line of flight in forms that resist representation. Deleuze's political metaphysics allows us to understand both reactionary and reformist aspects of the AGM that correspond more closely to typically modernist formulations, while at the same time also accounting for more open, fluid, and complex political experiments such as isocracy, inclusiveness and non-power.

The AGM is a complex thing. It is impossible to find even a mainstream or general view on what it is and what role it plays in world politics. For some it is anti-capitalist, for others it refers specifically to protests – very often only in

Western capitals. For some it is a direct theoretical descendent of Marx or a host of ideological descendants of Bakunin; for others it shares more similarities with local indigenous movements of the Global South such as the Adivasi movements in India. For some it is about global networks of solidarity, for others it is much more individualistic. The value of Deleuze's political philosophy when considering the AGM is that it allows us not only to think of the AGM in terms of a global system of which it is an ontologically equal part (with the state, IGOs, TNCs, and supranational bodies such as the UN or IMF), but also allows one to parse out all of the different variations in theory and practice which surround or rather form the AGM. Furthermore, with the method of transcendental empiricism or nomad science one can trace the morphogenic or genetic process which leads the AGM as a whole or any given aspect of the AGM to a state of affairs, and in turn analyse its line of flight.

Extending Deleuze's philosophy to world politics, territoriality and the individual political agent (as fostered by their scientific counterparts methodological nationalism and methodological individualism) are not only specific actualizations of immanent forces in various eras and locations, but as Chapters 3 and 4 showed, in fact are much more nebulous and heterogeneous in the times and places in which they putatively were at their apogee. The twentieth century provides a wealth of examples, where, despite rhetoric, boundaries were heterogeneous in practice and the modern individual with its rights and appetites was reserved for a relatively small number of people, mainly in Western regions.

In thinking about or studying world politics, any approach which incorporates a behaviouralistic metaphysics or foundationalist ontology – however slight – is inconsistent with the Deleuzian perspective developed in this book and especially in Chapter 4. Entities do not choose amongst an array of possibilities in a metric time that simply flows from one moment to the next. Taking Deleuze seriously, states of affairs are actualizations of immanent relations characterized by Events. They are not chosen by people or organizations, they are evolutions of complex systems. To play on Deleuze's distinction between destiny and necessity once more, one might say that states of affairs are *destined* to be actualized, but not *necessarily* so. In other words, the results or effects of complex interactions at the virtual level must be expressed in one and only one form (destiny). But this is not to say that they arrive at that state through any necessity, as if they were meant to be that way, or that there is some transcendent reason (from and essence or God) for it. Put another way, there is no stopping the eternal return, but this does not mean that its effects are predictable or inevitable; world politics is not deterministic.

However, to say that there is no Deleuzian politics would be inaccurate. As argued in Chapters 2 and 4, there clearly is. It is the Nietzschean one of value: good and bad as opposed to good and evil. This addresses, as has been shown in the last chapter, the significance of Deleuze's ontology and metaphysics for the individual political agent. Again, Chapters 2, 3, and 4 emphasize the way in which Deleuze's thought is a nomad science: not only can it be a political way of living, but perhaps more importantly, it provides an analytical framework with which to account for not only the static but also the fluid and complex. And it is such theoretical flexibility that is required to map the movements of the contemporary world of speed, emergence, and complexity that has been exposed, as the science of modernity, the Royal Science, crumbles under its own weight. There is a sense in which the limits set on the political subject by Deleuze are almost anti-utopian, as if it is simply not possible to attain a pure line of flight, to build the perfect Body without Organs, or become an *Übermensch*.[1] However, this subject-as-fold is the only notion of a subject consistent with Deleuze's ontological position of univocity which insists on immanence.

To come full circle from the discussion of desire at the beginning of Chapter 2, we can say that individual human beings may be seen as desiring machines, but desire here does not refer to the personal preferences of an autonomous individual, but rather designates the specific process of actualization. The human choice or volition that plays so prevalent a role – mostly implicitly – in contemporary social scientific discourse is a theoretical red herring. As Paul Veyne explains,

> [M]an has a 'will to power,' to actualisation, which is indeterminate: it is not happiness that he is seeking. He does not have a list of specific needs to satisfy, after which he would remain quietly in a chair in his room; he is the actualizing animal, and realizes the potentialities of all sorts that come his way.
>
> (1997: 163)

In terms of 'larger' entities or assemblages, the same holds true. States have no interests independent of the milieu in which they find themselves, just as NGOs are not acting autonomously nor on anyone's behalf. This is the ultimate statement of the principle of unintended consequences. This is not to say that thinking about individuals, states, and institutions as if they have volition and make choices is wrong – indeed, such methodological principles often do provide very productive results. It is merely to recognize that such an attribution of will to such entities is inconsistent with a comprehensive reading of Deleuze's political philosophy, as presented here. In the end one might reach a middle ground wherein for certain research questions (anything to do with demographics or polling, for example), positivistic methods as a necessary illusion or a useful fiction are appropriate. However, in order to arrive at a better understanding of the processes that make up world politics we need a nomad science that goes beyond approaches founded on discrete entities with essences that, as was argued in Chapter 3, are ill equipped to deal with emergence and complexity. Just as for the analysis of global assemblages, Deleuze provides an analysis of the individual which accounts for its paradoxes, shifts, inconsistencies, irrationality, and complexity.

Deleuze is important to the study of world politics because he is primarily engaged in the critique of the fundamentals of Western philosophy which have come to form the basis of contemporary social science investigation. His approach is intriguing in that he does not merely dismiss the project of Western philosophy out of hand, rather his work constitutes one of the finest engagements with it. There are, of course, other critics, but few are so well-versed in the tradition which they seek to criticize. Moreover, as we saw in Chapter 2, Deleuze does not merely dismantle this tradition. More than just to do away with metaphysics, he seeks to resuscitate an immanent and materialist one based on univocity. It must be stressed again that Deleuze is not denying or criticizing the actual nor representational forms of thinking as exemplified by the teacher (Socrates), or the private (Descartes), or State (Hegel) thinker. He simply argues, rather, that they are not – indeed they cannot – be primary. They are the result of events on the plane of immanence. This is a truly nomadic thought,

> A thought grappling with exterior forces instead of being gathered up in an interior form, operating by relays instead of forming an image; an event thought, a haecceity, instead of a subject-thought, a problem-thought instead of an essence-thought or theorem; a thought that appeals to a people instead of taking itself for a government ministry.
>
> (*ATP*: 378)

The conclusion of Chapter 1 listed five conditions of a comprehensive theory of world politics in general and the AGM in particular. The first was an account of globalization. From the analysis in Chapter 3, globalization must be understood as the intensified role of immanent relations. This can be seen in (but is not the result of) global flows of people, information, and technology in a space which is becoming smoother and a time that increasingly resembles that of the Aion. The second condition was an account for the push down to the level of the individual, but also global coordination. In Chapter 4 we saw how the process of neoliberalism uncovers and promotes the individual in perhaps unprecedented ways. But this does not preclude the possibility of coordinated action. On the contrary, because Deleuze's theory of multiplicity dissolves the barrier between the group and the individual, coordination is in fact part of global complexity. This covers the third condition, that of accounting for group action without recourse to identity or framing. That is not to say that these two parameters have ceased to function. However, their role cannot be seen as primary, but rather as one form of reterritorialization. Overall, the approach to world politics as developed from Deleuze's philosophy provides a sound model of organization and disorganization, the fourth condition. The two-poled approach presented in this book accounts for both the chaotic lines of flight (which are primary and determining) as well as the stratifications of representation and structure. The final condition was to show what a politics of non-power might look like. Chapter 4 described how the notion of becoming minoritarian and the ethic involved therein was in fact the only political position consistent with Deleuze's philosophy.

What makes Deleuze difficult to study is his penchant for what he refers to as 'intellectual buggery' (*N*: 6) out of which new 'monstrosities' are born. Where, in these couplings then, is the Deleuze that one might study? First of all prima facie one could object to the entire search for the author called 'Deleuze' with a philosophy containing certain meanings. This is why Boundas writes of the Hume series, the Nietzsche series, the Foucault series, and so on; and why Badiou likewise writes of the Leibniz–Deleuze and the Bergson–Deleuze. It is as if there were a variety of Deleuzes, or a room full of Deleuzes, each lost in conversation (or perhaps 'intercourse' is better) with other thinkers. It would be difficult indeed to take a passage from *Empiricism and Subjectivity*, first published in 1953 and, say, *The Fold* (in 1988), and distil a unity of Deleuze's thought. These books are written at different times in an almost half-century long career and serve different purposes. In short, they are different *machines*. But if we say there is not one Deleuze, no single author with intention and meaning, might we not nevertheless ask if there is not something in common amongst all the Deleuzes? The answer must be a commitment to univocity and thus immanence, implying, in turn, a commitment to empiricism. In contrast to Foucault, who continually and quite openly reworked his position over 25 years, the Deleuzian approach, the Deleuze-machine, came all at once and was subsequently deployed and differentiated amongst a number of thinkers (his own books) and cases (the main books with Guattari). In the former group it is almost as if Deleuze introduces the philosopher with the title role to *his* own philosophy – to see, for example, how the principle of association in Hume relates to individuation, or how forms of content and forms of expression in Foucault reinforce the idea of actualization.

The political metaphysics investigated in the last three chapters of this book should not be understood as running contrary to the research agendas of many fields of the social sciences, specifically IR, IPS, sociology, geography, and political science. Because it is empirically based, materialist, and non-discursive, it has many overlaps and points of engagement. It need not seem like a multitude of ambiguities and abstractions, but in fact lends itself to practical inquiry, even though there are not yet any high profile empirical research programmes. One of the arguments of this book is that Deleuze does present a positive and productive approach to questions of world politics and of social science in general, and, stopping far short of saying that this is the only worthwhile approach (that the twentieth century will be known as the Deleuzian one), approaches to world politics nevertheless have a lot to gain by engaging with Deleuze's nomad science. To be sure, some fields of study warrant an approach based more on relations amongst the actual. Demographic studies, for example, as well as economic policy and other quantitative-based research areas will naturally stay in the domain of representational thought. Indeed, representing something is what these studies are all about. However, in order to understand a world politics characterized by change, fluidity, and chaos it is hoped that this book has shown how Deleuze's philosophy can be invaluable.

The analysis given in these pages is admittedly far from comprehensive. A further step would involve more detailed empirical analyses of various aspects of the AGM as instances of world politics. One could call this an assemblage theory analysis and it would map the becomings of the entity in question – a social movement, network, or individual, for example – that is, how it combines and recombines on the plane of immanence and is actualized in specific forms of content and forms of expression. Such an analysis would be an immanent one and therefore could have no recourse to a fundamental structure or essential characteristics of bodies or individuals. It would investigate the AGM and its various elements, aspects, and expressions on a case by case basis. Such an approach would naturally be rather painstaking, resembling the archaeological works of Foucault such as *The Birth of the Clinic* (1989) and *Discipline and Punish* (1977) in size and scope, if not exactly in methodology owing to its strictly materialist ontology.

Deleuze does not offer a final lens through which to understand various phenomena, such as theories of Marx or Lévi-Strauss, behaviouralism, or any other paradigm that establishes some sort of independent variable against which we can map the world. Such charting or measuring can only deal with the metrics of the actual; Deleuze, in contrast, provides us with a calculus of the virtual. As Deleuze often writes, it is the universals that need to be explained – the trick is to find and understand processes in their specificity. In a broader sense, assemblage theory, fully grounded in Deleuze's political metaphysics, lends itself nicely to other empirical avenues, particularly those characterized by complexity. Candidates might include population movements, financial systems, or networks of (dis)organized violence. Moreover there are surely other aspects of Deleuze's thought that would be useful in such analyses including a deeper investigation of the roles of chance and power, an exploration of the mechanic phylum, as well as aspects which lend themselves to epistemological questions such as sense, nonsense, and paradox. These all suggest avenues of further research.

Deleuze's philosophy is an attempt to make theory worthy of the Event. This would involve a sensitivity to the singular nature of Events which are the results of true difference. There are many analogues of such an attempt. Authors such as Ruggie (1993: 158) and Harvey (1990: 240ff.) have observed the shift in notions of cartography and perspective that played a role in underwriting the rise of the territorial state in the Early Modern period. Similarly Deleuze writes that a turn to a truly immanent philosophy would entail a 'Copernican revolution' and involve, much like the earlier shift to perspective and scale, doing to thought what abstract painting did to art: 'The theory of thought is like painting: it needs that revolution which took it from representation to abstraction. This is the aim of a theory of thought without image' (*DR*: 346). Such a shift would be capable of moving us beyond the constraints of representational thought that characterizes the vast majority of contemporary theorizing, engendering a nomad science that could map the complexities of world politics that today find their ever-stronger expression.

Notes

Introduction

1 Some may be rather squeamish about using the notion of science or the scientific in a discussion of Deleuze and politics. All I mean here is a systematic approach with a rigorous and purposeful methodology applied to a clear field of inquiry, as distinct from the so-called literary readings of political phenomena, as will be addressed in the main text below.
2 To this end, and looking as it does at Deleuze's work as a whole, the book revisits some of the texts in their original French and makes some alterations to the available translations. This is justified for several reasons. First, some of the English terminology ('meanwhile' for *entre-temps*, for example) is rather distracting from what I take to be the central thrust of Deleuze's arguments. Second, there are some errors, including a key one in *Difference and Repetition* (writing 'systems' instead of 'series' on page 144 of the Continuum edition in a crucial passage on differentiation). Third, translations between books are terribly inconsistent. For example, Tom Conely often translates *actuellement* as 'currently', which would in standard parlance be correct, but in at least a number of important passages it would be better to adhere to the more consistent and, it must be said, accurate usage of 'the actual'. All changes are noted in the text.

1 World politics and the AGM

1 Of course within specific issues (particularly labour) there has been tremendous global connection.
2 'The idea that the United States had somehow dissolved as a centre of power into the impersonal "smooth space" of Empire seems, at best, premature. We are confronted with a hybrid form of sovereignty, in which appeals to universal principles coexist in complex ways with assertions of national interests.' (Callinicos 2002: 261).
3 Though some claim that this is more of an assertion than a reality. See for example Scholte (2000: 117).
4 See www.adbusters.org.
5 Even in Chiapas. See Marcos (2001: 248).
6 Writers such as Falk and George Monbiot are often criticized for being too cosy with the capitalist state and mainstream media establishment. See for example Jasiewicz (2008).
7 This exposes the danger of describing the AGM merely in terms of non-state actors as Karns and Mingst do (2004: 214).
8 They also distinguish between supporters and reformists.
9 For more on this 'revolutionary' strategy, see Marcos (2003).
10 For more, see Holloway (2002: 28ff.).
11 The topic of networks will be addressed in greater detail in Chapter 3.

12 Here I include most theoretical approaches including realist, neo-realist, neoliberal institutionalist, Marxist, and even constructivist, which for all its theoretical subtlety is mostly also in the final analysis concerned primarily with states. However I am not referring here to a putative theoretical unity nor suggesting that there are not enormous differences between different branches of IR. Only that as a legitimate field of study and in comparison to the others in this section it shares some defining characteristics, very real and potentially game-changing revolutions within the discipline notwithstanding. These include a concern with global affairs, at least some degree of distinction between the foreign and the domestic and thus a tacit acceptance of the state as object, and the international or global as a level of analysis. Similar guarded generalizing in order to make a theoretical comparison between disciplines can be found in, among others, Buzan and Little (2000: 18ff), Albert (2007), and Bigo and Walker (2007).
13 For more on Eurocentric ahistoricism in IR, see for example Buzan and Little (2000) and Teschke (2003).
14 This will receive considerable attention in Chapter 3.
15 See for example Tarrow (1998), and Oommen (2004), respectively.
16 With the exception of Marxists such as Waterman (see 1998).
17 See, for example, Bauman (2002), Beck and Beck-Gernsheim (2002), and Giddens (1991).
18 To be sure Deleuze himself did not invent or coin many of these words or expressions. For example, his usage of multiplicity comes from Georg Riemann (1919), plateau from Gregory Bateson (1972), and Carl Jung had already made use of rhizome (1965). Nor can it be properly said that he himself actually popularized them or put them into use. 'Nomad', for example, in social movement theory is perhaps most well-known from Alberto Melucci (1989). Yet when we trace the genealogies of these terms in the context of their productive theoretical use, particularly in the realm of politics, they inevitably seem to flow through Deleuze's work.

2 Deleuze and politics as becoming

1 See for example Heidegger's 'everyday hermeneutics' (1962: 76–8).
2 For a well-known reading that leans in this direction, see Patton (2000: 34ff.).
3 See for example Dillon (2000) and Patton (2003).
4 In other words, their use obscures assumptions made by the author, which very often, it is worth noting, in fact run contrary to Deleuze's ontological position.
5 Here and elsewhere the somewhat awkward word 'notion' will be used to denote Deleuzianisms or linguistic figures that refer to various elements of his philosophy. The simple reason for this is that he, like many philosophers, uses the common words 'idea' and 'concept' in very technical ways. So here I will refrain from talking about Deleuze's concepts in any general way, though I will talk about concepts (the 'notion' of concepts) in Deleuze.
6 This is italicized in the original.
7 In this context it is possible to contrast *Anti-Oedipus*, a characteristically Guattarian book, with *A Thousand Plateaus* which can be read as a much more Deleuzian work having jettisoned much of the psychoanalysis and focussing on Deleuzian 'cases' (see below).
8 Deleuze's Marxian credentials are far from clear.
9 For an assessment of this, see Kraniauskas (2003: 36–7).
10 It is a source of no small disappointment to many theorists that Hardt and Negri's follow-up books to *Empire*, the much-awaited *Multitude (2004)* as well as *Commonwealth* (2009), did not opt for a further explanation and clarification of some of the novel theoretical applications suggested in *Empire*.
11 Though it is worth pointing out that Deleuze more often than not applies his ontology to or explains it with examples from art (e.g. Klee) and especially literature (Melville,

Carrol, Fitzgerald). Additionally, in *What is Philosophy?* he and Guattari expound on their theory of science – as distinct from philosophy and art.
12 This will be addressed in greater detail below.
13 The text in question reads. *'Une fulguration s'est produite, qui portera le nom de Deleuze ... Un jour, peut-être, le siècle sera deleuzien.'* (1970: 886).
14 See also Tampio (2009).
15 Obviously Paul Patton's *Deleuze and the Political* (2000) would seem to fit the bill here, however Patton is more interested in teasing out specific Anglo-American political themes, which, as he makes clear, are difficult to find in Deleuze. In other words Patton is distinctly focussed on political theory, rather than a theory of politics. In a different vein Bonta and Protevi's (2004) glossary and brief case study goes some distance in the direction of a science of world politics.
16 When we move to compare the difference between a rock and a bird, for example, difference becomes less, not more, distinct. In such a case we are obliged to move to a higher category, saying that one is an animal and the other a mineral. Using granite (as a species of rock) in this comparison makes it no clearer.
17 I acknowledge my reliance on Widder (2001) in the following analysis of this ontological problem. His article is certainly the best I have read on difference in Deleuze and Aristotle.
18 This theme will come up again in the discussion of haecceity below.
19 Though it is interesting to note that Widder's argument is more readily sustainable in his use of the Tredennick translation: 'we can only apprehend them through intelligence or perception.' (see Widder 2001: 451, n13).
20 It is possible that from the perspective of contemporary Western scientific discourse, entrenched as it is in certain ways of thinking, such a fundamental critique sounds a little far-fetched. But such perspectives must be seen to lie within historical and geographical contexts. Thus in the history of Western thought, the Aristotelian conception of difference must have seemed strange and bewildering to, for example, the Stoics. One could undoubtedly trace the status of Being and analogy in other traditions, as well as deviations (what Deleuze sometimes calls minor sciences) shooting off from the Western mainstream.
21 Translation altered. See Deleuze (1968: 56–7).
22 Heidegger plays a somewhat ambiguous role in such a game. In one sense we can see him as inherently part of this lineage, and yet he surely belongs to the one following in several important respects. See Agamben (1999: 225, 239).
23 This will be explored in some detail in Chapter 3.
24 Though Widder (2001) gives the notion of simulacra considerable credence, as the title of his essay makes clear, Patton (2000: 35) argues that Deleuze later distances himself from it. This can be read simply, I think, as Deleuze's shift towards an exploration of rhizomatics and away from Plato in general. In any case, for Deleuze's concise critique of the Platonic notion of difference, see *The Logic of Sense*, page 291–320.
25 This is italicized in the original.
26 As we will see later on, Deleuze's approach dissolves the difference between structure and agency, as well as group and individual.
27 Here is another example of the contradictory readings of Deleuze. Contrast this quote with Boundas: 'difference is not a concept: concepts are not processes' (2006:4). In the broader sense I tend to agree with Boundas here.
28 For more on this, see Protevi (2001: 2ff.).
29 The difference has important implications, and an exploration of the encounter between representational and non-representational thought of some order would make an interesting study. It might be possible to read works by Lynn Mario de Souza (see for example 2002) in this light.
30 Though he certainly knows the difference between the two. Spivak's observation

(1994: 70) that this is a source of some confusion for Deleuze requires considerable reassessment.
31 This is italicized in the original.
32 The onus would have been on Hardt and Negri to explain such a relationship, something they have yet to do. For a detailed refutation of Badiou's criticism, see Widder (2001).
33 This makes William Connolly's appeals to Deleuzian figures (see for example 2005) rather problematic. See also Campbell and Schoolman (2008).
34 Though it is important to note he does sometimes use the word 'possible', though he has a specific meaning in mind, for example when he deals with incompossibility. See for example *The Fold,* page 68.
35 For more on this difference, see, for example, Nealon (2003).
36 In the face of doxa this alternative will employ paradox, as laid out in *The Logic of Sense*.
37 Of course there are other ways of overcoming this, for example Bell's Theorem (see for example Peat 1991). This is not what Deleuze proposes, however. See Delanda (2002: 39).
38 Translation altered. See Deleuze (1968: 56–7).
39 Beyond the substantive and critical evidence (see Badiou's notion of the cases below), Deleuze himself says as much in the preface to the English edition of *Difference and Repetition*, first published in 1994: '*Difference and Repetition* was the first book in which I tried to "do philosophy". All that I have done since is connected to this book, including what I wrote with Guattari (obviously, I speak from my own point of view).' *Difference and Repetition*, page xiii.
40 Nevertheless it is true that Deleuze often refers to the virtual as a 'sterile double' – most notably in *The Logic of Sense* but also in *Difference and Repetition*.
41 Some might object that there are important metaphysical differences between the virtual and the plane of immanence or the Body without Organs. These differences must be read, however, as practical differences that Deleuze often exploits, as in the notion of line of flight below. Virtual–actual are used here as they form the basic relationship of other, similar notions.
42 Notice how 'qualities' is used here; it is important for the discussion below.
43 For more on the Einstein–Bergson time debate and Deleuze's role within it, see Olma (2007).
44 For a good discussion on time, science, and Bergson, see *Cinema 1: The Movement Image*, Chapter 1.
45 Deleuze-inspired studies, including this one, might benefit from updated and consistent translations of key texts such as *Foucault, The Fold,* and *Difference and Repetition*.
46 Translation slightly altered. See Deleuze (1968: 286–7)
47 Again, repetition is a notion often overlooked by complexity-inspired Deleuze researchers and warrants further study.
48 This will be explored in more detail in Chapter 4.
49 He can thus read actualize, differenciate, integrate, and solve as synonymous. See *Difference and Repetition*, page 262.
50 Psychology would seem to share this drive for controls.
51 One could read, for example, *The Myth of 1648* (Teschke 2003) as an acknowledgement that the state system was never a perfectly closed (nor open) one.
52 Rendering '*un entre-temps*' as 'a meanwhile' is a bit misleading. *Meanwhile* in English is a somewhat less specific term, capable of designating, for instance, the notion of concurrence; in other words, one thing happening within the time of another. 'It is the event that is a meanwhile' (Deleuze and Guattari 1994: 160) risks being an indistinct notion, a kind of never-never land in a parallel time. I think we have to read Deleuze here with something much more specific in mind, by in effect taking him much more literally:

entre-temps meaning 'in this interval of time', or 'the interval of time between two actions or two occurrences': *'Dans cet intervalle de temps; Intervalle de temps entre deux actions, deux faits'* (Le Petit Robert 1991). Deleuze means that it is precisely the Event that is between two instants. This focuses on his notion, borrowed from Bergson, that the present is infinitely subdivided by the past and future in both directions.

53 That is: it is the Event, not time, that is between two instants.
54 Vice-diction is properly related to transcendental empiricism. 'The procedure capable of following and describing multiplicities and themes' *Difference and Repetition*, page 238.
55 This is a good example of the slight variation in terms: in this case from 'pure spatium' to 'plane of consistency'. Likewise the Body without Organs refers to an actualized entity which becomes dis-*organ*ized or more accurately de-*organ*ized. In this sense it is the achievement of the actualized thing: through schizoanalysis, for example, we can find our Body without Organs, that is, our place in the virtual, defined not by representation (or anything Oedipal) but by intensive quantities.
56 This is clearly expressed in *Dialogues II*, page 102.
57 See for example Currier (2003); Delanda (2006); Eriksson (2005); Legg (2009); Marcus and Saka (2006); Phillips (2006) and Venn (2006).
58 Presumably Deleuze and Guattari are thinking about Part II, Section 3. See Foucault (2002b: 49ff.)
59 See also *Desire and Pleasure*.
60 The third person limited point of view could only be described as loose at best, and only emphasizes the sense of the immanent series of the book. See Melville (2001).
61 For more on this topic and how it is related to morality, see *Nietzsche and Philosophy*, page 115.
62 For more on starting in the middle, see for example *A Thousand Plateaus*, page 293.
63 For Deleuze's own view on these cases, see *Difference and Repetition*, page 28: 'The examples invoked above concern the most diverse kinds of cases, from nominal concepts to concepts of nature and freedom'. Translation altered. See Deleuze (1968: 37).
64 See *What is Philosophy?*, page 160, as well as the discussion on counteractualization above.
65 Hardt and Negri's *Empire* is perhaps the best example of (rather inaccurately) equating multiplicity with virtuality or immanent relations (see 2000: 103).
66 'One is represented by space (or rather, if all the nuances are taken into account, by the impure combination of homogeneous time): it is a multiplicity of exteriority, of simultaneity, of juxtaposition, of order, or quantitative differentiation, of *difference in degree*; it is a numerical multiplicity, *discontinuous and actual*. The other type of multiplicity appears in pure duration: it is an internal multiplicity of succession, of fusion, or organisation, of heterogeneity, of quantitative discrimination, or of *difference in kind*; it is a *virtual and continuous* multiplicity that cannot be reduced to number.' *Bergsonism*, page 38. See also Bergson (2001: 87).
67 Deleuze and Guattari make it clear that both are equally important halves of a single reality. For just a few more examples in *A Thousand Plateaus*, see pages 20, 158, 161, 228, 337, 415, 423, 471, 482, 500, 506, 509, and 513. See also *Cinema 1*, pages 11, 17, 22, 59.
68 Contradiction, according to Deleuze, would form the basis of contemporary social science research only insofar as it is representational.
69 See for example Foucault (2002a: 18).
70 Though fresh translations could go some way towards dispelling this appearance.
71 Of course this is arguable, but there are very few engaging counter positions to date; perhaps Badiou's (see 2005) is the strongest.
72 For more, see Protevi (2001).
73 'Whether we are individuals or groups, we are made up of lines and these lines are very varied in nature' *Dialogues II*, page 93.

3 Deleuze and world politics

1 cf. Žižek (2002b: 311).
2 See *Nietzsche and Philosophy*, pp. 71–3.
3 Thus, somewhat paradoxically, from Deleuze's perspective the scientific advances of European modernity in fact technically *narrow* or *limit* the scope of knowledge about the world, though this by no means lowers their value in terms of productive capability.
4 Kobrin is here quoting Harvey (1990: 254).
5 Because Lipschutz moves so quickly here to a historical look at the term civil society, it is unclear whether global civil society is not state-centric in terms of granting a non-state-centric approach to the theoretician; or rather if global civil society as a plurality of agents is not state-centric.
6 The following analysis admittedly narrows its scope mostly to the realm of IR, or at least International Political Sociology. In the context of the present broader study, it must be noted that the vast majority of sociological and historical investigations – in broad terms, of course – suffer from the same methodological nationalism that has gripped IR since its founding.
7 For more on clientelism, see Roniger (1994) and especially Güneş-Ayata (1994).
8 As Ruggie writes, 'The Enlightenment was animated by the desire to demystify and secularize, to subject natural forces to rational explanation and control, as well as by the expectation that doing so would promote social welfare, moral progress, and human happiness.' To complete his argument about the significance of postmodernism, he continues: 'The optimism, certitude, and categorical fixity of this project were shattered by Nietzsche, Freud, Wittgenstein; Darwin, Einstein, Heisenberg; Braque, Picasso, Duchamp; Joyce, Proust, Becket; Schoenberg, Berg, Bartok; two world wars, a Great Depression, Nazi death camps, Stalin's Gulags, Hiroshima, and Nagasaki long before Lyotard, Foucault, and Derrida pronounced and celebrated its demise' (1993: 145).
9 The foundations of such a line argument are a little startling as they require us to be very hesitant about what the Romans actually said about themselves (or perhaps more accurately, what a very small group of elite citizens said about the Roman people). Such a methodological approach of dismissing what people say about themselves – in effect, ignoring their own discourse – would be quite tricky today. And yet Burns cautions against simplifying history into 'a Hegelian dichotomy of force and counter-force, a binary world, a "we versus them" scenario.' The Romans had a myopia about their relationship with the barbarians which was much the same. We must avoid their gaze, and not 'through their eyes look outward from a secure centre directly to a threatened periphery and overlook the mundane middle, where contrasts and compromise dominated the physical and psychological landscapes' (2003: 14). The hubs or 'monolithic poles' of inside and outside from which this middle drew reference were in fact in themselves 'mythical' (25).
10 This is the most common argument against territoriality. See also Jessop (2003) and Patomäki (2003), for example.
11 In particular the twelfth century Champagne Fairs. See Abu-Lughod (1989: 51–77)
12 For a discussion on this notion of cooling – another way of describing actualization or differenciation – see Deleuze, *Cinema 1*, page 63.
13 It is important to note that despite the rather dense philosophy presented so far in this book, Deleuze often takes up more 'earthly' matters. Early in his career – *Empiricisme et Subjectivité: Essai sur la Nature Humaine selon Hume* was first published in 1953 – Deleuze was interested in the nature of the institution as understood by Hume. From his perspective, one that serves as a foreshadowing of Foucault's work in particular, society is not defined by its laws in terms of contracts, but rather by its institutions. The former are purely negative whereas the latter are positive and are based on

not right but utility. 'The law cannot, by itself, be the source of obligation, because legal obligation presupposes utility. Society cannot guarantee preexisting rights: if people enter society, it is precisely because they do not have preexisting rights. ... Society is a set of conventions founded on utility, not a set of obligations founded on contract.' *Empiricism and Subjectivity*, pages 45–6.

14 In *A Thousand Plateaus*, Deleuze and Guattari form endless 'becoming-' words such as: becoming-woman, becoming-whale, wolf-becoming, and perhaps most importantly, especially for the discussion in Chapter 4, becoming-minoritarian.

15 I think the roots of this error can be seen in Delanda's previous work on Deleuze (2002: 166). For a further critique, see Legg (2009: 238).

16 Hirst and Woolley (1982: 119), to whom we will return in the next chapter, also sees Christianity as central to Western modernity.

17 This is not to say, however, that the virtual is only able to be seen through fast-paced cosmopolitan life. Far from it. Moreover, nor is this desirable: One of the major themes of *Capitalism and Schizophrenia* is that the capitalist axiomatic constantly re-territorializes flows.

18 This notion is largely drawn from Deleuze and Guattari's first co-volume, *Anti-Oedipus*.

19 'The schizophrenic is not, as is generally claimed, characterised by his loss of touch with reality, but by the absolute proximity to and total instantaneousness with things, this overexposure to the transparency of the world. Stripped of a stage and crossed over without the least obstacle, the schizophrenic cannot produce the limits of his very being, he can no longer produce himself as a mirror. He becomes a pure screen, a pure absorption and resorption surface of the influent networks.' Baudrillard (1988: 27).

20 See for example Stichweh (2003).

21 See for example Habermas (2005).

22 See for example Hardt and Negri (2000).

23 See for example Jarvis (2007), especially chapter seven.

24 'There is no such thing as either man or nature now, only a process that produces the one within the other and couples the machines together. Producing-machines, desiring machines everywhere, schizophrenic machines, all of species life: the self and the non-self, outside and inside, no longer have any meaning whatsoever.' *Anti-Oedipus*, page 2. See also Dillon (2000: 12–13).

25 For a classic discussion see for example Whitehead (1925: 25).

26 And art, incidentally.

27 'It could be said that science and philosophy take opposed paths, because philosophical concepts have events for consistency whereas scientific functions have states of affairs or mixtures for reference: through concepts, philosophy continually extracts a consistent event from the state of affairs – a smile without the cat, as it were – whereas through functions, science continually actualizes the event in a state of affairs, thing, or body that can be referred to' *What is Philosophy?*, p. 126.

28 See for example Cerny (1999); Demirovic (2000); Haas (1992); and Chesters and Welsh (2005).

29 Foucault is the great chronicler in the massive shifts that took place at the height of the modern period in terms of, for example medicine, health, the family, and madness. His goal as a historian is to explain the upheavals that took place during that era, and one of the characteristics that would mark them as complex to the contemporary reader is that he dismisses a simple, linear explanation of change. See for example, *The Archaeology of Knowledge*, (2002b: 44ff.).

30 Deleuze and Guattari here reference Prigogine and Stengers (1988: 162–3).

31 Indeed, many argue today that such closed-system analysis is not up to the task of understanding states and so-called state behaviours. See for example Albert, Jacobson, and Lapid (2001).

32 Deleuze never talks about modelling, which in most cases today involves setting up experiments wherein a number of variables interact in a rule-based environment to trace their development over an artificial time in order to see what patterns develop and what new properties emerge. Generally this is conducted on computers with extremely fast processing capacity. These powerful modelling computers – the kind social scientists have to wait months or years to have access to – were in their infancy during Deleuze's lifetime.
33 This problem is similar to the one Foucault faced in *The Archaeology of Knowledge*. He was dealing with statements, but the same could be said about emergence. He writes that a statement must be 'accepted, in its empirical modesty, as the locus of particular events, regularities, relationships, modification and systematic transformations; in short that is treated not as the result or trace of something else, but as a practical domain that is autonomous (although dependent), and which can be described at its own level (although it must be articulated on something other than itself)' (2002b: 137).
34 They write of a 'politically informed version' of complexity theory (2004: 5) and that the results of complexity theory 'prompted Deleuze to distinguish the actual/extensive, intensive, and virtual in his ontology' (2004: 16).
35 Quoted from Weizman (2007: 212).
36 Barabási notes that around 90 per cent of sites only have ten or fewer links. A few, however, have close to a million and are extremely visible (2002: 57–8).
37 Although to be accurate, in *Nietzsche and Philosophy* Deleuze is interested in the relationship between chance and necessity, not necessity and destiny. The distinction between necessity and destiny he attributes to the Stoics in *The Logic of Sense*, page 194. See also *Difference and Repetition*, page 353.
38 As Nietzsche writes, there is no doer behind the doing (1989: 45).
39 See *A Thousand Plateaus*, page 19.
40 Again, what Deleuze refers to in *The Logic of Sense* as an incorporeal change, in other words, actualizations brought about through the communication of disparate series.
41 Of course since no system can be completely closed, even the most rigid, stratified organization still has its line of flight.
42 For more on abstract machine, see *A Thousand Plateaus*, pages 109, 141, and 252.

4 Subjectivity and political agency

1 For this reason Deleuze, when talking about extensities, sometimes refers to 'dividuals'. See *Cinema 1*, page 14.
2 This ethic or aesthetic of a 'style of life' brings the analysis back to Nietzsche's will to power, which will be addressed below when we turn to ethics.
3 'They are not free to know: the decadents need the lie – it is one of the conditions of their preservation' (1989: 272).
4 It is interesting to note that Deleuze is almost completely left out of this account in Hirst and Woolley, as is often the case with other critical works including Peter Dews' *Logics of Disintegration* (1987) and Craig Calhoun's *Critical Social Theory; Culture, History, and the Challenge of Difference* (1995). What this points to is an awkwardness in trying to locate Deleuze among both his contemporaries and the collective impact their work had in the English-speaking world and in the humanities and social sciences in general. Such oversight underscores the need for more comprehensive re-enactments and deployments of Deleuze thought, as this book attempts to do.
5 For an overview, see Cusset (2003).
6 As will be argued in greater detail at the end of the chapter, it is somewhat ironic, then, that many critics of neoliberal globalization – many aspects of the AGM, that is – contend that we need *more* individualism (see for example Gray 1995: 55).

7 See for example Hardt and Negri (2000: 138); Jameson (1991: 48); Massumi (2002: xvi); and Žižek (1993: 216).
8 As Bains points out, sensing is an immanent process: there is no 'I' behind the seeing, or 'I' behind the eye. We do not experience ourselves seeing, we simply see. Sensory experience is existence itself rather than a 'representation of' it (2002: 108).
9 Already the *cogito* in *cogito ergo sum* – although Descartes never actually writes this in the *Meditations* (1960) – presumes the subject of the verb. In other words, as many have pointed out, the 'I think ...' cannot be a proof of existence, for it already assumes a thinking 'I' in the first place.
10 See for example Dews (1987: 223); Hays (1992: 80); Huyssen (1986: 26); and Jameson (1991: 15).
11 Translation altered. See Deleuze (1988b: 149).
12 Translation altered. See Deleuze (1988b: 26–7).
13 Deleuze here is drawing on Leibniz's distinction between three kinds of monads: perceptive (plants), sensory (animals), and thinking (humans – and angels). The overlap amongst Leibniz, Hume, Bergson, and Deleuze is striking here in that what distinguishes these thinking souls from their animal counterparts is memory: For Leibniz, the term monad should apply to 'simple substances which have perception only, and that the name of Souls should be given only to those in which perception is more distinct, and is accompanied by memory.' (1898: 230).
14 Tom Conley's translation here needs considerable revision. While normally *actuellement* would be rendered in English as 'currently' (in this passage Conley also uses 'authentically', and 'real' for *actuel*), from the full passage it is clear that Deleuze is referring to what we have designated here as the actual. Indeed, the temporal import of *actuellement* emphasizes the aspect of time in Deleuze's philosophy: the actual as the experience of the present time passing.
15 Translation altered. See Deleuze (1988b: 31–2).
16 'Thought is not a constant attribute, but a predicate passing endlessly from one thought to another.' *The Fold*, page 60.
17 This leads Deleuze to an interesting notion of what it means to learn (and to teach). 'The idea of the sea, for example, as Leibniz showed, is a system of liaisons or differential relations between particulars and singularities corresponding to the degrees of variation among these relations – the totality of the system being incarnated in the real movement of the waves. To learn to swim is to conjugate the distinctive points of our bodies with the singular points of the objective Idea in order to form a problematic field. This conjugation determines for us a threshold of consciousness at which our real acts are adjusted to our perceptions of the real relations, thereby providing a solution to the problem.' *Difference and Repetition*, pages 204–5.
18 Here the author must acknowledge inspiration from Bains, whose ideas informed the materials of this argument, the conclusions of which, however, differ substantially.
19 Actually, at points he refers to two kinds of multiplicities, both virtual and actual (*WP*: 126, 127) as mentioned in Chapter 2. But for the present purpose the significant aspect is the virtual multiplicity.
20 The problems of inaccessibility of Chesters and Welsh's work on complexity–Deleuze and the AGM stem largely from their difficulty in developing their Deleuzian intervention in any other terms, thus sadly rendering books such as *Complexity and Social Movements* (2006) rather self-referential and, as such, opaque to all but a few other readers.
21 As we shall see, according to Deleuze and Guattari, it is only the non-denumerable sets that do not seek entrance into the power of the axiomatic. See *A Thousand Plateaus*, page 470.
22 In Deleuzian terms, the post-Marxist notion of the social would refer to stratifications of the actual, the political to lines of flight. Deleuze would probably understand

fantasmatic logics or enjoyment as one form of stratification among others (political, social, etc.).
23 See also Laclau and Mouffe (1985: 101).
24 See also 'Desire and Pleasure', page 189.
25 One also notes the role of meaning here, which is explicitly absent in Deleuze.
26 The classic discussion of structure–agency in the realm of world politics remains Wendt (1987).
27 For an introduction into the relationship between the Enlightenment and constructivism, see Devetak (1995).
28 One might say that Deleuze got his ontology from Spinoza, his metaphysics from Bergson, his politics from Foucault, and his ethics from Nietzsche.
29 That is, physical areas which fall outside national jurisdiction. In these ultimate forms of 'non-place', as can be found at major international transit areas (major airports, for example) and conflict zones, individuals exists only as 'bare life'.
30 The status of ideology in Deleuze is determined by his commitment to immanence and the functioning of assemblages. His contempt for ideology is perhaps most strikingly highlighted by its absence from his writing. Some analysis can be found, however, in *Negotiations*, page 184, and *A Thousand Plateaus*, pages 89–90.
31 Arif Dirlik adds post-colonial thought as well (see 1994: 96–7).
32 Foreshadowing the basic tenor of Žižek's critique of liberalism, Brian Massumi puts it thus: 'More insidious than its institution-based propagation is the State-form's ability to propagate itself without centrally directed inculcation (liberalism and good citizenship). Still more insidious is the process presiding over our present plight, in which the moral and philosophical foundations of national and personal identity have crumbled, making a mockery of the State-form – but the world keeps right on going as if they hadn't (neo-conservatism and cynical greed).' (1992: 5).
33 'Today's liberal-democratic hegemony is sustained by a kind of unwritten *Denkverbot* similar to the infamous *Berufsverbot* in Germany in the late sixties; the moment one shows a minimal sign of engaging the political projects that aim to seriously challenge the existing order, the answer is immediately: "Benevolent as it is, this will necessarily end in a new gulag!" ... This is the point that one cannot and should not concede: *today, actual freedom of thought must mean the freedom to question the predominant liberal-democratic post-ideological consensus – or it means nothing.*' Žižek (2002a: 544–5).
34 That is, in the Foucauldian sense. 'I do not think that a society can exist without power relations, if by that one means the strategies by which individuals try to direct and control the conduct of others. The problem, then, is not to try to dissolve them in the utopia of completely transparent communication but to acquire the rules of law, the management techniques, and also the morality, the *ēthos*, the practice of the self, that will allow us to play these games of power with as little domination as possible.' Foucault (1997: 298).
35 See Lecercle (1996: 44).

Conclusion

1 On the other hand, the corollary of this is that we are always already perfectly free – that is without restriction or stratification – in so far as we exist virtually.

References

Abu-Lughod, J. (1989) *Before European Hegemony: The World System A.D. 1250–1350*, New York: Oxford University Press.
Agamben, G. (1998) *Homo Sacer: Sovereign Power and Bare Life*, trans. D. Heller-Roazen, Stanford: Stanford University Press.
—— (1999) *Potentialities: Collected Essays in Philosophy*, trans. D. Heller-Roazen, Stanford: Stanford University Press.
Agamben, G. and Raulff, U. (2004) 'An Interview with Giorgio Agamben', *German Law Journal*, 5: 609–14.
Agnew, J. (1994) 'The Territorial Trap: The Geographical Assumptions of International Relations Theory', *Review of International Political Economy*, 1: 53–80.
Albert, M. (2004) 'On the Modern Systems Theory of Society and IR', in M. Albert and L. Hilkermeier (eds) *Observing International Relations; Niklas Luhmann and World Politics*, London: Routledge, 13–29.
—— (2007) '"Globalization Theory": Yesterday's Fad or More Lively than Ever?', *International Political Sociology*, 1: 165–82.
Albert, M., Jacobson, D. and Lapid, Y. (2001) *Identities, Borders, Orders: Rethinking International Relations Theory*, Minneapolis: University of Minnesota Press.
Althusser, L. (1971) *Lenin and Philosophy, and other Essays*, London: New Left Books.
Amin, S. (2000) *Capitalism in the Age of Globalization*, London: Zed Books.
Anderson, J. (1996) 'The Shifting Stage of Politics: New Medieval and Postmodern Territorialities', *Environment and Planning D: Society and Space*, 14: 133–53.
Ansell Pearson, K. (1999) *Germinal Life; The Difference and Repetition of Gilles Deleuze*, London: Routledge.
Appadurai, A. (1990) 'Disjuncture and Difference in the Global Cultural Economy', *Theory, Culture & Society*, 7: 295–310.
—— (1996a) 'Sovereignty without Territoriality: Notes for a Postnational Geography', in P. Yaeger (ed.) *The Geography of Identity*, Ann Arbor: University of Michigan Press.
—— (1996b) *Modernity at Large: Cultural Dimensions of Globalisation*, Minneapolis: University of Minnesota Press.
—— (1999) 'Globalization and the Research Imagination', *International Social Science Journal*, 51: 229–38.
Aristotle (1984a) 'Metaphysics', in J. Barnes (ed.) *The Complete Works of Aristotle*, Princeton: Princeton University Press, 1552–758.
—— (1984b) 'Politics', in J. Barnes (ed.) *The Complete Works of Aristotle*, Princeton: Princeton University Press, 1986–2129.

Ashley, R. (1987) 'The Geopolitics of Geopolitical Space: Toward a Critical Social Theory of International Politics', *Alternatives*, 12: 403–34.
—— (1996) 'The Achievements of Post-structuralism', in S. Smith, K. Booth, and M. Zalewski (eds) *International Theory: Positivism and Beyond*, Cambridge: Cambridge University Press, 240–53.
ATTAC (1998) *Platform of the International Movement ATTAC* [online]. www.attac.org/en/whatisattac/international-platform (Accessed April 2010).
Augé, M. (1995) *Non-Places: An Introduction to the Anthropology of Supermodernity*, London: Verso.
Badiou, A. (1994) '*Gilles Deleuze, The Fold: Leibniz and the Baroque*', in C. Boundas and D. Olkowski (eds) *Gilles Deleuze and the Theatre of Philosophy*, London: Routledge, 51–69.
—— (1997) *Deleuze: the Clamour of Being*, trans. L. Burchill, Minneapolis: University of Minnesota Press.
—— (2005) *Being and Event*, London: Continuum.
Bains, P. (2002) 'Subjectless Subjectivities', in B. Massumi (ed.) *A Shock to Thought: Expression after Deleuze and Guattari*, London: Routledge, 101–16.
Baker, G. (2002) 'Problems in the Theorisation of Global Civil Society', *Political Studies*, 50: 928–43.
Barabási, A.-L. (2002) *Linked; The New Science of Networks*, Cambridge, Massachusetts: Perseus.
Bateson, G. (1972) *Steps to an Ecology of Mind; Collected Essays in Anthropology, Psychiatry, Evolution, and Epistemology*, San Francisco: Chandler.
Baudrillard, J. (1983a) *In the Shadow of the Silent Majorities*, trans. P. Foss, J. Johnston and P. Patton, New York: Semiotext(e).
—— (1983b) *Simulations*, trans. P. Foss, P. Patton, and P. Beitchman, New York: Semiotext(e).
—— (1988) *The Ecstasy of Communication*, trans. B. Schutze and C. Schutze, New York: Semiotext(e).
Bauman, Z. (1992) *Intimations of Postmodernity*, London: Routledge.
—— (2002) *Individually, Together*, London: Sage.
Beck, U. and Beck-Gernsheim, E. (2002) *Individualization*, trans. P. Camiller, London: Sage.
Bergson, H. (1929) *Matter and Memory*, trans. N. M. Paul and W. S. Palmer, London: G. Allen and Co.
—— (2001) *Time and Free Will: An Essay on the Immediate Data of Consciousness*, trans. F. L. Pogson, Mineolo: Dover.
Bhabha, H. (1994) 'How Newness Enters the World: Postmodern Space, Postcolonial Times and the Trials of Cultural Transition', *The Location of Culture*, 212–35.
Bigo, D. and Walker, R. (2007) 'Political Sociology and the Problem of the International', *Millennium: Journal of International Studies*, 35: 725–39.
Bigongiari, D. (1953) 'Introduction', in D. Bigongiari (ed.) *The Political Ideas of St. Thomas Aquinas*, London: Hafner Press, i–xxxvii.
Bonta, M. and Protevi, J. (2004) *Deleuze and Geophilosophy: A Guide and Glossary*, Edinburgh: Edinburgh University Press.
Boundas, C. (1994) 'Deleuze: Serialization and Subject Formation', in C. Boundas (ed.) *Gilles Deleuze and the Theatre of Philosophy*, 99–116.
—— (1996) 'Deleuze-Bergson: An Ontology of the Virtual', in P. Patton (ed.) *Deleuze: A Critical Reader*, Oxford: Blackwell, 81–106.

—— (2006) 'What Difference does Deleuze's Difference Make?', in C. Boundas (ed.) *Deleuze and Philosophy*, Edinburgh: Edinburgh University Press, 3–30.

Boy, A.-D. (2008) Anfang einer Welle. *Der Spiegel.* 51.

Brennan, T. (2003) 'The Empire's New Clothes', *Critical Inquiry*, 29: 337–67.

Brenner, R. (2002) *The Boom and the Bubble; The US in the World Economy*, London: Verso.

Brown, N. and Szeman, I. (2002) 'The Global Coliseum: On Empire', *Cultural Studies*, 16: 177–92.

Bryson, J. (2007) 'The "Second" Global Shift: The Offshoring or Global Sourcing of Corporate Services and the Rise of Distanciated Emotional Labour', *Geografiska Annaler* 89: 31–43.

Bull, H. (1977) *The Anarchical Society: A Study of Order in World Politics*, New York: Columbia University Press.

Burbach, R. (2001) *Globalization and Postmodern Politics: From Zapatistas to High-tech Robber Barons*, London: Pluto.

Burbach, R., Núñez, O., et al. (1997) *Globalisation and its Discontents: The Rise of Postmodern Socialisms*, London: Pluto.

Burns, T. (2003) *Rome and the Barbarians, 100 B.C.–A.D. 400*, Baltimore: Johns Hopkins University Press.

Buzan, B. (1994) 'The Level of Analysis Problem in International Relations Reconsidered', in K. Booth and S. Smith (eds) *International Relations Theory Today*, London: Polity Press.

Buzan, B. andand Little, R. (2000) *International Systems in World History; Remaking the Study of International Relations*, Oxford: Oxford University Press.

—— (2001) 'Why International Relations has Failed as an Intellectual Project and What to Do About It', *Millennium: Journal of International Studies*, 30: 19–39.

Byrne, D. (1998) *Complexity Theory and the Social Sciences: An Introduction*, London: Routledge.

Calhoun, C. (1995) *Critical Social Theory; Culture, History, and the Challenge of Difference*, Cambridge USA: Blackwell.

Callinicos, A. (2001) *Toni Negri in Perspective* [online]. *International Socialism Journal*. Available from: http:/pubs.socialistreviewindex.org.uk/isj92/callinicos.htm (accessed April 2010).

—— (2002) 'Marxism and Global Governance', in D. Held and A. McGrew (eds) *Governing Globalization; Power, Authority and Global Governance*, Cambridge: Polity, 249–266.

—— (2003) *An Anti-capitalism Manifesto*, Cambridge: Polity Press.

Campbell, D. and Schoolman, M. (eds) (2008) *William Connolly and the Contemporary Global Condition*, Durham: Duke University Press.

Castells, M. (1996) *The Rise of the Network Society*, London: Blackwell

Cerny, P. (1999) 'Globalization, Governance, and Complexity', in A. Prakash and J. Hart (eds) *Globalization and Governance*, London: Routledge, 188–212.

Chandler, D. (2004) 'Building Civil Society from Below?', *Millennium: Journal of International Studies*, 33: 313–39.

Chatterton, P. and Hodkinson, S. (2006) *Autonomy in the City; Reflections on the UK Social Centres Movement* [online]. www.autonomousgeographies.org/files/socialcentrespamphlet.pdf (accessed June 2010).

Chesters, G. and Welsh, I. (2005) 'Complexity and Social Movement(s): Process and Emergence in Planetary Action Systems', *Theory, Culture & Society*, 22: 187–211.

—— (2006) *Complexity and Social Movements: Multitudes at the Edge of Chaos*, London: Routledge.
Colebrook, C. (2002) *Gilles Deleuze*, London: Routledge.
Connolly, W. E. (2005) *Pluralism*, Durham: Duke University Press.
Cox, R. (2005) 'Civil Society at the Turn of the Millennium; Prospects for an Alternative World Order', in L. Amoore (ed.) *The Global Resistance Reader*, London: Routledge, 103–23.
Cresswell, T. (2006) *On the Move: Mobility in the Modern Western World*, New York: Routledge.
Currier, D. (2003) 'Feminist Technological Futures: Deleuze and Body/Technology Assemblages', *Feminist Theory*, 4: 321–38.
Cusset, F. (2003) *French Theory; Foucault, Derrida, Deleuze & Cie et les mutations de la vie intellectuelle aux États-Unis*, Paris: Éditions la découverte.
Cutler, C., Haufler, V., and Porter, T. (eds) (1999) *Private Authority and International Relations*, Albany: SUNY.
Dale, G. (2001) '"Merging Rivulets of Opposition": Perspectives of the Anti-Capitalist Movement', *Millennium: Journal of International Studies*, 30: 365–69.
Day, R. (2004) 'From Hegemony to Affinity: The Political Logic of the Newest Social Movements', *Cultural Studies*, 18: 716–48.
—— (2005) *Gramsci is Dead: Anarchist Currents in the Newest Social Movements*, London: Pluto.
De Souza, L. M. T. M. (2002) 'A Case among Cases, a World among Worlds: The Ecology of Writing Among the Kashinawá in Brazil', *Journal Of Language Identity And Education*, 1: 261–78.
Delanda, M. (2002) *Intensive Science and Virtual Philosophy*, London: Continuum.
—— (2006) *A New Philosophy of Society*, London: Continuum.
Deleuze, G. (1968) *Différence et répétition*, Paris: Presses universitaires de France.
—— (1986) *Cinema 1: The Movement-Image*, trans. H. Tomlinson and B. Habberjam, Minneapolis: Athlone Press.
—— (1988a) *Bergsonism*, trans. H. Tomlinson and B. Habberjam, New York: Zone Books.
—— (1988b) *Le Pli. Leibniz et le Baroque*, Paris: Les Éditions de Minuit.
—— (1991) *Empiricism and Subjectivity: An Essay on Hume's Theory of Human Nature*, trans. C. Boundas, New York: Columbia University Press.
—— (1992) *Expressionism in Philosophy: Spinoza*, trans. M. Joughin, New York: Zone Books.
—— (1995) *Negotiations. 1972–1990*, trans. M. Jougin, New York: Columbia University Press.
—— (1997) 'Desire and Pleasure', in A. I. Davidson (ed.) *Foucault and His Interlocutors*, Chicago: University of Chicago Press, 183–92.
—— (2004a) *Difference and Repetition*, trans. P. Patton, London: Continuum.
—— (2004b) *The Logic of Sense*, trans. M. Lester and C. Stivale, London: Continuum.
—— (2005) *Nietzsche and Philosophy*, trans. H. Tomlinson, London: Continuum.
—— (2006a) *The Fold: Leibniz and the Baroque*, trans. T. Conley, London: Continuum.
—— (2006b) *Foucault*, trans. S. Hand, London: Continuum.
Deleuze, G. and Guattari, F. (1983) *Anti-Oedipus*, trans. R. Hurley, M. Seem, and H. R. Lane, London: Athlone Press.
—— (1986) *Kafka: Towards a Minor Literature*, trans. D. Polan, Minneapolis: University of Minnesota Press.

—— (1987) *A Thousand Plateaus*, trans. B. Massumi, London: Continuum.

—— (1994) *What is Philosophy?*, trans. G. Burchell and H. Tomlinson, London: Verso.

Deleuze, G. and Parnet, C. (2006) *Dialogues II*, trans. H. Tomlinson and B. Habberjam, London: Continuum.

Della Porta, D. and Kriesi, H. (1999) 'Introduction', in D. Della Porta, H. Kriesi, and D. Rucht (eds) *Social Movements in a Globalizing World*, New York: St. Martin's Press, 1–22.

Demirovic, A. (2000) 'NGOs and Social Movements: A Study in Contrasts', *CNS*, 11: 131–40.

Der Derian, J. and Shapiro, M. (1989) *International/Intertextual Relations. Postmodern Readings of World Politics*, New York: Lexington.

Derrida, J. (1977) *Of Grammatology*, trans. G. Spivak, Baltimore: Johns Hopkins University Press.

—— (1983) *Dissemination*, trans. B. Johnson, Chicago: University of Chicago Press.

—— (1992) *Given Time I: Counterfeit Money*, trans. P. Kamuf, Chicago: Chicago University Press.

—— (1997) *The Politics of Friendship*, London: Verso.

Desai, M. and Said, Y. (2001) 'The New Anti-Capitalist Movement: Money and Global Civil Society', in H. Anheier, M. Glasius, and M. Kaldor (eds) *Global Civil Society 2001*, Oxford: Oxford University Press, 51–78.

Descartes, R. (1960) *Meditations on First Philosophy*, trans. L. Lafleur, New York: Macmillan.

Devetak, R. (1995) 'The Project of Modernity and International Relations Theory', *Millennium: Journal of International Studies*, 24: 27–51.

Dews, P. (1987) *Logics of Disintegration*, London: Verso.

Dillon, M. (2000) 'Poststructuralism, Complexity and Poetics', *Theory, Culture and Society*, 17: 1–26.

Dillon, S. (2006) *Schools Cut Back Subjects to Push Reading and Math* [online]. www.nytimes.com/2006/03/26/education/26child.html?ex=1301029200en (Accessed December 2009).

Dirlik, A. (1994) *After the Revolution: Waking to Global Capitalism*, Hanover: Wesleyan University Press.

Dodds, E. A. (1973) *The Greeks and the Irrational*, Berkeley: University of California Press.

Egyed, B. (2006) 'Counter-Actualisation and the Method of Intuitions', in C. Boundas (ed.) *Deleuze and Philosophy*, Edinburgh: Edinburgh University Press, 74–84.

Eriksson, K. (2005) 'Foucault, Deleuze, and the Ontology of Networks', *European Legacy*, 10: 595–610.

Eschle, C. and Stammers, N. (2004) 'Taking Part: Social Movements, INGOs, and Global Change', *Alternatives*, 29: 333–372.

Etzioni, A. (2004) 'The Capabilities and Limits of the Global Civil Society', *Millennium: Journal of International Studies*, 33: 341–43.

Eve, R., Horsfall, S. , and Lee, M. (eds) (1997) *Chaos, Complexity, and Sociology*, London: Sage.

Falk, R. (2005) 'Global Civil Society: Perspectives, Initiatives, Movements', in L. Amoore (ed.) *The Global Resistance Reader*, London: Routledge, 124–35.

Fisher, W. and Ponniah, T. (eds) (2003) *Another World Is Possible: Popular Alternatives to Globalization at the World Social Forum*, London: Zed Books.

Foucault, M. (1969) *Les mots et les choses: une archéologie des sciences humaines*, Paris: Gallimard.
—— (1970) 'Theatrum philosophicum', *Critique*, 282: 885–908.
—— (1977) *Discipline and Punish*, trans. A. M. S. Smith, New York: Vintage.
—— (1983) 'Preface', in G. Deleuze and F. Guattari *Anti-Oedipus*, London: Athlone Press, xi–xiv.
—— (1989) *The Birth of the Clinic; An Achaeology of Medical Perception*, trans. A. M. Sheridan, London: Routledge.
—— (1994a) 'Two Lectures', in M. Kelly (ed.) *Critique and Power; Recasting the Foucault/Habermas Debate*, Cambridge: MIT Press, 17–46.
—— (1994b) 'Critical Theory/Intellectual History', in M. Kelly (ed.) *Critique and Power; Recasting the Foucault/Habermas Debate*, Cambridge: MIT Press, 109–37.
—— (1997) 'The Ethics of the Concern for Self as a Practice of Freedom', in P. Rabinow (ed.) *Ethics, Subjectivity and Truth*, New York: The New Press, 281–301.
—— (2002a) *The Order of Things*, London: Routledge.
—— (2002b) *The Archaeology of Knowledge*, London: Routledge.
Fukuyama, F. (1992) *The End of History and the Last Man*, New York: Free Press.
Gaerber, D. (2002) 'The New Anarchists', *New Left Review*, 13: 61–73.
Giddens, A. (1984) *The Constitution of Society: Outline of the Theory of Structuration*, Cambridge: Polity Press.
—— (1991) *Modernity and Self-Identity. Self and Society in the Late Modern Age*, Cambridge: Polity Press.
Gill, S. (2003) *Power and Resistance in the New World Order*, Basingstoke: Palgrave Macmillan.
Glynos, J. and Howarth, D. R. (2007) *Logics of Critical Explanation in Social and Political Theory*, London: Routledge.
Goodchild, P. (1996) *Deleuze and Guattari: An Introduction to the Politics of Desire*, London: Sage.
Gray, J. (1995) *Liberalism*, 2nd edn, Buckingham: Open University Press.
Güneş-Ayata, A. (1994) 'Clientelism: Premodern, Modern, Postmodern', in L. Roniger and A. Güneş-Ayata (eds) *Democracy, Clientelism, and Civil Society*, Boulder: Lynne Rienner Publishers 19–28.
Haas, P. M. (1992) 'Introduction: Epistemic Communities and International Policy Coordination', *International Organization*, 46: 1–35.
Habermas, J. (2005) 'Interpreting the Fall of a Monument', in M. Pensky (ed.) *Globalizing Critical Theory*, Oxford: Rowman and Littlefield, 19–26.
Hacking, I. (1990) *The Taming of Chance*, Cambridge: Cambridge University Press.
—— (2002) *Historical Ontology*, Cambridge: Harvard University Press.
Halliday, F. (2000) 'Getting Real About Seattle', *Millennium: Journal of International Studies*, 29: 123–9.
Hallward, P. (2006) *Out of This World: Deleuze and the Philosophy of Creation*, London: Verso.
Hardt, M. and Negri, A. (2000) *Empire*, Massachusetts: Harvard University Press.
—— (2004) *Multitude; War and Democracy in the Age of Empire*, London: Penguin.
—— (2009) *Commonwealth*, Cambridge: Harvard University Press.
Harvey, D. (1990) *The Condition of Postmodernity; An Enquiry into the Origins of Cultural Change*, Oxford: Blackwell.
—— (1999) *The Limits to Capital*, London: Verso.
—— (2000) *Spaces of Hope*, Berkeley: University of California Press.

—— (2007) 'Neoliberalism as Creative Destruction', *The Annals of the American Academy of Political and Social Science*, 610: 21–44.

Hayden, P. and el-Ojeili, C. (2005) 'Confronting Globalisation: An Introduction', in P. Hayden and C. el-Ojeili (eds) *Confronting Globalization; Humanity, Justice and the Renewal of Politics*, Basingstoke: Palgrave Macmillan, 1–22.

Hays, K. M. (1992) *Modernism and the Posthumanist Subject: The Architecture of Hannes Meyer and Ludwig Hilberseimer*, Cambridge, Mass.: MIT Press.

He, B. and Murphy, H. (2007) 'Global Social Justice at the WTO? The Role of NGOs in Constructing Global Social Compacts', *International Affairs*, 4: 707–27.

Hegel, G. W. F. (1967) *Philosophy of Right*, London: Oxford University Press.

Heidegger, M. (1962) *Being and Time*, trans. J. Macquarrie and E. Robinson, San Francisco: Harper and Row.

—— (1977) 'The Age of the World Picture', *The Question Concerning Technology and Other Essays*, New York: Harper and Row, 115–54.

—— (1984) *The Metaphysical Foundation of Logic*, trans. M. Heim, Bloomington: Indiana University Press.

Held, D. (1995) *Democracy and the Global Order: From the Modern State to Cosmopolitan Governance*, Stanford: Stanford University Press.

—— (2004) 'Democratic Accountability and Political Effectiveness from a Cosmopolitan Perspective', *Government and Opposition*, 39: 364–91.

—— (ed.) (2005) *Global Governance and Accountability*, Oxford: Blackwell.

Held, D. and McGrew, A. (2002) 'Introduction', in D. Held and A. McGrew (eds) *Governing Globalization; Power, Authority, and Global Governance*, Cambridge: Polity Press, 1–21.

Heller, T. and Wellbery, D. (1986) 'Introduction', in T. Heller, M. Sosna, and D. Wellbery (eds) *Reconstructing Individualism; Autonomy, Individuality, and the Self in Western Thought*, Stanford: Stanford University Press, 1–15.

Hirst, P. (2005) *Space and Power: Politics, War and Architecture*, Cambridge Polity.

Hirst, P. and Woolley, P. (1982) *Social Relations and Human Attributes*, London: Tavistock Publications.

Hobbes, T. (1967) *Leviathan*, London: Oxford University Press.

Holloway, J. (1998) 'Dignity's Revolt', in J. Holloway and E. Paláelz (eds) *Zapatista! Reinventing Revolution in Mexico*, London: Pluto, 159–98.

—— (2002) *Change the World Without Taking Power: The Meaning of Revolution Today*, London: Pluto.

Hopgood, S. (2000) 'Reading the Small Print in Global Civil Society: The Inexorable Hegemony of the Liberal Self', *Millennium: Journal of International Studies*, 29: 1–25.

Hudock, A. C. (1999) *NGOs and Civil Society: Democracy by Proxy?*, Oxford: Polity Press.

Huntington, S. (1993) 'The Clash of Civilizations?', *Foreign Affairs*, Summer: 22–49.

Huyssen, A. (1986) *After the Great Divide: Modernism, Mass Culture, Postmodernism*, Bloomington: Indiana University Press.

Indymedia (2005) *G8 Protest Worth It? Critique of Summit Protest Strategy: Re-presented Notes on Summits and Counter Summits* [online]. www.indymedia.org.uk/en/2005/12/330579.html (accessed December 2008).

Jameson, F. (1983) 'Postmodernism and Consumer Society', in H. Foster (ed.) *Postmodern Culture*, London: Pluto, 111–25.

—— (1991) *Postmodernism, Or the Cultural Logic of Late Capitalism*, London: Verso.

Jarvis, P. (2007) *Globalisation, Lifelong Learning and the Learning Society: Sociological Perspectives*, Abingdon: Routledge.

Jasiewicz, E. (2008) *Time for a Revolution* [online]. *Guardian*. Available from: www.guardian.co.uk/commentisfree/2008/aug/21/climatechange.kingsnorthclimatecamp?gusrc=rssandfeed=commentisfree (accessed December 2009).

Jessop, B. (2003) *Globalization: It's About Time Too!*, Vienna: Institute for Advanced Studies.

Jung, C. (1965) *Memoirs, Dreams, Reflections*, New York: Vintage.

Juniper, J. and Jose, J. (2008) 'Foucault and Spinoza: Philosophies of Immanence and the Decentred Political Subject', *History of the Human Science*, 21: 1–20.

Karns, M. and Mingst, K. (2004) *International Organizations; The Politics and Process of Global Governance*, Boulder: Lynne Rienner Publishers.

Klein, N. (2000) *No Logo*, London: Flamingo.

—— (2002a) 'The Unknown Icon', in J. Schalit (ed.) *Anti-capitalism Reader; Imagining a Geography of Opposition*, New York: Akashic, 89–100.

—— (2002b) *Fences and Windows*, London: Flamingo.

Kobrin, S. (1999) 'Back to the Future; Neomedievalism and the Postmodern Digital World Economy', in A. Prakash and J. Hart (eds) *Globalization and Governance*, London: Routledge, 165–87.

Kraniauskas, J. (2003) 'Empire, or Multitude; Transnational Negri', *Radical Philosophy*, 103: 29–39.

Kratochwil, F. (1986) 'Of Systems, Boundaries, and Territoriality: An Inquiry Into the Formation of the State System', *World Politics*, 39: 27–52.

Lacey, A. (2005a) 'Spaces of Justice: The Social Divine of Global Anti-Capital Activists' Sites of Resistance', *Canadian Review of Sociology and Anthropology*, 42: 403–20.

—— (2005b) 'Networked Communities; Social Centres and Activist Spaces in Contemporary Britain', *Space and Culture*, 8: 286–301.

Lachernmann, G. and Dannecker, P. (eds) (2008) *Negotiating Development in Muslim Societies; Gendered Spaces and Translocal Connections*, Plymouth: Lexington.

Laclau, E. (1990) *New Reflections on the Revolution of Our Time*, London: Verso.

Laclau, E. and Mouffe, C. (1985) *Hegemony and Socialist Strategy: Towards a Radical Democratic Politics*, London: Verso.

Lash, S. (2002) 'Individualization in a Non-Linear Mode', *Individualization*, London: Sage, vii–xiii.

—— (2006) 'Life (Vitalism)', *Theory, Culture and Society*, 23: 323–9.

Le Petit Robert (1991) *Dictionnaire de la Langue Française*, Paris: Le Robert.

Lecercle, J.-J. (1996) 'The Pedagogy of Philosophy', *Radical Philosophy*, 75: 44–6.

Lee, M. (1997) 'From Enlightenment to Chaos; Toward Nonmodern Social Theory', in R. Eve, S. Horsfall, and M. Lee (eds) *Chaos, Complexity, and Sociology*, London: Sage, 15–29.

Legg, S. (2009) 'Of Scales, Networks and Assemblages: The League of Nations Apparatus and the Scalar Sovereignty of the Government of India', *Transactions of the Institute of British Geographers*, 34: 234–253.

Leibniz, G. W. (1898) *The Monadology and Other Philosophical Writings*, trans. R. Latta, Oxford: Clarendon.

Lipschutz, R. (1992) 'Restructuring World Politics: The Emergence of Global Civil Society', *Millennium: Journal of International Studies*, 21: 389–420.

Mac Sheoin, T. (2007) 'Transnational Activism', *Global Social Policy*, 7: 105–110.

References

Mandelbrot, B. (1993) 'Fractals', in J. Holte (ed.) *Choas: The New Science*, Maryland: University Press of America, 1–34.

Marcos (2001) *Our Word is Our Weapon: Selected Writings*, ed. J. P. de León, London: Serpent's Tail.

—— (2003) *I Shit on All the Revolutionary Vanguards of this Planet* [online]. http://struggle.ws/mexico/ezln/2003/marcos/etaJAN.html (accessed June 2011).

Marcus, G. E. and Saka, E. (2006) 'Assemblage', *Theory, Culture and Society*, 23: 101–106.

Marcuse, P. (2005) 'Are Social Forums the Future of Social Movements?', *International Journal of Urban and Regional Research*, 29: 417–24.

Massumi, B. (1992) *A User's Guide to Capitalism and Schizophrenia: Deviations from Deleuze and Guattari*, Cambridge: MIT Press.

—— (2002) 'Like A Thought', in B. Massumi (ed.) *A Shock to Thought: Expression After Deleuze and Guattari*, London: Routledge, xiii–xxxix.

May, T. (1993) 'The System and its Fractures: Gilles Deleuze on Otherness', *The Journal of the British Society for Phenomenology*, 24: 3–14.

—— (2005) *Gilles Deleuze: An Introduction*, Cambridge: Cambridge University Press.

McAdam, D., Tarrow, S., and Tilly, C. (2001) *Dynamics of Contention*, Cambridge: Cambridge University Press.

McDonald, K. (2002) 'From Solidarity to Fluidarity: Social Movements Beyond "Collective Identity" – The Case of Globalization Conflicts', *Social Movement Studies*, 1: 109–28.

McNeill, W. (1982) *The Pursuit of Power: Technology, Armed Force, and Society Since A.D. 1000*, Chicago: University of Chicago Press.

Melucci, A. (1985) 'The Symbolic Challenge of Contemporary Social Movements', *Social Research*, 52: 798–816.

—— (1989) *Nomads of the Present*, London: Hutchinson Radius.

Melville, H. (2001) *Moby-Dick, or, The Whale*, New York: Penguin Books.

Meyer, J. et al. (1997) 'World Society and the Nation-State', *American Journal of Sociology*, 103: 144–81.

Micheletti, M. (2003) *Political Virtue and Shopping: Individuals, Consumerism, and Collective Action*, New York: Palgrave Macmillan.

Mihata, K. (1997) 'The Persistence of "Emergence"', in R. Eve, S. Horsfall, and M. Lee (eds) *Chaos, Complexity, and Sociology*, London: Sage, 30–38.

Monbiot, G. (2003) *Stronger than Ever* [online]. *The Guardian*. Available from: www.guardian.co.uk/politics/2003/jan/28/greenpolitics.eu (accessed January 2009).

Naím, M. (2007) 'What Is a Gongo? How Government-sponsored Groups Masquerade as Civil Society', *Foreign Policy*, 160: 96.

Nealon, J. (2003) 'Beyond Hermaneutics: Deleuze, Derrida and Contemporary Theory', in P. Patton and J. Protevi (eds) *Between Deleuze and Derrida*, London: Continuum, 158–168.

Nietzsche, F. (1966) *Beyond Good and Evil*, trans. W. Kaufmann, New York: Vintage.

—— (1989) *On the Genealogy of Morals*, trans. W. Kaufmann and R. J. Hollingdale, New York: Vintage.

—— (1990) *Twilight of the Idols and The Antichrist*, trans. R. J. Hollingdale, London: Penguin.

O'Brien, R. (2000) *Contesting Global Governance: Multilateral Economic Institutions and Global Social Movements*, Cambridge: Cambridge University Press.

Ó Tuathail, G. (1996) *Critical Geopolitics*, London: Routledge.

Ogden, S. (2002) *Inklings of Democracy in China*, Cambridge: Harvard University Asia Center.
Olesen, T. (2005) 'World Politics and Social Movements: The Janus Face of the Global Democratic Structure', *Global Society*, 19.
Olma, S. (2007) 'Physical Bergsonism and the Worldliness of Time', *Theory, Culture and Society*, 24: 123–37.
Oommen, T. (2004) *Nation, Civil Society and Social Movements; Essays in Political Sociology*, London: Sage.
Parr, A. (ed.) (2005) *The Deleuze Dictionary*, Edinburgh: Edinburgh University Press.
Patomäki, H. (2003) 'Problems of Democratizing Global Governance: Time, Space and the Emancipatory Process', *European Journal of International Relations*, 9: 347–76.
Patomäki, H. and Teivainen, T. (2004) 'The World Social Forum: An Open Space or a Movement of Movements?', *Theory, Culture and Society*, 21: 145–54.
Patton, P. (2000) *Deleuze and the Political*, London: Routledge.
—— (2003) 'Future Politics', in P. Patton and J. Protevi (eds) *Between Deleuze and Derrida*, London: Continuum, 15–29.
—— (2005) 'Deleuze and Democracy', *Contemporary Political Theory*, 4: 400–13.
Peat, F. D. (1991) *Einstein's Moon: Bell's Theorem and the Curious Quest for Quantum Reality*, New York: Contemporary Books.
Pefanis, J. (1991) *Heterology and the Postmodern: Bataille, Baudrillard and Lyotard*, Durham: Duke University Press.
Peiten, H.-O. (1993) 'The Causality Principle, Deterministic Laws and Chaos', in J. Holte (ed.) *Chaos: the New Science*, Maryland: University Press of America, 36–43.
Penksy, M. (2005) 'Globalizing Theory, Theorizing Globalization: Introduction', in M. Pensky (ed.) *Globalizing Critical Theory*, Oxford: Rowman and Littlefield, 1–15.
People's Global Action (2001) *What is PGA?* [online]. www.nadir.org/nadir/initiativ/agp/pga_leaflet_a5.pdf (accessed April 2010).
Petrarca, F. (1904) *Secretum*, trans. E. Mills, New York: E.P. Dutton and Company.
Phillips, J. (2006) 'Agencement/Assemblage', *Theory, Culture and Society*, 23: 108–109.
Pieterse, J. (2004) *Globalization and Culture*, Boulder: Rowman and Littlefield.
Plant, S. (1993) 'Nomads and Revolutionaries', *The Journal of the British Society for Phenomenology*, 24: 88–101.
Polanyi, K. (1968) *The Great Transformation: The Political and Economic Origins of Our Time*, Boston: Beacon Press.
Polletta, F. and Jasper, J. (2001) 'Collective Identity and Social Movements', *Annual Review of Sociology*, 27: 283–305.
Ponniah, T. and Fisher, W. (2003) 'Introduction: The World Social Forum and the Reinvention of Democracy', in W. Fisher and T. Ponniah (eds) *Another World is Possible: Popular Alternatives to Globalization at the World Social Forum*, London: Zed Books, 1–20.
Prigogine, I. and Stengers, I. (1983) *La Nouvelle alliance: métamorphose de la science*, Paris: Gallimard.
—— (1984) *Order Out of Chaos; Man's New Dialogue with Nature*, New York: Bantam.
—— (1988) *Entre le temps et l'éternité*, Paris: Fayard.
Protevi, J. (2001) *Political Physics; Deleuze, Derrida and the Body Politic*, London: Athlone Press.
Rawls, J. (1972) *A Theory of Justice*, Oxford: Clarendon Press.
Reid, J. (2003) 'Deleuze's War Machine: Nomadism Against the State', *Millennium: Journal of International Studies*, 32: 57–85.

References

Rescher, N. (1996) *Process Metaphysics; An Introduction to Process Philosophy*, New York: State University of New York Press.

Riemann, B. (1919) *Über die Hypothesen, welche der Geometrie zu Grunde liegen*, Berlin: Springer.

Robertson, R. (1990) 'Mapping the Global Condition', in M. Featherstone (ed.) *Global Culture: Nationalism, Globalization and Modernity*, London: Sage, 15–28.

—— (1992) *Globalisation: Social Theory and Global Culture*, London: Sage.

—— (1995) 'Glocalization: Time–Space and Homogeneity–Heterogeneity', in M. Featherstone, S. Lash, and R. Robertson (eds) *Global Modernities*, London: Sage, 25–44.

Robinson, A. and Tormey, S. (2005) '"Horizontals", "Verticals" and the Conflicting Logics of Transformative Politics', in P. Hayden and C. el-Ojeili (eds) *Confronting Globalization; Humanity, Justice and the Renewal of Politics*, Basingstoke: Palgrave Macmillan, 208–26.

Roniger, L. (1994) 'Conclusions: the Transformation of Clientelism and Civil Society', in L. Roniger and A. Güneş-Ayata (eds) *Clientelism: Premodern, Modern, Postmodern*, Boulder: L. Rienner 207–14.

Rosenau, J. (1990) *Turbulence in World Politics; A Theory of Change and Continuity*, Hemel Hempstead: Harvester Wheatsheaf.

—— (2002) 'Governance in a New Global Order', in D. Held and A. McGrew (eds) *Governing Globalization; Power, Authority and Global Governance*, Cambridge: Polity, 70–86.

—— (2003) *Distant Proximities: Dynamics Beyond Globalization*, Princeton: Princeton University Press.

Rosenberg, J. (2005) 'Globalisation Theory: A Post Mortem', *International Politics*, 42: 2–74.

Rucht, D. (1999) 'The Transnationalization of Social Movements; Trends, Causes, Problems', in D. D. Porta, H. Kriesi, and D. Rucht (eds) *Social Movements in a Globalizing World*, Basingstoke: Palgrave Macmillan, 206–22.

Ruggie, J. (1993) 'Territoriality and Beyond: Problematizing Modernity in International Relations', *International Organization*, 47: 139–74.

Said, E. (1995) *Orientalism; Western Conceptions of the Orient*, London: Penguin Books.

Saul, J. R. (2005) *The Collapse of Globalism; And the Reinvention of the World*, Toronto: Penguin Group, Canada.

Saunders, J. J. (2001) *The History of the Mongol Conquests*, Philadelphia: University of Pennsylvania Press.

Schaub, M. (2003) *Gilles Deleuze im Wunderland: Zeit als Ereignisphilosophie*, München: Fink.

Scholte, J. A. (2000) 'Cautionary Reflections on Seattle', *Millennium: Journal of International Studies*, 29: 115–21.

—— (2004) 'Civil Society and Democratically Accountable Global Governance', *Government and Opposition*, 39: 211–33.

—— (2005) *Globalization; A Critical Introduction*, 2nd edn, London: Palgrave Macmillan.

Schrift, A. (2000) 'Nietzsche, Foucault, Deleuze, and the Subject of Radical Democracy', *Angelaki*, 5: 151–61.

—— (2006) 'Deleuze Becoming Nietzsche Becoming Spinoza Becoming Deleuze; Toward a Politics of Immanence', *Philosophy Today*: 187–194.

Second Declaration of La Realidad (1996) [online]. www.cedoz.org/site/index.php (Accessed May 2011).

Smith, A. D. (1990) 'Toward a Global Culture?', *Theory, Culture and Society*, 7: 171–91.

Smith, D. (2003) 'Deleuze and Derrida, Immanence and Transcendence: Two Directions in Recent French Thought', in P. Patton and J. Protevi (eds) *Between Deleuze and Derrida*, London: Continuum, 46–66.
Snell, B. (1953) *The Discovery of the Mind*, Oxford: Blackwell.
Spinoza, B. (1992) *The Ethics*, Indianapolis: Hacking.
Spivak, G. (1994) 'Can the Subaltern Speak?', in P. Williams (ed.) *Colonial Discourse and Post-Colonial Theory: A Reader*, Urbana: University of Illinois Press, 271–313.
—— (1999) *A Critique of Postcolonial Reason; Toward a History of the Vanishing Present*, Harvard: President and Fellows of Harvard College.
Spruyt, H. (2002) 'The Origins, Development, and Possible Decline of the Modern State', *Annual Review of Political Science*, 5: 127–49.
Steger, M. (2005) *Globalism: Market Ideology Meets Terrorism*, 2nd edn, Lanham: Rowman and Littlefield.
Stichweh, R. (2003) *Die Weltgesellschaft: Soziologische Analysen*, Frankfurt: Suhrkamp.
Stratton, J. (1984) 'Book Reviews : Social Relations and Human Attributes', *Journal of Sociology*, 20: 129–33.
Tampio, N. (2009) 'Assemblages and the Multitude', *European Journal of Political Theory*, 8: 383–400.
Tarrow, S. (1998) *Power in Movement; Social Movements and Contentious Politics*, 2nd edn, Cambridge: Cambridge University Press.
Teschke, B. (2003) *The Myth of 1648: Class, Geopolitics, and the Making of Modern International Relations*, London: Verso.
Thatcher, M. and Keay, D. (1987) Aids, Education and the Year 2000! *Woman's Own*, 8–10.
Thoburn, N. (2003) *Deleuze, Marx and Politics*, London: Routledge.
Toffler, A. (1984) 'Science and Change', *Order Out of Chaos*, New York: Bantam, xiv–xxiv.
Tormey, S. (2005a) 'After Gleneagles: Where Next?', in D. Harvie *et al.* (eds) *Shut Them Down!*, Leeds: Dissent, 337–49.
—— (2005b) 'A "Creative Power"?: The Uses of Deleuze. A Review Essay', *Contemporary Political Theory*, 4: 414–30.
—— (2006) '"Not in My Name": Deleuze, Zapatismo and the Critique of Representation', *Parliamentary Affairs*, 59: 138–54.
Trimble, W. (1946) 'The Embassy Chapel Question, 1625–1660', *The Journal of Modern History*, 18: 97–107.
Turner, F. (1997) 'Forward: Chaos and Social Science', in R. Eve, S. Horsfall, and M. Lee (eds) *Chaos, Complexity, and Sociology*, London: Sage, xi–xxvii.
Tyler, P. (2003) 'A New Power in the Streets', *New York Times*, 17 February.
United Nations (1948) The Universal Declaration of Human Rights.
Urry, J. (2003) *Global Complexity*, Malden Polity.
—— (2005a) 'The Complexities of the Global', *Theory, Culture and Society*, 22: 235–54.
—— (2005b) 'The Complexity Turn', *Theory, Culture and Society*, 22: 1–14.
Valentin, J. (2006) 'Gilles Deleuze's Political Posture', in C. Boundas (ed.) *Deleuze and Philosophy*, Edinburgh: Edinburgh University Press, 185–201.
Venn, C. (2006) 'A Note on Assemblage', *Theory, Culture and Society*, 23: 107–8.
Veyne, P. (1997) 'Foucault Revolutionizes History', in A. Davidson (ed.) *Foucault and His Interlocutors*, Chicago: University of Chicago Press, 147–82.
Villani, A. (2006) 'Why Am I Deleuzian?', in C. Boundas (ed.) *Deleuze and Philosophy*, Edinburgh: Edinburgh University Press, 227–49.

Wagner, G. (1999) *Herausforderung Vielfalt: Plädoyer für eine kosmopolitische Soziologie*, Konstanz: Universitätsverlag Konstanz.
Walker, R. (1993) *Inside/Outside: International Relations as Political Theory*, Cambridge: Cambridge University Press.
—— (2005) 'Social Movements/World Politics', in L. Amoore (ed.) *The Global Resistance Reader*, London: Routledge, 136–49.
Waterman, P. (1998) *Globalization, Social Movements, and the New Internationalisms*, London: Mansell.
Weber, M. (2005) '"Alter-Globalisation" and Social Movements: Towards Understanding Transnational Politicization', in P. Hayden and C. el-Ojeili (eds) *Confronting Globalization; Humanity, Justice and the Renewal of Politics*, Basingstoke: Palgrave Macmillan, 191–207.
Weizman, E. (2007) *Hollow Land: Israel's Architecture of Occupation*, London: Verso.
Wendt, A. (1987) 'The Agent-Structure Problem in International Relations Theory', *International Organization* 41: 335–70.
White, L. T. (1966) *Medieval Technology and Social Change*, Oxford: Clarendon
Whitehead, A. N. (1925) *Science and the Modern World. Lowell Lectures*, New York: Macmillan.
Widder, N. (2001) 'The Rights of Simulacra: Deleuze and the Univocity of Being', *Continental Philosophy Review*, 34: 437–53.
Williams, J. (2003) *Gilles Deleuze's Difference and Repetition: A Critical Introduction and Guide*, Edinburgh: Edinburgh University Press.
WSF (2001) *World Social Forum Charter of Principles* [online]. www.forumsocialmundial.org.br/main.php?id_menu=4andcd_language=2 (accessed November 2006).
—— (2006) *See the general objectives defined for WSF 2007* [online]. www.forumsocialmundial.org.br/noticias_01.php?cd_news=2253andcd_language=2 (accessed December 2008).
Wuthnow, J. (2002) 'Deleuze in the Postcolonial: On Nomads and Indigenous Politics', *Feminist Theory*, 3: 183–200.
Žižek, S. (1990) 'Beyond Discourse Analysis', in E. Laclau *New Reflections on the Revolution of Our Time*, London: Verso, 249–60.
—— (1993) *Tarrying with the Negative; Kant, Hegel, and the Critique of Ideology*, Durham: Duke University Press.
—— (1999) *The Ticklish Subject; The Absent Centre of Political Ontology*, London: Verso.
—— (2002a) 'A Plea for Leninist Intolerance', *Critical Inquiry*, 28: 542–66.
—— (ed.) (2002b) *Revolution at the Gates; Selected Writings of Lenin from 1917; V.I. Lenin*, London: Verso.
—— (2003) *Organs without Bodies; Deleuze and Consequences*, London: Routledge.
—— (2005) 'Against Human Rights', *New Left Review*, 34: 115–31.

Index

Page numbers in **bold** denote figures.

A Thousand Plateaus 2, 46, 90–1, 154, 187, 195n7
actualization 77, 80–1, 132, 157–8, 197n49; *see also* differenciation
Agamben, G. 176
Aion 82, 116–17, 119, 129
Alice in Wonderland 89
alter-globalization movement (AGM); aims 16, 18–19; and complexity 127, 129–31, 138, 140; definition 19–20, 23; diversity 14–15; effects 10; hierarchy 142; formation 12–14; media attention 10, 16, 18; newness 11, 13; organization of 24, 26, 139–40; subversion technique 16; violence 16, 23
Althusser, L. 36, 150
analogy of judgment 55–6
Anglo–American literature 186
anti-capitalism 20–2
Anti-Oedipus 46, 136, 153, 195n7
Aristotle 53–60, **54**, 105
art 99, 116–17, 195n11
assemblage (*agencement*) 87–8, 115, 142–3
atheism 56
attributes 160
axiomatic 178

Badiou, A. 47, 62, 69, 90–1, 155
Barabási, A.-L. 130
becoming 89–90, 94, 103, 113, 121, 123, 138, 164–5, 183, 200n14; becoming-minoritarian 165, 183
Being 53–6, 63
Bergson, H. 5, 70, 82
Bergsonism 70–1
borders 101, 107–12

Boundas, C. 71–2
brain 162–3
Burns, T. 108
butterfly effect 125
Buzan, B. and Little, R. 102

capitalism 20–1, 177–80
cause 83, 106–7, 136; *see also* Event
chance 133–4
chaos 125–6, 132
chess 91
Chesters, G. and Welsh, I. 138–9
China 109, 131–2
Christianity 148, 172
Chronos 82–3, 116–17
cinema 116
citizenship 108
civil society 105; global 29–30, 99–100
Classical Greece 158
clientelism 108
cogito 61, 64; *see also* Descartes, R
Cold War 8, 110
common sense 55, 65
complexity 71, 87, 98, 123–30, 133–4, 140–1, 173
concept 52–5, 84, 140
contraction 163
counteractualization 85–7, 132; *see also* deterritorialization; line of flight
counterhegemony 34–5

dark precursor 75; *see also* cause; Event
Delanda, M. 50–1, 71–2, 115
Deleuze, G. comprehensive reading of 49, 94, 175; dangers of jargon 49; Deleuzian century 51, 196n13; dissastifaction with readings of 50; liberal reading of 51;

Deleuze, G. *continued*
    terminology 50–1; translation problems 163, 194n2, 197n45n52, 202n14
Derrida, J. 57, 63
Descartes, R. 65, 202n9
desire 46
determinism 67, 132–3
deterritorialization 86–7, 106–7, 124; *see also* counteractualization; line of flight
Dews, P. 152
difference 3, 44, 52–6, **54**, 73, 76; perfect 53
Difference and Repetition 71, 73, 79
differenciation 73, 75–8, 80–2, 159
differentiation 76, 84
digital media 17–18, 141
discourse 151, 199 n 9
disparity 78
drama 77
duration–matter **70**, 162

embassy chapel 111
emergence 81, 87, 120–1, 124; *see also* newness
Empire 63, 195n10
empiricism 93–4, 97
Englightenment, the 106, 199n8
entre-temps 83
enveloping–enveloped **79**, 159
epistemology 135, 147–8
equivalence 166
equivocity 55–6
eternal return 84, 174, 182; *see also* repetition
ethics 174–5
European Union 113
Event 74–5, 83–4, 157, 160, 174
experimentation (versus interpretation) 45

far right 21
felt 91
fold, the 155–61
Foucault, M. 25, 87–8, 93, 135, 146–7, 115, 167, 200n29, 201n33
free will 172

G8, 10
Global Governance 28–31
Global South 21
globalization 20–1, 101, 104, 107, 112–13, 131, 150, 178
Glynos, J. and Howarth D. 165–9
go 91

good sense 55, 65
government organized non-governmental organizations (GONGOs) 139
Guattari, F. 195n7
Gulliver Fallacy 113–14

haecceity 164, 166–7; *see also* specificity
Hayden, P. and el-Ojeili, C. 101
Hegel, G.F.W. 58, 104–5
Hegemony and Socialist Strategy 36–7
Heidegger, M. 146, 161, 171, 196n22
Held, D. 29
Hirst, P. and Woolley, P. 148–9, 151–2
history 117
Hobbes, T. 104–5, 149
Homer 152
homosexuality 180
human rights 176, 180–1
humanism 121–2, 169
hylomorphism 121, 132

identity 15, 21, 25, 33–4, 135, 148, 166, 170–1, 180
ideology 168, 177
immanence 5, 68–9, 129, 132, 147
individualization 9, 15, 162, 179
individuals 151–2, 154, 160
individuation 74–5, **76**, 89
intellectual buggery 191–2
intensity 70, 74–5, 78–80
intensive qualitites 70
intensive quantity 74, **76**, 80
International Relations 31–2, 113, 123, 199n6, 201n31
Internet 17, 131, 201n36
Israeli Defense Forces 130

Jessop, B. 112–13
Julius Caesar 108
jurisprudence 175–6

Kobrin, S. 118
Kratochwil, F. 108–10

lack 46, 167
Laclau, E. and Mouffe, C. 36, 166
Leibniz, G.W. 58, 79, 156, 160
level of analysis 115
liberal values 158
liberalism 150, 181, 203n32n33
limit 124
line of flight 85, 125, 167; *see also* counteractualization; deterritorialization
Lipschutz, R. 99–101

Index

machines 121, 163, 200n24
maps 99
Marxism 35–6
materialism 52, 143, 144
matter 121
meaning 174
Melucci, A 22
Melville, H. 89–90, 198n60
memory 162, 202n13
metaphors, use of in theory 44–5
metaphysics 52, 60
methodological nationalism 102, 199n6
model–copy 67, 126
modeling 128, 201n32
modernity 105–6, 116–17, 199n3
monad 156–7, 202n13
Mongol Empire 109
morality 175
Mothers Against Driving Drunk (MADD) 34
multi-perspectivism 110; *see also* post-colonialism
multiplicity 64, 88, 91–2, 113, 163–4, 202n19

negative theology 57; *see also* lack
neo-liberalism 177–80
neo-medievalism 118–20
networks 130
newness 89, 124; *see also* emergence
Nietzsche, F. 75, 84–5, 90, 146, 149
non-governmental organizations (NGOs) 30–1, 139
non-linear outcomes 124, 127
notion 91, 195n5; relative 92, 120; *see also* two poles
numbers, the numerable 63

order 126

pantheism 56
People's Global Action (PGA) 12, 25–6
perplication 78
phenomenology 43, 147
philosophy 44, 48, 57, 65–6, 200n27
Plato 57–8
pluralism 63, 163
populations 88–9, 114
positivism 39, 97
possible, the 66–8, 134
post-colonialism 110, 171
post-Marxism 36–8, 165–70
post-structuralism 43, 57, 93, 107, 120–1, 145, 152

postmodernism 66, 124–5
postmodernity 118–20, 150
power 24–5, 182, 203n34
predictability 124, 132, 173–4
Prigogine, I. and Stengers, I. 115–16, 121–2
protests 13–14; anti-war 14

quasi-causes 107

rational actor 170
Rawls, J. 150
real, the 65–6
Reclaim the Streets 34
reflexive modernity 162, 170
repetition 77–8, 84, 174; *see also* eternal return
representation 58–62, 113–14, 135; infinite 58
Rescher, N. 128
rhizome 81, 128, 184; *see also* systems, open
Robertson, R. 105
Roman Republic/Empire 108

schizophrenia 117, 200n19
science 97, 122–3, 125–6, 194n1, 200n27; nomad 3, 132, 134–5; Royal 102, 121, 137
Seattle, 'Battle of' 13
Second Declaration of La Realidad 12; *see also* Zapatismo, Subcommandante Marcos
series 75, 154
simulacrum 57, 59, 196n24
singularities 76–7, **76**, 154, 156–7
Smith, the 49
smooth–striated 120
social centres 17
social movement theory 32–5
society 149, 199–200n13
sovereignty 104
space 98–9, 112–14, 118–20
spatio–temporal dynamisms 75, 77–8
specificity 135, 164, 166
Spivak, G. 196–7 n 30
state, the 34, 100–5, 107, 111–13
stirrup 88
Subcomandante Marcos 26
subject, the 129, 146–55, 167, 170; death of 169; larval 75
subjectification 158, 185
subjectivitiy 149, 153, 158, 170
systems 129–32; closed 81, 132; open 81, 129, 131; *see also* rhizome

tacit rule 110
taxonomic essentialism 58, 122
technology 141
territory 32, 107–12
Teschke, B. 106
The Logic of Sense 86
theoretical challenges 4, 11, 27, 39–40, 96–7
Thomas Aquinas 56, 105
thought 61–2, 160–1; *see also cogito*
time 72, 81–5, 115–19, 129; *see also* Chronos and Aion
transcendence 62–4
transcendental empiricism 94, 128, 134–8
transcendental illusion 55, 65, 76, 81, 129
transnationalism 9
two poles 87, 92–4, 104, 106, 120, 161

Übermensch 84–5, 165, 175
unfolding 158–9
unintended consequences 136
univocity 56, 63, 155
Urry, J. 130–1, 140

values 170, 174
vice-diction 85, 198n54
virtual–actual 71, 73, 76–7, 91, 94, 131, 157; *see also* two poles
virtual, the 73–4, 81, 83, 86, 162, 167
vitalism 121

Walker, R. 31, 106
Washington Consensus 2
Weizman, E. 130
What is Philosophy? 51, 86
Whitehead, A. 173
Widder, N. 53
work 118–19
World Social Forum 14, 17
World Wide Web 131

Xinjiang 109

Zapatismo 22, 24–5; *see also* Subcomandante Marcos
Žižek, S. 69, 85–6, 150–1